The Economics of Contract Law

Editorial Advisory Board

Little, Brown
and Company
Law Book Division

The Economics of Contract Law

Anthony T. Kronman
Richard A. Posner
Professors of Law, University of Chicago

Little, Brown and Company Boston and Toronto

Library of Congress Catalog Card No. 78-70055

Seventh Printing

HAL

Published simultaneously in Canada
by Little, Brown & Company (Canada) Limited

Printed in the United States of America

Contents

Preface *ix*

Chapter 1
Introduction: Economic Theory and Contract Law **1**

Chapter 2
The Economic Basis of Contracts **10**

Hobbes, Leviathan 10
Umbeck, A Theory of Contract Choice and the California Gold Rush 11
Birmingham, Game Theory and Contract Law 16
Tullock, The Logic of the Law 22
Hardy, Risk and Risk-Bearing 26
Holmes, The Common Law 28
Coase, The Nature of the Firm 31
Notes and Questions 32

Chapter 3
Consideration and Assent **40**

Fuller, Consideration and Form 40
Posner, Gratuitous Promises in Economics and Law 46
Landes & Posner, Unilateral and Implied Contracts and Restitution 58
Notes and Questions 64

Chapter 4
Duress and Unconscionability 67

Dalzell, Duress by Economic Pressure 67
Goldberg, Institutional Change and the Quasi-Invisible Hand 72
Coase, The Choice of the Institutional Framework: A Comment 77
Trebilcock, The Doctrine of Inequality of Bargaining Power 78
Epstein, Unconscionability: A Critical Reappraisal 93
Kennedy, Form and Substance in Private Law Adjudication 100
Notes and Questions 107

Chapter 5
Mistake and Impossibility 114

Kronman, Mistake, Disclosure, Information, and the Law of Contracts 114
Posner & Rosenfield, Impossibility and Related Doctrines in Contract Law 122
Schwartz, Sales Law and Inflations 138
Joskow, Commercial Impossibility, the Uranium Market and the Westinghouse Case 143
Notes and Questions 149

Chapter 6
Remedies 154

Barton, The Economic Basis of Damages for Breach of Contract 154
Priest, Breach and Remedy for the Tender of Nonconforming Goods 167
Leff, Injury, Ignorance and Spite—The Dynamics of Coercive Collection 175
Kronman, Specific Performance 181
Goetz & Scott, Liquidated Damages, Penalties and the Just Compensation Principle 194
Speidel & Clay, Seller's Recovery of Overhead 208
Note, Microeconomics and the Lost-Volume Seller 213

Grossfeld, Money Sanctions for Breach of Contract in a Communist Economy 220
Notes and Questions 223

Chapter 7
Freedom of Contract: Philosophical Perspectives on Economic Analysis 230

Weber, Freedom and Coercion 230
Baker, The Ideology of the Economic Analysis of Law 233
Nozick, Anarchy, State, and Utopia 240
Marx, The Buying and Selling of Labor-Power 245
Horwitz, The Transformation of American Law 250
Note on Paternalism 253
Notes and Questions 261

Index *269*

Preface

Recent years have seen an outpouring of scholarly literature analyzing law from an economic standpoint.[1] The question arises how the insights of this literature can be communicated most effectively to law students. Special courses on the economics of law, co-teaching of law courses by economists, the inclusion of economic materials in casebooks, and the preparation of supplementary reading materials are among the possible approaches. The last is the one followed in this book, as in two previous works which Little, Brown has published.[2] This is a book of readings on the economics of contract law that is designed to supplement the casebook in a first-year course on contracts. The selections are (with a few exceptions) nontechnical, and no previous acquaintance with economics is assumed on the part of the reader.

Although the book is intended primarily for law-school instruction, we hope it will also find an audience among economists, philosophers, and others interested in the social role of contract.[3] While all of the principal readings have previously appeared elsewhere, the introduction and the notes at the end of each chapter add to the literature on the economics of contract law in some respects.

We are indebted to our colleagues Richard A. Epstein, Gareth Jones, William M. Landes, and Antonin Scalia for suggestions, to Donna Patterson and Sharon Wallace for research, editorial, and

1. See Richard A. Posner, Economic Analysis of Law (2d ed. 1977), and references cited there.

2. Economic Foundations of Property Law (Bruce A. Ackerman ed. 1975), and Perspectives on Tort Law (Robert Rabin ed. 1976). The latter book is not limited to, but is heavily weighted toward, economic analysis of tort law.

3. In particular, economists interested in comparing contract with other methods of economic organization (such as regulation and vertical integration) may benefit from a greater familiarity with the law and economics of the contract process. See Note 10, p. 39 infra.

clerical assistance, and to the Law and Economics Program at the University of Chicago Law School for financial assistance.[4]

Anthony T. Kronman
Richard A. Posner

June 1978

4. Editorial note: Deletions from the original text are indicated in the usual way, except that some subheadings have been deleted or renumbered without indication. Deletions of footnotes are not indicated, and remaining footnotes have been renumbered. Footnotes added by the editors are bracketed.

The Economics of Contract Law

Chapter 1

Introduction: Economic Theory and Contract Law

The law of contracts regulates, among other kinds of transactions, the purchase and sale of goods (including real estate) and services. Since buying and selling—and related transactions, such as leasing and borrowing, which are also governed by contract law—are quintessentially economic activities, it would seem that economics should have something useful to say to students of contract law. For example, economics may be able to tell us why people make contracts and how contract law can facilitate the operation of markets. And to the extent that contract doctrines reflect judicial efforts, whether deliberate or unconscious, to achieve efficiency, economics may help toward an understanding of the meaning of the doctrines and their appropriate limits.

The essays reprinted in this book are a sample of the efforts that have been made, both by economists and by lawyers having a bent for economics, to apply economic principles to contracts and contract law. The reader will have to decide, after reading these essays, whether, as we believe, economics has a substantial contribution to make to the study of contract law. This chapter offers an overview of the economic approach to contracts and contract law and a guide to the readings.

I

The fundamental economic principle with which we begin is that if voluntary exchanges are permitted—if, in other words, a market is allowed to operate—resources will gravitate toward their most valuable uses. If *A* owns a good that is worth only $100 to him but $150 to *B*, both will be made better off by an exchange of *A*'s good for *B*'s money at any price between $100 and $150; and if they realize this, they will make the exchange. By making both of them better off, the exchange will also increase the wealth of the society (of which they are members), assuming the exchange does not reduce the welfare of nonparties more than it increases *A*'s and *B*'s welfare.[1] Before the exchange—which, let us say, takes place at a price of $125—*A* had a good worth $100 to him and *B* had $125 in cash, a total of $225. After the exchange, *A* has $125 in cash and *B* has a good worth $150 to him, a total of $275. The exchange has increased the wealth of society by $50 (ignoring, as we have done, any possible third-party effects).

The principle is the same whether we are speaking of the purchase of a string of pearls, a lawyer's time, a machine for making shoes, or an ingot of aluminum. The existence of a market—a locus of opportunities for mutually advantageous exchanges—facilitates the allocation of the good or service in question to the use in which it is most valuable, thereby maximizing the wealth of society.

This conclusion may be questioned on various grounds. For example, it may be argued that since "value" in this analysis is measured by willingness to pay, which in turn is affected by the distribution of income and wealth (one cannot offer to buy a good without having money or the means to obtain it), the maximization of value cannot be regarded as an uncontroversially proper goal for society to pursue. An introductory chapter is not the place to explore the philosophical basis of the economist's concept of value. For our purposes it is enough that the reader understand the technical meaning of the concept. The reader (assisted by some of the selections in this book)[2] can then decide whether there is any "value," in an ultimate social sense, to the *economic* concept of value which the system of free exchanges promotes.

The principle that voluntary exchange should be freely permitted in order to maximize value is frequently summarized in the concept (or slogan) of "freedom of contract." This is something of a misnomer, for the concept of *contract* typically plays an insignificant role in elucidations and critiques of the principle of voluntary exchange. Many value-maximizing exchanges occur without contracts, or with contracts so rudimentary or transitory as to have little interest for economists studying the phenomenon of voluntary exchange. If *A*

1. Many contracts have third-party effects but they are normally studied in courses in environmental law, property law, and torts rather than in courses on contract law. We shall therefore ignore them.

2. See especially Chapter 7.

buys the Chicago Tribune from *B*, a news vendor, paying 20¢ for it on the spot, this is a value-maximizing exchange; but it would be pretentious to speak of a contract between *A* and *B*, though technically there is one (if a section of the paper is missing, *A* can probably rescind the contract and get his 20¢ back). One can talk about the principle or system of voluntary exchange for quite some time before it becomes necessary to consider the role of contracts and contract law in facilitating the process.

In the newspaper example, the exchange is virtually (though not completely) instantaneous; and this provides a clue to the role of contracts in the process of voluntary exchange. It is true that, although money and good cross at the same moment, the actual *use* of the good—the reading of the newspaper—occurs after the exchange and takes some time; so really the process of exchange is not complete until the paper has been opened and inspected. Only then can the buyer be satisfied that he got what he paid for (that no pages are missing or illegible, etc.). Still, the time required to complete the exchange in the newspaper example is quite short. Where the time is long, contracts and contract law become important.

Suppose that *A* promises to build a house for *B*, construction to take six months to complete and *B* to pay either periodically or on completion. With construction so time-consuming, there is a significant likelihood that something will occur to frustrate the exchange—insolvency, changes in the price of inputs, labor troubles, etc. Nor is *A*'s performance complete when construction of the house is finished. A durable good like a house by definition yields services to the purchaser over a period of time, a long one in the case of a house; and it is these services rather than the physical structure itself that the purchaser is hoping to acquire. If the house wears out long before the purchaser reasonably believed it would, the exchange will be effectively thwarted long after nominal completion of performance by the promisor.

Economists have pointed out that the cost of an undertaking tends to be inversely related to the time allowed for completion.[3] Stated differently, it is costly to accelerate completion of a time-consuming task. It would also be costly to make goods less durable in order to compress the period in which the full exchange of the goods could be completed. These observations suggest that a system of contract rights, and not merely one of property rights, may be necessary to minimize the costs of production in a market system.

Thus far we have been attempting to elucidate the concept of a

3. See Armen A. Alchian, Costs and Outputs, in Readings in Microeconomics 159, 165 (William Breit & Harold M. Hochman eds., 2d ed. 1971).

contract and explain its economic significance. We have said nothing about the economic function of contract *law*. Its basic function is to provide a sanction for reneging, which, in the absence of sanctions, is sometimes tempting where the parties' performance is not simultaneous. During the process of an extended exchange, a point may be reached where it is in the interest (though perhaps only the very narrow, short-run interest) of one of the parties to terminate performance. If *A* agrees to build a house for *B* and *B* pays him in advance, *A* can make himself better off, at least if loss of reputation (which, depending on *A*'s particular situation, may be unimportant to him) is ignored, by pocketing *B*'s money and not building the house. The problem arises because the nonsimultaneous character of the exchange offers one of the parties a strategic advantage which he can use to obtain a transfer payment that utterly vitiates the advantages of the contract to the other party.[4] Clearly, if such conduct were permitted, people would be reluctant to enter into contracts and the process of economic exchange would be retarded.

A noninstantaneous or extended exchange creates not only strategic opportunities that parties might try to exploit in the absence of legal sanction, but also uncertainty with regard to the conditions under which performance will occur. This uncertainty exposes the parties to the risk that the costs and benefits of their exchange will turn out to be different from what they expected. An important function of contract law is to enforce the parties' agreed-upon allocation of risk.

A related function is to reduce the costs of the exchange process by supplying a standard set of risk-allocation terms for use by contracting parties. Many substantive rules of contract law are simply specifications of the consequences of some contingency for which the contract makes no express provision. If the parties are satisfied with the way in which the rule allocates the risk of that contingency, they have no need to incur the expense of writing their own risk-allocation rule into the contract.

Besides (1) imposing costs on people who try to exploit the other party to the contract by refusing to abide by its terms and (2) providing a stock of standard contractual provisions, the law of contracts (3) imposes costs on, and thereby discourages, *careless* behavior in the contracting process—behavior that unnecessarily increases the costs of the process itself. Suppose *A* promises to give *B* a boat if *B* stops smoking, *B* complies with this condition (at some cost to himself), but *A* refuses to give him the boat. *A* proves that *B* misun-

4. The parallel problem that would be created by the absence of property rights has long been known. See, e.g., William Blackstone, 2 Commentaries on the Laws of England 4, 7 (1766).

derstood him—he never meant to promise him a boat. *B* in turn proves that he was reasonably induced by *A*'s words and conduct to believe that *A* had indeed promised him the boat. If we believe that *A* did not in fact intend such a promise, then enforcement of the promise cannot be justified as necessary to prevent frustration of a value-maximizing exchange; there is no basis for presuming that an exchange will make the parties better off if one of them never intended to make it. But we may still want to enforce the contract in order to give people in *A*'s position an incentive to avoid carelessly inducing others to incur costs in reliance on the existence of a contract. This problem may seem to belong to the law of torts rather than contracts, since enforcement serves not to promote a mutually beneficial exchange but instead to deter careless behavior. But enforcement does promote the contractual process by discouraging a costly form of carelessness that would tend to impede it.

The foregoing discussion suggests a resolution along economic lines of the old dispute in contract law over whether the basis of contract formation is a "subjective" or "objective" one—whether the law requires an actual meeting of minds or whether it is enough that the parties use words or conduct that would signify agreement to an impartial observer. Only a contract that involves an actual meeting of minds satisfies the economist's definition of a value-maximizing exchange; but the economist allows a place for rules designed to prevent people from misleading others into thinking they have a contract with them; hence both the subjective and objective theories have a place in contract law.

The discussion to this point has emphasized the economic role of contract and has outlined the economic functions of contract law. It is, however, one thing to show that contract law *could* promote economic efficiency and another thing to prove that it *does*. A number of scholars in recent years have claimed that the common law, including the law of contracts, has an implicit economic logic—the purpose, or in any event the effect, of many common law doctrines is, they believe, to increase economic efficiency.[5] One of the points emphasized by those skeptical of this theory is the implausibility of supposing that judges have been able to work out the economics of legal obligations and liabilities correctly. To be sure, one observes business firms behaving "correctly" from an economic standpoint (i.e., maximizing profits by equating marginal revenue to marginal cost) without being conscious of, or at least articulate about, what they are doing. But this can be explained by the com-

5. The fullest statement of this point of view appears in Richard A. Posner, Economic Analysis of Law pt. II (2d ed. 1977). For its application to contract law see id. ch. 4.

petitive process: firms that do not maximize profits will be unable to attract capital from competing demanders and so will eventually be driven out of business. The survivors, the firms we observe, are those that pursue, whether unwittingly or deliberately, profit-maximizing strategies. But it is unclear what the mechanism is that drives judges to discover and apply correct microeconomic principles.

In the case of contract law, however, a competitive mechanism is at hand to explain why the rules of contract law might be expected to be generally efficient. As we have seen, many rules of contract law are designed simply to supply contract terms where the parties have not done so expressly. If prospective contracting parties do not like the terms supplied by contract law, normally they are free to supplant them with their own express terms. The parties will prefer efficient terms because those are the terms that minimize the costs of the transaction to them, and accordingly the tendency will be to contract around any inefficient rules of contract law.[6] The efficient rules will survive; the inefficient will be progressively ignored and eventually forgotten.

This competitive or evolutionary process is reinforced by two other factors. The first is the willingness of the courts to honor the parties' designation of the law to be applied to resolve any dispute arising from a contract between them.[7] The second is the right of contracting parties to agree to submit any disputes arising out of the contract to a private arbitrator. Because of these factors, courts that apply inefficient rules of contract law will tend to lose cases to tribunals that apply efficient rules. Even if a court system does not "mind" losing contract business, one will observe a body of cases heavily concentrated in tribunals that apply efficient rules.

The foregoing discussion does not, of course, prove that the

6. This is an application of the famous "Coase theorem"—that given zero transaction costs, the law's assignment of rights or liabilities will not affect efficiency. See Ronald H. Coase, The Problem of Social Cost, 3 J. Law & Econ. 1 (1960). The costs of contracting around an inefficient contract doctrine are not zero, but are probably low enough to permit the Coase theorem to apply, at least approximately, to contract law.

Coase's article, and economists generally, emphasize large numbers of parties as one source of high transaction costs, as in the typical pollution case. From here it is easy, but incorrect, to jump to the conclusion that where only two parties are involved, as in the ordinary contracting situation, the transaction costs must be so low that contract law "can't matter" from an economic standpoint. While it is true that legal doctrines stipulating contractual terms that the parties are free to waive, or to offset by a change in price or in some other contract term, probably do not have significant long-run economic effects on the exchange process, they do affect the costs of the process; moreover, to provide no legal sanction at all for breach of contract could, as suggested in the text, distort the exchange process substantially.

7. See American Law Institute, Restatement of Law Second, Conflict of Laws §§186-188 (1968).

rules of contract law are efficient; it simply makes the idea a bit less shocking. It should be noted, however, that the relevance of economics to contract law does not depend on proving that the logic of that law is economics. Since efficiency is an important value in our society (we need not decide here how important), a critique of contract law based on efficiency is a potentially powerful tool of legal reform.

II

Having sketched the general nature of the economic approach to contracts and contract law, we shall now indicate the areas covered by the readings in this book. The aim in Chapter 2 is to give the reader some idea of the economic functions of contracts in general. In searching for items to include in Chapter 2, we were struck by the paucity of economic writings on contracts.[8] The near absence, until very recently, of an economic literature on contracts seems surprising given the centrality of exchange in the economic analysis of markets—not to mention the large polemical as well as scientific literature on freedom of contract. But as we have pointed out, exchange and contract are not synonymous concepts. When economists speak of free exchange or freedom of contract they are speaking of a system of transferable property rights. They are not interested in the mechanics of the process of exchange when a durable good or service is involved, yet it is those mechanics that are the concern of contract and contract law.

With Chapter 3, we turn to the substantive rules of contract law itself, beginning with the doctrine of consideration. At first glance, the requirement that a promise, to be enforceable, must be supported by consideration may seem an obvious corollary of the exchange function of contract—if no exchange is contemplated, what could be the economic basis for enforcing a promise? However, at

8. There are two exceptions to this generalization. One is the literature on the choice among contract, firm, and regulation as methods of resource allocation and, relatedly, on the problems of shirking, monitoring, and enforcement created by particular types of contract such as sharecropping contracts and long-term contracts. Although this is an important literature, it is more germane to the study of industrial organization than to the study of contract law, in part because it assumes rather than analyzes the legal framework. A flavor of the literature is given in the Coase excerpt in Chapter 2, and additional discussion and references appear in the Notes and Questions at the end of the chapter. The second exception is a growing literature on specialized contracts, especially insurance contracts. For a recent example see Milton Harris & Artur Raviv, Some Results on Incentive Contracts with Applications to Education and Employment, Health Insurance, and Law Enforcement, 68 Am. Econ. Rev. 20 (1978). This literature also does not focus on the problems of interpretation and legal enforcement that are central to the economic analysis of contract law.

second glance, it becomes evident that even completely gratuitous promises can increase value—indeed, that they would not be made otherwise. This makes the economic role of consideration problematic. Fuller in his paper offers a mixture of economic and paternalistic reasons for the doctrine; Posner takes issue with the latter reasons. Chapter 3 also addresses the economic basis for the enforceability of unilateral contracts and of promises implied in law.

Chapter 4 considers the defense of duress and its modern extension, unconscionability. The notion of inequality of bargaining power, which underlies the concept of unconscionability, is an economic one which scholars such as Professor Goldberg have used to challenge the traditional view that, in the absence of fraud or duress (in the sense of physical threat or the equivalent), a bargain between adults represents a value-enhancing exchange. Economic thinking has also been used, by Coase and Epstein among others, to criticize the inequality-of-bargaining-power argument and to attempt to rehabilitate the traditional legal position. Chapter 4 attempts to convey the flavor of this debate.

Chapter 5 asks whether the defenses of mistake (mutual or unilateral) and impossibility represent merely sympathetic judicial responses to the plight of individual promisors tripped up by unforeseen contingencies that prevent performance on the anticipated terms, or whether they represent economically motivated, or at least economically intelligible, implied terms in contracts involving significant uncertainties. This area of contract law has some of the most colorful cases in the contracts repertoire, ranging from Sherwood v. Walker (the case of the pregnant cow, Rose 2d of Aberlone) to the pending Westinghouse uranium case, one of the largest contract cases in history; both cases are discussed in Chapter 5.

The coverage of substantive contract doctrine in Chapters 3-5 is incomplete. Among the important topics omitted entirely are the Statute of Frauds, the doctrine of conditions, third-party beneficiaries, and assignments. Other important doctrines are touched on only lightly. The resulting unevenness of coverage reflects the state of the economic literature. Perhaps this book will stimulate economic research in the neglected areas.

Chapter 6 takes up remedies, an area where the economic literature is especially rich. John Barton's pathbreaking article sets forth an economic model of contract damages and examines the conformity of the law to the model. Priest's article on rejection of nonconforming goods, in a similar vein, asks whether the legal rules governing rejection conform to economic theory; like Barton, he finds the answer to be generally "yes." Other questions addressed by the papers in this chapter include the insufficiency of simple damages to assure performance, the role of specific performance, and the desirability of enforcing penalty clauses. The picture which emerges from the chapter is one of impressive congruence between law and economics in some areas of contract remedy law and puzzling discrepancies in others.

Chapter 7 attempts to place the economic analysis of contract law in a broader, more philosophical perspective than that of the earlier chapters. The idea of freedom of contract as embodied in contract law itself is the focus of this chapter, and a variety of contrasting viewpoints is presented. In a note on paternalism the editors take a stab at identifying those areas in contract law where paternalism has displaced efficiency as the force shaping the development of doctrine.

This reader will have served its purpose if it persuades the student (and teacher) of contract law that the economic perspective on contract law can broaden the lawyer's intellectual and professional horizons by placing recurrent questions of law and social policy in a different and interesting light.

Chapter 2

The Economic Basis of Contracts

*Leviathan**

Thomas Hobbes

The mutual transferring of Right, is that which men call CONTRACT.

There is difference, between transferring of Right to the Thing; and transferring, or tradition, that is, delivery of the Thing itself. For the Thing may be delivered together with the Translation of the Right; as in buying and selling with ready money; or exchange of goods, or lands: and it may be delivered some time after.

Again, one of the Contractors, may deliver the Thing contracted for on his part, and leave the other to perform his part at some determinate time after, and in the mean time be trusted; and then the Contract on his part, is called PACT, or COVENANT: Or both parts may contract now, to perform hereafter: in which cases, he that is to perform in time to come, being trusted, his performance is called *Keeping of Promise*, or Faith; and the failing of performance (if it be voluntary) *Violation of Faith*. . . .

If a Covenant be made, wherein neither of the parties perform presently, but trust one another; in the condition of mere Nature, (which is a condition of War of every man against every man), upon any reasonable suspicion, it is Void: But if there be a common Power set over them both, with right and force sufficient to compell performance; it is not Void. For he that performeth first, has no assurance the other will perform after; because the bonds of words are too weak to bridle men's ambition, avarice, anger, and other Passions, with-

*Reprinted from Chapter 14, pp. 192-196, of the Blackwell edition.

out the fear of some coercive Power; which in the condition of mere Nature, where all men are equal, and judges of the justness of their own fears cannot possibly be supposed. And therefore he which performeth first, does but betray himself to his enemy; contrary to the Right (he can never abandon) of defending his life, and means of living.

But in a civil estate, where there is a Power set up to constrain those that would otherwise violate their faith, that fear is no more reasonable; and for that cause, he which by the Covenant is to perform first, is obliged so to do.

*A Theory of Contract Choice and the California Gold Rush**

John Umbeck

I. Theory

Assume that a number of wealth-maximizing individuals are placed on a limited quantity of land which contains the scarce resource gold. The gold is distributed randomly throughout and can be acquired only by adding labor effort to land—an input which is related to the final output through a linear homogeneous production function.[1] However, there is no government or state to assign exclusive ownership rights to the gold-bearing land. If the individuals, each of whom is trying to acquire as much land as possible, are to avoid violent conflicts, they must agree, through contract, upon how the land or gold will be divided. By assumption, these agreements are limited to two alternatives: a sharing contract or a land allotment contract.

Under the sharing contract, a group of miners would agree not to fight among themselves for the rights to mine gold. Instead, they would claim, as a group, a certain amount of land from which nongroup members would be excluded. Within the group, no individual has the right to exclude another member from any of the gold-bearing land. Each miner agrees to work a certain number of hours out of each production period. At the end of this period, all of the individual's gold is placed in a common pool where it is measured and then divided up among all members according to an agreed-upon formula. The contract further provides that the group

*Reprinted from 20 J. Law & Econ. 421 (1978), with permission. Copyright © 1978 by the University of Chicago Law School.

1. [That is, there are no economies of scale in production.]

will punish anyone found guilty of violating the terms of the agreement.

Under the land allotment contract, a group of miners would claim a certain amount of land from which nongroup members would be excluded. However, unlike the sharing arrangement, each individual is alloted a particular piece of this land. This alloted land becomes private property and, as such, the individual owner can exclude all other miners, including members of the contracting group. Each miner works his own land with as much labor as he chooses to supply and keeps for himself all the gold he finds. Violators of the contractual provisions will be punished by the group.

Regardless of their choice of contract, individuals claiming exclusive rights to scarce resources will incur costs in keeping others from stealing this property. There is little reason to suppose that the costs of excluding outsiders will vary significantly with the contract choice; however, stealing among group members is a different matter.

In the land allotment contract, each person is given a measured amount of land to work for himself. If anyone violates that agreement and trespasses on another's property, it can be determined at a relatively low cost, as the trespasser is observed to be within the boundary markers of another person's land. On the other hand, under the sharing agreement each individual has a right to a share of the final product produced by everyone else. The costs of enforcing these rights will depend on the characteristics of the good itself. For example, if the good is small it will be relatively easy to conceal and avoid sharing, thereby raising the costs of enforcing the contract. Similarly, the more valuable the good, the greater is the gain from the avoidance of sharing and the greater the costs of enforcement. In the mining example, even small quantities of gold would be of significant value and easily concealed, thus making the costs of sharing enforcement relatively high when compared to the alternative allotment contract.

On the basis of the above discussion alone, I would conclude that the costs of the sharing contract would probably exceed the costs of the land allotment contract in the gold mining case. [This conclusion is reinforced by the fact that] the sharing contract has one additional cost which the land allotment contract does not have. . . . [U]nder the sharing contract, some resources will have to be allocated to enforcing the work requirement. Under the land allotment scheme this cost does not exist at all since each miner keeps one hundred per cent of the gold he finds.

If the costs of the share contract are greater than the costs of the land allotment contract, cost minimization dictates that the latter will always be chosen. So why use the sharing contract? In the mining example, assume that the gold is not distributed evenly throughout the land claimed by the contracting group. Two individuals working their own piece of land under the allotment contract could experience significantly different income streams. By sharing the actual gold yield, the average expected income per miner would not change but the variance would be reduced. If miners prefer a lower to a higher income variance, given the same average, and if contracting costs were the same under both arrangements, then a share contract would always be chosen.

In choosing between these two contracts, both the variance in income and the costs of contracting must be considered. To be more explicit, *in choosing between contracts, each individual will attempt to minimize the variance in his income subject to the constraint of contracting costs.*

This hypothesis becomes refutable when the effect of some observable variable on either income or contracting costs can be determined. [For example, as] the population in a contracting group increases, the differences between the costs associated with the two contractual forms will increase, thereby leading to a reduction in the observed incidence of sharing contracts. . . .

It is in the area of enforcement that the population increase will have significantly different effects on the rate of change in the individual's contracting costs. Notice that under the land allotment contract each individual will have more potential trespassers to exclude from his property. This cost increase will be offset, at least partially, by two factors: the individual will have less land area to defend, thus reducing his total enforcement costs and, having less land, his property is a less valuable theft target to potential trespassers. Even with these offsetting factors, I expect that there will be some increase in the costs of enforcing an individual's property rights to land. However, I do not expect that it will be as great an increase as that associated with the sharing contract. In the sharing agreement, each miner has rights to a share of the gold found by everyone else. As the population increases, there are more miners to be watched, and the cost of enforcing these rights will probably rise. This cost increase will not be offset by a decline in the value of the good being stolen as in the case of the land allotment contract. To the contrary, the incentive to steal by concealing the gold discovery will increase with the population. . . .

II. Evidence

Prior to the year 1846, the land we now call California was governed by Mexican laws and customs. Most of the country was uninhabited and an individual could acquire rights to a tract of land merely by filing a request, along with a rough map showing location and boundaries, with the local government representative. Mexican authority came to an end when President Polk declared war and American troops occupied California. The land was under military rule from 1846 until 1848 when the Treaty of Peace, Friendship, Limits and Settlement, between the United States and the Mexican Republic, ended the war. According to this treaty all Mexican laws not in conflict with the Constitution of the United States were to be continued in force. All nonprivately owned land, and this included all of the gold-mining areas, became the property of the United States Federal Government, which at this time *had no law regulating the acquisition of privately owned mining rights in federal lands.*

On January 24, 1848, just nine days before the signing of the peace treaty, gold was discovered on the American River near the present site of Sacramento. It was probably in response to this discovery and the uncertain legal position on California mineral lands that led to the following decree by the military governor, Colonel Mason: "From and after this date, the Mexican laws and customs now prevailing in California relative to the acquisition of mining rights on public lands are hereby abolished." Colonel Mason offered no alternative legal system by which private property rights to mineral lands could be obtained. With Mexican laws abolished and no federal, state, or territorial law to replace it, California mineral lands remained the property of the United States Government. All individuals who claimed private mining rights were trespassers.

Had there been a legal framework to regulate private mining rights, it is doubtful that it could have been enforced. Reportedly, before the gold discovery, there were 1,059 soldiers in California. Shortly after, this number was reduced to about 660, primarily by desertion. . . .

While all California gold land legally belonged to the federal government, it appears that there was no economical mechanism with which to enforce their exclusive rights. Gold-bearing land was, for all practical purposes, a nonexclusive resource.

Contrary to the television westerns which claim to depict this period of American history, the reported incidence of violence in the California gold fields was remarkably low. Instead of fighting over the rights to mineral land, the miners entered into contractual arrangements which assigned mining rights in an orderly and . . . predictable fashion. These contracts took one of two general forms: land allotment and sharing. The gold land which was claimed as exclusive property by the group of contracting miners was called a "mining district," and between 1848 and 1866 it is estimated that over 500 separate districts were organized, ranging in population from four individuals to 8,000. . . .

Around the pan-and-cradle technology, the first contracts emerged in early 1848. With rare exception they took a form of sharing. Typically, the groups, ranging in size from two to eight, would agree to work a certain number of hours per day at one or more of the various mining operations; hauling dirt or water, rocking the cradle, and so forth. At the end of the day, the total gold yield was measured and divided evenly among the members. The contracts allowed for one exception to the sharing rule. Any nugget weighing more than one-half ounce that was found before it went into the cradle belonged to the discoverer. . . .

The observed variance in the actual gold yield of any given piece of land was significant. It is not unusual to read accounts of one group averaging over one hundred dollars a day per man, while their neighbors averaged only three or four dollars over the same time period. The costs of reducing this variance by sharing were apparently not too high within the small groups which were formed during 1848. With rare exception, sharing was the only contract form chosen. I can find no evidence that the land allotment contract appeared prior to the summer of 1849. . . .

Judging from the observed behavior of the California miners throughout 1848 and the first part of 1849, the sharing contract worked quite well. As long as gold land was relatively abundant, a small group of individuals could maintain exclusive rights to a piece of land and enforce the sharing arrangement at a nonprohibitive cost. However, when the group size exceeded about sixteen members, this contractual form ran into difficulties.

By the summer of 1849, the tremendous influx of miners was having an impact in the mining districts. Because there was little offsetting increase in the size of the gold fields, it was not unusual to read reports of hundreds or even thousands of newcomers converging on a river bank where previously there had been only four or five miners. Of course, the original miners had alternatives. They could have tried to maintain exclusive rights by keeping away all outsiders. At odds of one hundred or more to one, their chances of success approached zero. They could have left the area in search of other rich deposits, but these were becoming increasingly scarce. Or, they could admit some of the outsiders until their numbers were large enough to successfully defend their rights against future claimants. Survival in the gold fields dictated the latter choice, and group size increased.

With an increase in group size, the use of the sharing contract as a means of assigning rights to mine gold encountered difficulties. As predicted, the sharing arrangement was replaced by the land allotment contract. Each individual group member was given a particular piece of land, or "claim," along with the rights to all the gold it contained. . . .

*Game Theory and Contract Law**

Robert L. Birmingham

I. The Prisoner's Dilemma

Assume two individuals, 1 and 2, have robbed a bank. They have been apprehended by the police and isolated in separate cells. The district attorney tells each that although he is certain of their guilt he has insufficient evidence to convict them of robbery. He asserts, however, that even without further information he will be able to secure their conviction on a lesser charge carrying a penalty of imprisonment for one year. He urges each of the prisoners to confess, promising that if one cooperates and the other remains silent, he will escape punishment, while his recalcitrant partner will be incarcerated for ten years. If both confess, each will receive a sentence of six years. 1 and 2 accept the accuracy of this outline of possible consequences and must decide whether to confess.

	a_2	b_2
a_1	(1, 1)	(−2, 2)
b_1	(2, −2)	(−1, −1)

Figure 1

Results of choices which confront the prisoners are depicted in figure 1. The first and second numbers in each set of parentheses measure on an ordinal scale the worth or utility of designated outcomes to 1 and 2 respectively. An ordinal scale is one which "allows only the determination of the rank of a set of objects, but not the 'distances' between them." Following Bentham, we may define "utility" as "that property in any object, whereby it tends to produce benefit, advantage, pleasure, good, or happiness (all this in the

*Reprinted from Robert L. Birmingham, Legal and Moral Duty in Game Theory: Common Law Contract and Chinese Analogies, 18 Buffalo L. Rev. 99, 103-110 (1969), with permission.

present case comes to the same thing)." The values of solutions to each individual is here assumed to vary inversely with the length of the prison sentence imposed on him.

By choosing a_1 (remaining silent) or b_1 (confessing) player 1 can select the outcomes of either the first row or the second row. Similarly 2 can choose between the first and second columns. For example, joint silence yields a utility of 1 to each prisoner, which can be determined from the upper left set of solutions.

Since $2 > 1 > -1 > -2$, individual 1 will prefer the outcome at the lower left. The upper left is more desirable to him than the lower right, while the upper right is least satisfactory. Outcomes may be similarly ranked in order of decreasing desirability to individual 2: upper right, upper left, lower right, lower left.

Obviously each prisoner can maximize his own well-being through confession. Assume that player 1 chooses to confess. Then, if player 2 remains silent, 1's choice yields to him a utility of 2, greater than the level 1 which he could obtain through silence. On the other hand, if player 2 confesses, player 1's confession gives a utility of -1, rather than the -2 which 1 would obtain if he had remained silent. Player 2 faces a similar outcome pattern.

Thus, each prisoner, acting rationally, will confess. Their joint confessions will dictate the outcome in the lower right corner, a utility of -1 to each. If both had remained silent, each would have obtained a utility of 1. Rational decision paradoxically results in incarceration of each prisoner for five more years than would be necessary if both had irrationally remained silent.

A generalization of the example of the preceding section is shown in figure 2, where unidentified letters replace the more specific values of figure 1. So long as

$$s < p < r < t$$

for each player, rational behavior will induce equilibrium at the lower right values. A Pareto Optimum is a set of imputations such that it is impossible to increase the utility of any one individual without reducing the utility of some other. All outcomes except that resulting from the anticipated independent decisions of the players are Pareto optimal. . . .

	a_2	b_2
a_1	(r_1, r_2)	(s_1, t_2)
b_1	(t_1, s_2)	(p_1, p_2)

Figure 2

. . . II. Contract and Promise

The law of contract may be viewed as a means of resolving a class of situations involving the Prisoner's Dilemma. We may reinterpret figures 1 and 2 to illustrate a choice between acceptance and refusal of the obligations of an agreement.

Generally, both the individual and his community profit from the honoring of at least certain types of promises:

> Now, as much of the business of human life turns or moves upon conventions, frequent disappointments of those expectations which conventions naturally excite, would render human society a scene of baffled hopes, and of thwarted projects and labours. To prevent disappointments of such expectations, is therefore a main object of the legal and moral rules whose direct and appropriate purpose is the enforcement of pacts or agreements.[1]

Let a_1 and a_2 in the figures represent decisions to form and fulfill an agreement. Then b_1 and b_2 would stand for refusal either to enter into an agreement or to honor an obligation already undertaken. The benefit to the parties of making and carrying out a set of promises rather than not establishing the relationship is thus the difference between the utilities of the upper left and lower right solutions.

That each player prefer the former to the latter outcome is a necessary condition for agreement. Even after promises are exchanged, moreover, discovery that both will lose from the transaction will motivate rescission. Difficulties arise because in the absence of legal or moral sanctions one party will frequently find advantage in breach of an agreement honored by the other. It is likely, in other words, that either player 1 or player 2 can gain by selection of alternative "*b*" if the other can be persuaded to adhere to alternative "*a*." Such action would induce either the upper right or the lower left outcomes. Since these are least satisfactory to the player honoring his promise, under these conditions one would expect either no agreement or violation by both parties. The equilibrium solution is thus the lower right, although both players would prefer the upper left outcomes in any situation where agreement would occur if the upper right and lower left alternatives were excluded.

The function of the law of contract is simply to make possible equilibrium at a_1a_2 by rendering outcomes b_1a_2 and a_1b_2 unattractive to players 1 and 2 respectively. . . .

Occasionally the undesirable solutions b_1a_2 and a_1b_2 are excluded directly through requiring specific performance of contractual obligations. Such relief is at least in theory broadly available in civil law

1. J. Austin, Lectures on Jurisprudence 299-300 (2d ed. 1861).

jurisdictions. Generally, however, the common law seeks not to eliminate these undesirable outcomes but to compensate the player choosing solution "*a*" for the loss which would otherwise result from selection of "*b*" by his partner:

> The duty to keep a contract at common law means a prediction that you must pay damages if you do not keep it—and nothing else. If you commit a tort, you are liable to pay a compensatory sum. If you commit a contract, you are liable to pay a compensatory sum unless the promised event comes to pass. . . .[2]

Such a remedy may not only protect the innocent player when a contract is breached, but may also prevent breach by reducing the attractiveness of repudiation to the dishonoring party.

Both common law and civil law courts normally protect the expectation interest of an obligee: "In awarding compensatory damages, the effort is made to put the injured party in as good a position as that in which he would have been put by full performance of the contract. . . ." At times, however, the Anglo-American remedy protects only the reliance interest by restoring the innocent party to his position prior to contracting rather than placing him where he would be if the contract had been fulfilled. French law appears similarly variable: "It would be surprising if French judges did not, in practice, consider the reliance measure more appropriate in certain circumstances than the expectancy measure." In German law recovery is limited to the reliance interest where there is error, unauthorized agency, certain types of initial impossibility of performance, and certain types of statutory prohibition.

The impact of damage remedies may be readily assessed. Let the numbers of figure 1 represent cardinal values, for instance, dollars. Protection of the expectation interests of the parties entails assurance that each will receive the benefit of his bargain even if the other does not fulfill his obligations. In our illustration, therefore, adherence to choice "*a*" guarantees the adhering player a gain of 1 if a contract is initially formed. Combined actions a_1b_2 and b_1a_2 yield a joint product of 0. Since players 1 and 2 must obtain 1 in the first and second of these situations respectively, the breaching party receives only −1. Legal controls thus transform the game of figure 1 in the manner shown in figure 3. Choice "*a*" is now clearly advantageous to each participant; the new equilibrium solution entails formation and performance of the contract. The outcomes no longer conform to the Prisoner's Dilemma pattern. Figure 4 restates these results in terms of the more general symbols of figure 2.

The effect of protection of the reliance interest on the game of

2. Holmes, The Path of the Law, 10 Harv. L. Rev. 457, 462 (1897).

	a_2	b_2
a_1	$(1,\ 1)$	$(-2,\ 2)$
b_1	$(2,\ -2)$	$(-1,\ -1)$

$\longrightarrow$

	a_2	b_2
a_1	$(1,\ 1)$	$(1,\ -1)$
b_1	$(-1,\ 1)$	$(-1,\ -1)$

Figure 3

	a_2	b_2
a_1	$(r_1,\ r_2)$	$(s_1,\ t_2)$
b_1	$(t_1,\ s_2)$	$(p_1,\ p_2)$

$\longrightarrow$

	a_2	b_2
a_1	$(r_1,\ r_2)$	$(r_1,\ t_2 + s_1 - r_1)$
b_1	$(t_1 + s_2 - r_2,\ r_2)$	$(p_1,\ p_2)$

Figure 4

figure 1 is illustrated in figure 5. Here legal controls assure each party that breach by the other will not leave him in a position less satisfactory than that he would have occupied if he had not contracted. Player 1 when a_1b_2 is selected and player 2 when b_1a_2 is selected are therefore guaranteed a return of -1. Since the amount to be divided among them remains 0, the breaching party obtains 1. In this example the satisfaction of each player is independent of his actions. Given initial agreement, presumably each solution is equally probable.

	a_2	b_2
a_1	$(1,\ 1)$	$(-2,\ 2)$
b_1	$(2,\ -2)$	$(-1,\ -1)$

$\longrightarrow$

	a_2	b_2
a_1	$(1,\ 1)$	$(-1,\ 1)$
b_1	$(1,\ -1)$	$(-1,\ -1)$

Figure 5

	a_2	b_2
a_1	$(r_1,\ r_2)$	$(s_1,\ t_2)$
b_1	$(t_1,\ s_2)$	$(p_1,\ p_2)$

$\longrightarrow$

	a_2	b_2
a_1	$(r_1,\ r_2)$	$(p_1,\ t_2 + s_1 - p_1)$
b_1	$(t_1 + s_2 - p_2,\ p_2)$	$(p_1,\ p_2)$

Figure 6

These results are generalized in figure 6. It is obvious that effectiveness of protection of the reliance interest in assuring fulfillment of contractual obligations requires that:

$$r_1 > t_1 + s_2 - p_2$$
$$r_2 > t_2 + s_1 - p_1.$$

Breach will be avoided, in other words, so long as legal sanctions cause loss to a party violating his agreement.

Parallel conditions are applicable where the expectation interest is protected:

$$r_1 > t_1 + s_2 - r_2$$
$$r_2 > t_2 + s_1 - r_1.$$

Here the constraints are trivial. The inequalities may be rewritten as follows:

$$r_1 + r_2 > t_1 + s_2$$
$$r_1 + r_2 > s_1 + t_2$$

thus the breaching party will lose unless the sum of the gains to both players is increased by his actions. This would violate the assumptions underlying figure 2. If it is nevertheless possible, the parties would find advantage in revising the contract to permit such nonfulfillment.

Ineffectiveness of the legal sanction may be much more frequent where only the reliance interest is safeguarded. The marginal case is illustrated by the game of figure 5, where

$$r_1 = t_1 + s_2 - p_2$$
$$r_2 = t_2 + s_1 - p_1.$$

Any increase in r_1, r_2, p_1, or p_2 or any decrease in s_1, s_2, t_1, or t_2 would induce breach of contract by at least one player. Nevertheless $r_1 + r_2$ is significantly larger than either $t_1 + s_2$ or $s_1 + t_2$.

The possibility that the reliance measure will prove more advantageous to the innocent party is unrealistically precluded in our model by neglect of uncertainty: if r were not greater than p for each player, agreement would not occur.

Morris and Felix Cohen have stated: " 'The law of contract,' as Pollock and Maitland warned us, has, on occasion, 'threatened to swallow up all public law. . . .' Certainly there are few legal transactions that have not, at one time or another, been treated on a contract basis." The Prisoner's Dilemma principle is similarly relevant to a profusion of problems of legal theory. It has been most frequently applied in analysis of economic organization. Much basic antitrust legislation, for example, may be viewed as promoting efficiency by preventing concerns from establishing agreements permitting movement from lower right to upper left solutions. Statutes encouraging joint action by workers or establishing controls over farm output, on the other hand, are designed to facilitate achievement of equilibrium at the upper left by groups so large that unaided coordination is difficult. Prisoner's Dilemma patterns may be interpreted as explaining law in general if one adopts the analytically productive fiction of the social contract.

*The Logic of the Law**

Gordon Tullock

A simple contract involves a promise by *A* to do something tomorrow in return for *B's* doing something today. A promise, however, can be broken. Would it be sensible to favor the establishment of a system for enforcing selected promises? Simply from [the] assumption that the individual will choose to extend his range of choice, it follows that it would. If confronted with the choice between situation *A*, in which promises are not "enforced" and situation *B* in which promises may either be "enforced" or not, as the maker chooses, it would be rational to take the latter. It does not, after all, compel you to make enforceable promises, it only makes it possible. Situation *A*, on the other hand, limits you to unenforceable promises. Situation *B* is, of course, the existing law.

The fact that most legal codes permit the making of unenforceable promises is, for some reason, normally overlooked in discussions of the law. Since courts are largely engaged in dealing with enforceable contracts, the fact that not all promises are enforceable at law or in equity tends to be ignored. In fact, it is very easy to make an unenforceable promise. It seems likely that most promises that are made in day-to-day life are lacking in the technical characteristics that would give a court power to enforce them. If a promise might be enforceable, a simple statement that it is not to be legally binding will normally make it unenforceable.

Thus we have demonstrated that people should favor the establishment of a mechanism to make it possible for them to make enforceable promises. It is clear that situations in which making such an enforceable promise is desirable are fairly frequent. I wish to buy a house and do not have enough money to do so. Borrowing the money will improve my satisfaction, but in order to borrow I have to convince the lender that I will repay. Perhaps I can get away with an unenforceable promise, but for most people such loans are only possible if there is some mechanism to enforce the repayment. . . .

The possibility of erroneous court decisions must be taken into account in any discussion of the desirability of "enforcing" contracts. Someone must decide that the contract has been violated and take steps to enforce it. If that "someone" should be prone to frequent mistakes, then this fact must be taken into account when deciding whether or not contracts should be "enforced," and the extent to

*Reprinted by permission from The Logic of the Law by Gordon Tullock, pp. 35-47 (1971).

which that enforcement should be carried. Since judges are human, they will always make mistakes, although the number of these mistakes may possibly be reduced. What effect will this have on the desirability of making "enforcements" of contracts possible?

We can distinguish two main classes of error into which judges may fall in "enforcing" contracts. They may negatively fail to enforce a clause of a contract, or (positively) they may enforce a nonexistent clause. Thus, suppose *A* pays *B* a sum of money for some future act by *B*, and *B* refuses to carry out his promise. *A* goes to court and the court errs by agreeing with *B* that he has no legal liability. This is a negative error. For an example of a positive error, assume that *A* demands that *B* perform some additional act not provided for in the contract. The court errs by ordering *B* to carry out his nonexistent contractual obligation. Placed in this schematic form, these errors do not seem very likely. In fact, of course, contracts may be almost impossibly involved and the occurrence of errors is certain. Simple cases are likely to be decided correctly, but not all cases are simple. . . .

Suppose that I contract with a builder to add an extension to my house. After agreement on the plans and formal signature of the contract, a flood sweeps the town and, in addition to doing other damage, it destroys my house. On re-examining the architectural drawings, I realize that by simply closing off the end of the "addition," which would normally face my house with a few sheets of plywood, I will have housing that will serve to at least keep me warm until my house is rebuilt. I, therefore, appear in court and ask that the builder be forced to proceed with the contract. As a result of the flood, the builder, on the other hand, faces much higher costs because of the shortage of labor and materials, the changes of the topography of the site, the unavoidable delay in starting; hence, he can only finish by the contract date through the use of expensive overtime labor. He has also lost his own machinery in the flood and will have to buy or rent the necessary equipment.

He, therefore, argues that the contract called for the construction of an "addition," and that there is now nothing to be added to. I argue that I want him to produce the structure shown in the architect's drawings, and that the fact that there is now no longer a building located directly adjacent is irrelevant. Obviously, the judge is presented with a difficult problem. The two parties certainly were not thinking about the flood when they entered into the original contract. There are no specific provisions in the contract that clearly cover the problem in dispute.

Any decision of the court will contain an element of arbitrariness, and it would be more or less impossible to say that any decision was, in the eyes of God, right or wrong. The court must somehow or other supplement the original contract. For this purpose it is likely, in the real world, to turn to some general rule for such cases. The rule chosen would depend mainly upon the nationality of the court. Let us, however, examine some of the possible rules.

The simplest rule would be to flip a coin, and there is an element of this in all other rules. No modern legal system, however, openly adopts this expedient. A second rule would be to say that if the contract did not directly refer to the circumstances that arose, it has no present effect. This would lead the court to give a decision in favor of the defendant. In this particular case, such an outcome does not seem to be bad, but in most cases of this sort the difference between the situation that actually occurred and the one anticipated by the parties at the time the contract was signed is less extreme. Invalidating the contract because there is some minor difference does not seem very sensible.

A third possibility is to try to get some hint from the contract itself as to what the parties would have decided if the flood came (if they had any thought of it when they were making the original contract). Technically, this is "resolution by analogy." Thus, if the contract contained a provision canceling the entire arrangement if the house burned down, it would seem reasonable to assume that the parties would have put in a similar clause regarding floods if they had thought of it. Here again, we would get a decision for the defendant. Again, however, the relative ease of such a decision is a result of the simplicity of the case. Normally, no clause is as close to the contingency that actually occurs as fire is to flood. Courts trying to apply this general approach are frequently driven into the most extreme contortions in their attempts to find something in the contract that can be extended to cover the new situation.

A fourth possibility would be to try to find other evidence of the parties' intent. If, for example, in looking over the diagrams, I had said, "Gee, if the house burned down, I could actually live in the addition," and the contractor had replied, "You sure could," it would seem likely that the court would decide to force the contractor to build the addition. Once again, however, there is normally no such clear evidence of intent. Lastly, the rule actually followed by most courts in the world is simply to apply general legal norms to the matter. Stated more simply, this approach assumes that the written contract between the two parties is only a part of their agreement. A body of legal decisions, statutes, and codes that provides a set of rules for what should be done in cases where there are no specific provisions in the contract will be in existence. Thus, the court assumes that the contract was drawn up with the parties in actual, if not express, agreement that in any contingency not specifically covered by the contract, the rules provided by law will apply.

This approach also has the drawback that the contingency that arises may not be at all clearly covered by the existing laws. Thus, here again considerable contortions may be necessary to apply the procedure. The problem, however, is not as significant with this general approach. The contracting parties to the innumerable contracts that do exist tend to forget somewhat the same possible contingencies, with the result that rules originally developed for contracts of the past may very well fit. This procedure, of course, relieves the court from having to make up its mind on a difficult problem, which probably accounts for its popularity with judges.

Another advantage of this way of interpreting contracts when there is nothing in the text covering a contingency that has arisen is that it permits great economies in drawing up the contracts. The law of bills and notes, for example, is an extremely elaborate set of rules that fills many volumes. The contracts with which these rules deal may well take the form of one or two sentences printed on one side of a small piece of paper. If it were necessary to put into the actual contract all of the conditions that the law implies, no bill would be less than 100 pages long. Thus, the present situation provides a simple and quick contract, but it also provides definite rules that in effect elaborate that quick contract into a lengthy and complicated one. . . .

[Let us now consider] the amount of detail that the contracting parties should put into their contract in a situation in which everything that they clearly express in the contract will be carried out; those things that the contract clearly does not cover but in fact occur are dealt with in a stochastic manner that we may represent by the image of the flipped coin, and those issues that are related to the language but are not clearly covered by it will be dealt with by a mixture of certain and stochastic elements.

Suppose that I am buying a house and the seller and I have agreed on the price and a few other general matters, but have not completely and totally exhausted the possible items we could put into the contract of sale. Under these circumstances, I can weigh, on the one hand, the possibility that if some contingency not now covered by the contract occurs, I will lose in the essentially stochastical decision against the advantages and disadvantages of continuing the negotiations to get an additional clause covering the given contingency. The first thing to note, of course, is that the time spent in negotiations is a cost and clearly if the contingency is unlikely enough, I would be well advised to leave the matter in the lap of the gods. Furthermore, it is by no means obvious that if I negotiate with my bargaining partner the certain clause that we end up with will be more to my advantage than flipping the coin. This might or might not be true, depending on whether there is some mutually advantageous way of dealing with this particular problem. If there is some provision that could be reached with respect to this particular problem that will be to both of us ex ante better than flipping a coin, we would, of course, do it; but there is no intrinsic reason to believe that this would be so for all the details of a contract. Furthermore, even if such a possibility for profit did exist, it might also exist after the contingency itself had occurred and, therefore, we could make an agreement at that time rather than using the coin-flipping process. . . .

The same line of reasoning may be used to decide in general the proper degree of detail in the interpretive part of the law of contracts. The only real point of this part of the law is to save the parties the inconvenience of making their own contracts very long. Thus, it permits them to leave certain provisions out of their contract because they are covered by the law. Furthermore, since this technique in and of itself is more efficient than actually negotiating each contract clause step by step, one would assume that the parties would count it as a lower-cost way of obtaining certainty and, therefore, would prefer more details in this legally specified portion of the contract than in the part they actually negotiate between themselves.

*Risk and Risk-Bearing**

Charles O. Hardy

Risk may be defined as uncertainty in regard to cost, loss, or damage. In this definition, emphasis is on the word *uncertainty*. . . . [Market risks are the most important kind of risk facing the business manager.] By market risks we mean the unavoidable uncertainties due to the fact that *time* elapses between the purchase and the sale of commodities, during which time unpredictable changes often occur in the prices and other market conditions surrounding the commodities dealt in. Rarely is it possible to conclude both the buying and the selling part of a given transaction simultaneously, so as to relieve the business man of risk, and even when it can be done there is risk that he will be held to one contract and be unable to enforce the other. . . .

*Reprinted by permission from Risk and Risk-Bearing pp. 1-5, 60-61 (University of Chicago Press 1923).

It will be noted that from the standpoint of risk it makes no difference whether the buying or the selling occurs first. In many cases the business man contracts to deliver a certain commodity at a given price, then purchases the things he needs to fulfil his contract. The sale of a newspaper subscription, a building contract, the collection of university tuition, are all transactions of this character. More frequent are the transactions where something is bought first with the idea of selling it, or some product into which it enters, at a profit. Sometimes both elements are present in the same transaction, as when a tailor first buys cloth, then after taking an order for a suit, buys the labor to make it up. In all transactions of either of these types, and it must be repeated that practically all business is of one type or the other, the longer the *time* involved in the fulfilment of obligations entered into, or in the disposal of commodities bought, the greater the risk of adverse changes, either in price or in other market conditions. . . .

[One] way of transferring risk is what is known as "contracting out," a method similar to hedging, but not involving the use of a speculative futures market. Contracting out may be explained briefly as follows:

> The work of the organized exchanges has certain sensational elements, and volumes have been written upon these exchanges where sentences have not been written upon the vastly greater volume of speculative contracts entered into outside the limits of the organized exchange. These speculative contracts are so well known that a simple illustration will suffice. I decide to build a house. A contractor assumes the task. He then proceeds to make sub-contracts with the purveyors of lumber, bricks, and other materials to the effect that these materials shall be delivered to him at a certain future time and at a certain price. The main contractor has thus contracted himself out of risk with reference to price changes in these materials.
>
> Our contractor has thus been relieved of much of his risk.
>
> The foregoing illustration is typical. A man agrees to do a certain thing. He then contracts himself out of certain phases of the risk involved. True, the burden is merely transferred to someone else, but presumably this someone else is a specialist, and therein is the social defense.[1]

In the building industry and in some lines of manufacturing, it is practicable to pass on in this way the risk of price changes in nearly all the important cost items except labor; this latter risk the manager must ordinarily himself assume if he contracts in advance to sell his product at a given price. During the war, however, it was not uncommon for building contractors to rid themselves of this risk by

1. Adapted by permission from L. C. Marshall, Industrial Society, pp. 501-2. [Footnote in original.]

stipulations that the contract price should be readjusted in case changes in wage rates should occur before the completion of the job.

In many lines of commercial and manufacturing enterprise, risks can be passed on by coupling advance sales with advance purchases; in other lines, the risks must be assumed but can be kept at a minimum by keeping inventories and advance orders low. Quick turnovers give relatively little chance for profit or loss from price changes.

It is usually the case, however, that at some point in the chain of successive buyers and sellers the possibility of contracting out or coupling purchases and sales disappears. Someone must assume the risks; the fact that the one who assumes them is a specialist means that he has superior facilities for judging the situation, if a basis for judgment exists, but it also means, as a rule, that he does not secure a good distribution of risks.

*The Common Law**

Oliver Wendell Holmes, Jr.

An assurance that it shall rain to-morrow, or that a third person shall paint a picture, may as well be a promise as one that the promisee shall receive from some source one hundred bales of cotton, or that the promisor will pay the promisee one hundred dollars. What is the difference in the cases? It is only in the degree of power possessed by the promisor over the event. He has none in the first case. He has equally little legal authority to make a man paint a picture, although he may have larger means of persuasion. He probably will be able to make sure that the promisee has the cotton. Being a rich man, he is certain to be able to pay the one hundred dollars, except in the event of some most improbable accident.

But the law does not inquire, as a general thing, how far the accomplishment of an assurance touching the future is within the power of the promisor. In the moral world it may be that the obligation of a promise is confined to what lies within reach of the will of the promisor (except so far as the limit is unknown on one side, and misrepresented on the other). But unless some consideration of public policy intervenes, I take it that a man may bind himself at law that any future event shall happen. He can therefore promise it in a legal sense. It may be said that when a man covenants that it shall rain

*Reprinted from The Common Law, pp. 298-305 (1881).

to-morrow, or that *A* shall paint a picture, he only says, in a short form, I will pay if it does not rain, or if *A* does not paint a picture. But that is not necessarily so. A promise could easily be framed which would be broken by the happening of fair weather, or by *A* not painting. A promise, then, is simply an accepted assurance that a certain event or state of things shall come to pass.

But if this be true, it has more important bearings than simply to enlarge the definition of the word *promise*. It concerns the theory of contract. The consequences of a binding promise at common law are not affected by the degree of power which the promisor possesses over the promised event. If the promised event does not come to pass, the plaintiff's property is sold to satisfy the damages, within certain limits, which the promisee has suffered by the failure. The consequences are the same in kind whether the promise is that it shall rain, or that another man shall paint a picture, or that the promisor will deliver a bale of cotton.

If the legal consequence is the same in all cases, it seems proper that all contracts should be considered from the same legal point of view. In the case of a binding promise that it shall rain to-morrow, the immediate legal effect of what the promisor does is, that he takes the risk of the event, within certain defined limits, as between himself and the promisee. He does no more when he promises to deliver a bale of cotton.

If it be proper to state the common-law meaning of promise and contract in this way, it has the advantage of freeing the subject from the superfluous theory that contract is a qualified subjection of one will to another, a kind of limited slavery. It might be so regarded if the law compelled men to perform their contracts, or if it allowed promisees to exercise such compulsion. If, when a man promised to labor for another, the law made him do it, his relation to his promisee might be called a servitude ad hoc with some truth. But that is what the law never does. It never interferes until a promise has been broken, and therefore cannot possibly be performed according to its tenor. It is true that in some instances equity does what is called compelling specific performance. But, in the first place, I am speaking of the common law, and, in the next, this only means that equity compels the performance of certain elements of the total promise which are still capable of performance. For instance, take a promise to convey land within a certain time, a court of equity is not in the habit of interfering until the time has gone by, so that the promise cannot be performed as made. But if the conveyance is more important than the time, and the promisee prefers to have it late rather than never, the law may compel the performance of that. Not literally compel even in that case, however, but put the promisor in prison unless he will convey. This remedy is an exceptional one. The only universal consequence of a legally binding promise is, that the law makes the promisor pay damages if the promised event does not come to pass. In every case it leaves him free from interference until the time for fulfilment has gone by, and therefore free to break his contract if he chooses. . . .

. . . As the relation of contractor and contractee is voluntary, the consequences attaching to the relation must be voluntary. What the event contemplated by the promise is, or in other words what will amount to a breach of contract, is a matter of interpretation and construction. What consequences of the breach are assumed is more remotely, in like manner, a matter of construction, having regard to the circumstances under which the contract is made. Knowledge of what is dependent upon performance is one of those circumstances. It is not necessarily conclusive, but it may have the effect of enlarging the risk assumed.

The very office of construction is to work out, from what is expressly said and done, what would have been said with regard to events not definitely before the minds of the parties, if those events had been considered. The price paid in mercantile contracts generally excludes the construction that exceptional risks were intended to be assumed. The foregoing analysis is believed to show that the result which has been reached by the courts on grounds of practical good sense, falls in with the true theory of contract under the common law. . . .

But now suppose that there is no element of uncertainty except in the minds of the parties. Take, for instance, a wager on a past horse-race. It has been thought that this would amount to an absolute promise on one side, and no promise at all on the other. But this does not seem to me sound. Contracts are dealings between men, by which they make arrangements for the future. In making such arrangements the important thing is, not what is objectively true, but what the parties know. Any present fact which is unknown to the parties is just as uncertain for the purposes of making an arrangement at this moment, as any future fact. It is therefore a detriment to undertake to be ready to pay if the event turns out not to have been as expected. This seems to be the true explanation why forbearance to sue upon a claim believed by the plaintiff to be good is a sufficient consideration, although the claim was bad in fact, and known by the defendant to be bad. Were this view unsound, it is hard to see how wagers on any future event, except a miracle, could be sustained. For if the happening or not happening of the event is subject to the law of causation, the only uncertainty about it is in our foresight, not in its happening.

*The Nature of the Firm**

Ronald H. Coase

Our task is to attempt to discover why a firm emerges at all in a specialised exchange economy. The price mechanism (considered purely from the side of the direction of resources) might be superseded if the relationship which replaced it was desired for its own sake. This would be the case, for example, if some people preferred to work under the direction of some other person. Such individuals would accept less in order to work under someone, and firms would arise naturally from this. But it would appear that this cannot be a very important reason, for it would rather seem that the opposite tendency is operating if one judges from the stress normally laid on the advantage of "being one's own master." Of course, if the desire was not to be controlled but to control, to exercise power over others, then people might be willing to give up something in order to direct others; that is, they would be willing to pay others more than they could get under the price mechanism in order to be able to direct them. But this implies that those who direct pay in order to be able to do this and are not paid to direct, which is clearly not true in the majority of cases. Firms might also exist if purchasers preferred commodities which are produced by firms to those not so produced; but even in spheres where one would expect such preferences (if they exist) to be of negligible importance, firms are to be found in the real world. Therefore there must be other elements involved.

The main reason why it is profitable to establish a firm would seem to be that there is a cost of using the price mechanism. The most obvious cost of "organising" production through the price mechanism is that of discovering what the relevant prices are. This cost may be reduced but it will not be eliminated by the emergence of specialists who will sell this information. The costs of negotiating and concluding a separate contract for each exchange transaction which takes place on a market must also be taken into account. Again, in certain markets, e.g., produce exchanges, a technique is devised for minimising these contract costs; but they are not eliminated. It is true that contracts are not eliminated when there is a firm but they are greatly reduced. A factor of production (or the owner thereof) does not have to make a series of contracts with the factors with whom he is co-operating within the firm, as would be necessary, of course, if this co-operation were as a direct result of the

*Reprinted from 4 Economica 386, 390-392 (1937), by permission of the London School of Economics and Political Science.

working of the price mechanism. For this series of contracts is substituted one. At this stage, it is important to note the character of the contract into which a factor enters that is employed within a firm. The contract is one whereby the factor, for a certain remuneration (which may be fixed or fluctuating), agrees to obey the directions of an entrepreneur *within certain limits.* The essence of the contract is that it should only state the limits to the powers of the entrepreneur. Within these limits, he can therefore direct the other factors of production.

There are, however, other disadvantages—or costs—of using the price mechanism. It may be desired to make a long-term contract for the supply of some article or service. This may be due to the fact that if one contract is made for a longer period, instead of several shorter ones, then certain costs of making each contract will be avoided. Or, owing to the risk attitude of the people concerned, they may prefer to make a long rather than a short-term contract. Now, owing to the difficulty of forecasting, the longer the period of the contract is for the supply of the commodity or service, the less possible, and indeed, the less desirable it is for the person purchasing to specify what the other contracting party is expected to do. It may well be a matter of indifference to the person supplying the service or commodity which of several courses of action is taken, but not to the purchaser of that service or commodity. But the purchaser will not know which of these several courses he will want the supplier to take. Therefore, the service which is being provided is expressed in general terms, the exact details being left until a later date. All that is stated in the contract is the limits to what the persons supplying the commodity or service is expected to do. The details of what the supplier is expected to do is not stated in the contract but is decided later by the purchaser. When the direction of resources (within the limits of the contract) becomes dependent on the buyer in this way, that relationship which I term a "firm" may be obtained. A firm is likely therefore to emerge in those cases where a very short-term contract would be unsatisfactory. It is obviously of more importance in the case of services—labour—than it is in the case of the buying of commodities. In the case of commodities, the main items can be stated in advance and the details which will be decided later will be of minor significance.

NOTES AND QUESTIONS

1. As Umbeck's paper illustrates, even in the absence of a state-maintained legal system—i.e., in a situation which approxi-

mates the Hobbesian state of nature—there will be private contracts. But unless there is some enforcement mechanism, these contracts may be terribly expensive. For example, each party to a contract in the state of nature may require substantial security to assure the other party's performance (it was once common practice to offer a close relative as a "hostage" to secure the performance of a promise). And there will be great pressure to reduce or eliminate the time interval between the performance of one party and the performance of the other—to make all exchanges simultaneous ones. See pp. 3-4 supra.

Individuals in the state of nature may attempt to reduce the costs of contracting (along with the costs of physical insecurity) by establishing protective associations which provide enforcement services to their members. The "mining districts" established in California during the gold rush illustrate protective associations of this sort. As such associations increase in size, it will become more and more costly for an individual who wants to make contracts of his own to refrain from joining a protective association. So there will be a tendency for everyone to join one association or another. And—in the long run—there may even be a tendency for a single association to emerge as the preeminent one (why?). Viewed in this way, the state itself (an all-encompassing protective association) may be regarded as a market phenomenon which emerges from a competitive process in the market for protection. See Robert Nozick, Anarchy, State, and Utopia (1974).

2. Umbeck's analysis builds, to a considerable extent, on Steven N. S. Cheung's study of the choice of contractual arrangements in agriculture. Cheung focuses on the different types of contracts chosen by landlords and tenants in China and Southeast Asia prior to the agrarian reforms of the last thirty years. See Transaction Costs, Risk Aversion, and the Choice of Contractual Arrangements, 12 J. Law & Econ. 23 (1969), and The Theory of Share Tenancy (1969). Cheung argues that of the three basic types of agricultural contract—the fixed-rent contract, the wage contract, and the sharecropping contract—the sharecropping contract is the most costly to negotiate (since it contains many complex terms which the landlord and tenant must agree on) and to enforce (since the landlord must expend resources to determine the yield of the land in question before the sharing provisions of the contract can be applied). If this is so, Cheung asks, why are share contracts ever chosen? He offers the following answer (12 J. Law & Econ. at 26-27):

> Suppose the transaction cost is zero or the same for all forms of contract. Let us employ a behavioral postulate of risk aversion, defined here to mean that an individual, given the same expected average income, prefers a lower to a higher variance. In agriculture, variables

> exogenous to the production function, such as weather conditions and pests, are risk factors which are difficult to forecast and which may significantly affect the variance of the value of output. Under a fixed-rent contract, the tenant bears most, if not all, of the risk; under a wage contract, the landowner bears most, if not all, of the risk. Share tenancy may then be regarded as a device for risk sharing (or risk dispersion); that is, the variance of the output yield is distributed among the contracting parties. Given the postulate of risk aversion, a share contract will be mutually preferred by the landowner and the tenant.

According to Cheung, a share contract will be chosen "if the higher transaction cost [of negotiating and enforcing such a contract] is at least compensated for by the gain from risk dispersion" which a share contract affords. Id. at 27. For more on the role of risk aversion in choice of contractual arrangements see Notes 5-7 and p. 122 infra.

3. John Barton, in The Economic Basis of Damages for Breach of Contract, 1 J. Legal Studies 277 (1972), presents a variant of Birmingham's game-theoretic model of contract adherence. Barton uses as his example a contract to sell grain at price p on a date fixed in the contract. When the time for delivery comes, the price is s, which may be either lower or higher than p. If it is lower, the seller will gain and the buyer lose from contract adherence. If it is higher, the buyer will gain and the seller lose from adherence.

Barton describes the "game" as follows (id. at 279):

> [Figure 7 shows] a zero-sum game, whose equilibrium solution will be the dishonor-dishonor point, so long as the losing party has an incentive to avoid the contract.
>
> The law of damages changes this result by modifying the off-diagonal blocks, interpreted as those in which a party seeks to dishonor the contract but is subject to suit by the other party [as shown in Figure 8]. (Buyer's and seller's damages are both encompassed here by allowing d to be negative.) This is again a zero-sum game, but one in which at $d = s - p$, the conventional measure of damages, the equilibrium solution becomes the honor-honor point. Thus, this measure of damages serves to make it possible to contract with the expectation that the contract will be binding.

In a footnote (id. at 279 n.5), Barton, after summarizing Birmingham's game-theoretic model, states:

> I believe, however, that the model outlined in text which shows the market contract as a zero-sum game is more appropriate. First, it corresponds to the actual win-lose character of the market bet. Second, it allows more explicit contrast with the clearly non-zero sum features of the "non-market" transaction.

		Seller: Honor	Seller: Dishonor
Buyer	Honor	(s − p, p − s)	(0, 0)
	Dishonor	(0, 0)	(0, 0)

[Figure 7]

		Seller: Honor	Seller: Dishonor
Buyer	Honor	(s − p, p − s)	(0, 0)
	Dishonor	(d, −d)	(d, −d)

[Figure 8]

What is the difference between Birmingham's and Barton's models? Is the market contract, where the parties are in effect betting on future prices (see p. 154 infra), a "zero-sum game" because the gain to the party who guesses right is exactly offset by the loss to the party who guesses wrong? Would inclusion of collection costs make it a non-zero-sum game? What is a *nonmarket* contract and how might it be appropriately modeled in game-theoretic terms? Cf. Chapter 6. Is the game-theoretic perspective a useful one, or can the analysis be restated with greater clarity in simple economic language? Cf. p. 4 supra. Another portion of Barton's article is reprinted in Chapter 6.

4. What are the advantages of being able to make an *un*enforceable promise? This question is related to another one: why are gratuitous promises (promises unsupported by consideration) usually held to be unenforceable? See pp. 50-54 infra.

5. According to both Hardy and Holmes, an important function of contracting is to allocate the risk associated with uncertain future events. Suppose, for example, that a contractor agrees to build a house and then makes a series of subcontracts with suppliers of various materials. Hardy asserts that, by subcontracting, the principal contractor "passes on" the risk of a price change in the materials he requires. Before contracting, the price the principal will have to pay for his materials is uncertain. After contracting, it is fixed (unless of course, the subcontracts contain variable price terms). In this way, the principal contractor substitutes a single known outcome (the contract price) for a range of possible outcomes—the prices he might have to pay if he were to purchase his own materials. Whenever the range or variance of a set of possible outcomes is reduced (either to a more restricted range or to a single known outcome), the result is a reduction in risk in the economic sense.

To illustrate, compare a 10 percent chance of winning $100 with a 20 percent chance of winning $50. The actuarial or expected value of these bets is the same—$10—and an individual who was risk neutral would be indifferent between them. But although the expected values are the same, the amount of risk is different. In the first bet, the range of possible outcomes is from zero to $100; in the second, from zero to $50. The variance or risk is thus smaller in the second bet, so a risk-averse individual would derive greater utility from it. What would his preference be as between the second bet and just being given $10?

The purchase of insurance illustrates risk aversion, while gambling illustrates risk preference (why?). Risk aversion is deducible from the economic principle of diminishing marginal utility. That principle, which has considerable intuitive appeal, teaches that if an individual has one car and then buys another, and another, the second will yield the owner less utility than the first and the third less than the second. And so with money: the last $10,000 of annual income is worth less to the earner than the previous $10,000.

Where the parties to a contract differ in their aversion to risk, the assignment of the various risks that might, if they materialized, interfere with the performance of the contract (e.g., a strike, bad weather, death) to the party who is less risk averse offers the possibility of increasing the welfare generated by the contract. Indeed, the sole *raison d'être* of some contracts—contracts for insurance—is to shift risk from a risk-averse to a risk-neutral party (why and in what sense is an insurance company risk neutral?). Other contracts have an insurance component (can you think of examples?). But risk aversion cannot be the sole criterion used by the parties in assigning a risk; they must also consider the relative costs to each of them of preventing the risk from materializing. Prevention is a method, alternative to shifting risk to the less risk-averse party, of reducing the disutility of risk in the contract process. For further discussion of risk aversion see pp. 122-125 infra, and for analysis by economists see Armen A. Alchian, The Meaning of Utility Measurement, 43 Am. Econ. Rev. 26 (1953); Kenneth J. Arrow, Essays in the Theory of Risk-Bearing ch. 3 (1971); Milton Friedman, Price Theory ch. 4 (1976).

To return to our building-contract example, even if the builder reduces the riskiness of his enterprise by subcontracting with suppliers, he may still be disappointed by the way things turn out and may even end up worse off than if he had not subcontracted in the first place. For example, if, in the interim between the time he subcontracts and the time he requires the materials, the price of the materials declines below the contract price, the builder would prefer to be able to buy on the open market. This illustrates the important point that the risk-averse individual gives up upside as well as downside risk; in the example given, the builder trades a range for a point equal to the mean of that range.

6. According to John Barton, Note 3 supra, at 278, the market contract is a "bet," in which "each party enters the contract in the hope that he is guessing the market more accurately than the other, or, if the parties differ in their willingness to bear risks, in the judgment that the certain price set by the contract is more desirable than the uncertainty of the market price." Is Barton suggesting that some people make market contracts because they are risk avoiders while others make them for precisely the opposite reason—because they are risk *takers* (gamblers)? What is the difference between a "bet" and a "hedge"?

7. The risk-shifting function of contractual agreements is especially striking in the case of output and requirements contracts. The economic characteristics of such contracts are described in Harold C. Havighurst & Sidney Berman, Requirement and Output Contracts, 27 Ill. L. Rev. 1, 1-3 (1932), as follows:

> The ordinary type of agreement for the sale of goods specifies a fixed quantity for a fixed price. Buyers and sellers of goods in a community where production and distribution are on a small scale and for a limited market find such arrangements sufficient for their dealings. Large-scale production and expanding markets create greater uncertainties and more business hazards. There has arisen a demand for a more complex allocation of these new risks determined by the ability of the parties to bear certain risks conveniently and by their respective bargaining positions. To meet this demand many types of contracts have come into use containing various provisions for the fixing of terms with reference to future events. Among these we find contracts to supply raw materials for manufacture or finished products for resale in which the quantity term is subject to variation according to the needs of the buyer's business. A similar variable quantity term is to be found in contracts for all the products which a manufacturer or producer may turn out in his business during a specified period.
>
> The advantages of contracts without a fixed quantity term are most apparent in the case of a manufacturer who makes a contract for his requirements of raw material. If he is manufacturing for a market whose demand is incapable of certain prediction, the task of correlating his supply of materials with his sales may prove something of a burden if he is compelled to contract for fixed quantities. If his supply is assured and at the same time variable, he is relieved of the necessity of providing against insufficiency or of disposing of a surplus in a market with which he is unfamiliar and in which he has no regular customers. These reasons hold also to some extent when the buyer is a jobber. He is relieved of the necessity of predicting his sales over a period. The advantage to the seller is not so clear. The press of competition and the large quantities usually involved lead him to accede to provisions of this type in order to make his proposition more attrac-

> tive. Furthermore the fact that he is usually dealing with the commodity in question in larger quantities and is acquainted with the market makes it easier for him to effect the adjustments necessary because of the variations in the needs of the buyer's business.
>
> Output contracts have much in common with those for requirements, but there are differences. The seller's position is comparable to that of the buyer in the requirement contract, but his motives are not precisely the same. The purpose here seems to be to turn over the marketing of the product to the buyer, thus effecting a greater division of labor. Buyers do not enter into such contracts so much because of the competition of other prospective buyers, but because of the lower price the seller is able to make due to the elimination of marketing expense. The buyer's increased profit is for assuming the market risk and performing the marketing service with the attendant expense.
>
> The risks of price fluctuation are of course also present in these contracts as in the ordinary contract of sale over a period. But whereas in the contract for a fixed amount the parties stand to lose or gain in equal amounts according to whether the market rises or falls, the requirement buyer and the output seller have a distinct advantage in that they have a measure of control over the quantity. The market price of finished products usually bears a direct relation to the market price of raw materials. But in a rising market the requirement buyer, whose costs are in a measure stabilized by the contract, enjoys an advantage that will probably be reflected in business expansion. The output seller, operating at a higher cost but selling at the contract price, will tend to produce less. On the other hand, in a falling market the requirement buyer, who is obliged to pay the contract price for his materials, will purchase less goods and the output seller will increase his production. This aspect is even more marked when the buyer of requirements is a jobber. Business men without doubt are fully conscious of this inequality. But the party thus at a disadvantage is usually led to take his chances by the pressure of competition and the commercially desirable features already discussed. It is this effect of price fluctuation, however, that has led to much friction and litigation under these contracts. Doubtless from a commercial standpoint the loss from this source has not been sufficient to outweigh the advantages that are realized by the use of such agreements. [Reprinted by permission.]

See also Note 10 infra, and Victor P. Goldberg, Toward an Expanded Economic Theory of Contract, 10 J. Econ. Issues 45 (1976).

8. The role of contract law in supplying implied contract terms, noted by Tullock, was (to our knowledge) first remarked by Jeremy Bentham:

> . . . [O]bligations may be distinguished into original and adjective. I call those original, of which express mention is made in the contract itself: I call those adjective, which the law thinks proper to add to the first. The first turn upon events which the contracting parties have foreseen; the others upon events which they could not foresee.
>
> It is thus that in every country the law has supplied [sic] the shortsightedness of individuals, by doing for them what they would

have done for themselves, if their imagination had anticipated the march of nature.[1]

9. According to Holmes, the concept of risk is useful as a guide in interpreting contracts. For example, suppose that one party breaches his promise. Which consequences of the breach is he responsible for? If the contract itself is silent on this question, the court must determine which risks the breaching party agreed to bear. Often, this "agreement" will have to be extrapolated from a variety of sources: other terms in the contract, the behavior of the parties, unstated but widely shared assumptions about the meaning of a term in the context of a particular industry, and so on. "The very office of construction," Holmes tells us, "is to work out, from what is expressly said and done, what would have been said with regard to events not definitely before the minds of the parties, if those events had been considered." For a famous statement of the same proposition by Holmes the judge, see Globe Refining Co. v. Landa Cotton Oil Co., 190 U.S. 540 (1903).

To what extent should a court also use efficiency considerations to determine how the parties to a contract would have allocated a particular risk if they had considered the matter at the time of contracting? For a discussion of this question in the context of the doctrine of impossibility see p. 122 infra.

10. Coase's article on the nature of the firm directs attention to costs of the contracting process that might make it more efficient to organize production through a firm rather than through a series of contracts. What is really involved is a change in the nature of the contractual relationships among the participants in the productive process. The substitution of firm for contract is the substitution of employment contracts, whereby the entrepreneur pays the worker for the right to direct his work, for contracts specifying price and output but leaving the details of the work to the worker, unsupervised by the entrepreneur who is purchasing his output.

Each method of production—firm and contract—involves its own problems. These are the subject of an extensive literature. See, e.g., Armen A. Alchian & Harold Demsetz, Production, Information Costs, and Economic Organization, 62 Am. Econ. Rev. 777 (1972). On the related question of the choice between contract and regulation as methods of preventing monopolistic exploitation of consumers, see, e.g., Oliver E. Williamson, Franchise Bidding for Natural Monopolies—In General and with Respect to CATV, 7 Bell J. Econ. 73 (1976). And, for a brief overview of these questions, see Richard A. Posner, Economic Analysis of Law 283-285, 289-290 (2d ed. 1977).

1. A General View of a Complete Code of Laws, in 3 Works of Jeremy Bentham 157, 191 (John Bowring ed. 1843).

Chapter 3

Consideration and Assent

*Consideration and Form**

Lon L. Fuller

Reasons for Refusing to Enforce the Gratuitous and Unrelied-on Promise.—*A* promises to give *B* $100; *B* has in no way changed his position in reliance on this promise, and he has neither given nor promised anything in return for it. In such a situation enforcement of the promise is denied both in the common law and in the civil law. . . .

Looking at the case from the standpoint of the substantive bases of contractual liability we observe, first of all, that there is here neither reliance nor unjust enrichment. Furthermore, gratuities such as this one do not present an especially pressing case for the application of the principle of private autonomy, particularly if we bear in mind the substantive deterrents to judicial intervention. While an exchange of goods is a transaction which conduces to the production of wealth and the division of labor, a gift is, in Bufnoir's words, a "sterile transmission."[1] If on "substantive" grounds the balance already inclines away from judicial intervention, the case against enforcement becomes stronger when we draw into account the desiderata underlying the use of formalities. That there is in the instant

*Reprinted from 41 Colum. L. Rev. 799, 814-815 (1941), with permission.

1. Propriété et Contrat (2nd ed. 1924) 487. This remark of Bufnoir's cannot be taken too literally; the element of exchange is a variable one, and there are few human relationships which do not involve a degree of reciprocity. It should be recalled that the practice of exchanging goods has commonly emerged in primitive societies out of a system of donations with, as Llewellyn says, "a felt obligation to reciprocate."

case a lack of evidentiary and cautionary safeguards is obvious. As to the channeling function of form, we may observe that the promise is made in a field where intention is not naturally canalized. There is nothing here to effect a neat division between tentative and exploratory expressions of intention, on the one hand, and legally effective transactions, on the other. In contrast to the situation of the immediate gift of a chattel (where title will pass by the manual tradition), there is here no "natural formality" on which the courts might seize as a test of enforceability.

The Contractual Archetype—The Half-Completed Exchange.—*A* delivers a horse to *B* in return for *B*'s promise to pay him ten dollars; *B* defaults on his promise, and *A* sues for the agreed price. In this case are united all of the factors we have previously analyzed as tending in the direction of enforcement of a promise. On the substantive side, there is reliance by *A* and unjust enrichment of *B*. The transaction involves an exchange of economic values, and falls therefore in a field appropriately left to private autonomy in an economy where no other provision is made for the circulation of goods and the division of labor, or where (as perhaps in primitive society) an expanding economy makes the existing provision for those ends seem inadequate. On the side of form, the delivery and acceptance of the horse involve a kind of natural formality, which satisfies the evidentiary, cautionary, and channeling purposes of legal formalities. . . .

The Wholly Executory Exchange.—*B* promises to build a house for *A*, and *A*, in return, promises to pay *B* $5,000 on the completion of the house. *B* defaults on his promise, and *A*, without having had occasion to pay anything on the contract, sues *B* for damages. . . .

Where a bilateral contract remains wholly executory the arguments for judicial intervention have been considerably diminished in comparison with the situation of the half-completed exchange. There is here no unjust enrichment. Reliance may or may not exist, but in any event will not be so tangible and direct as where it consists in the rendition of the price of the defendant's performance. On the side of form, we have lost the natural formality involved in the turning over of property or the rendition and acceptance of services. There remains simply the fact that the transaction is an exchange and not a gift. This fact alone does offer some guaranty so far as the cautionary and channeling functions of form are concerned, though, except as the Statute of Frauds interposes to supply the deficiency, evidentiary safeguards are largely lacking. This lessening of the factors arguing for enforcement not only helps to explain why liability in this situation was late in developing, but also explains why even today the executory bilateral contract cannot be put on complete parity with the situation of the half-completed exchange.

In the situation of the half-completed exchange, the element of exchange is only one factor tending toward enforcement. Since that element is there reinforced by reliance, unjust enrichment, and the natural formality involved in the surrender and acceptance of a tangible benefit, it is unnecessary to analyze the concept of exchange closely, and it may properly be left vague. In the executory bilateral contract, on the other hand, the element of exchange stands largely alone as a basis of liability and its definition becomes crucial. Various definitions are possible. We may define exchange vaguely as a transaction from which each participant derives a benefit, or, more restrictively, as a transaction in which the motives of the parties are primarily economic rather than sentimental. Following Adam Smith, we may say that it is a transaction which, directly or indirectly, conduces to the division of labor. Or we may take Demogue's notion that the most important characteristic of exchange is that it is a situation in which the interests of the transacting parties are opposed, so that the social utility of the contract is guaranteed in some degree by the fact that it emerges as a compromise of those conflicting interests. The problem of choosing among these varying conceptions may seem remote and unimportant, yet it underlies some of the most familiar problems of contract law. For example, suppose a nephew promises his uncle that he will not smoke until he is twenty-one, and the uncle promises him $5,000 as a reward if he will keep his promise. Where the nephew sues after having earned the reward by following the prescribed line of conduct recovery has been permitted. But would such an agreement be enforced as an executory bilateral contract? Could the uncle, for example, sue the nephew for smoking a cigarette? In answering this question it is at once apparent that we are faced with the necessity of defining the particular kind of exchange which is essential to the enforcement of a bilateral contract. A similar problem underlies many of the cases involving "illusory promises."

Like consideration, exchange is a complex concept. To the problem of the executory exchange we may, within a narrower compass, apply the same general approach that we have applied to the problem of consideration as a whole. Here our "archetype" is the business trade of economic values in the form of goods, services, or money. To the degree that a particular case deviates from this archetype, the incentives to judicial intervention decrease, until a point is reached where relief will be denied altogether unless the attenuated element of exchange is reinforced, either on the formal side by some formal or informal satisfaction of the desiderata underlying the use of legal formalities, or on the substantive side by a showing of reliance or unjust enrichment, or of some special need for a regulation of the relations involved by private autonomy.

Transactions Ancillary to Exchanges.—There are various transactions which, though they are not themselves immediately directed toward accomplishing an exchange, are necessary preliminary steps toward exchanges, or are ancillary to exchanges in process of realization. Among these we may mention offers, promises of unpaid sureties, and what Llewellyn has described as "going-transaction adjustments" such as are involved in unilateral concessions or promises of extra compensation granted during performance of a bilateral contract.

Because of their connection with exchanges, these transactions, in varying degrees, participate in the underlying grounds, both "formal" and "substantive," which justify the enforcement of exchanges. Thus, for example, if it were thought that exchanges could in practice only be arranged through the device of preliminary offers and that offers could be effective only if made irrevocable, then the substantive grounds for enforcing bilateral contracts of exchange would extend to offers. Again, a promise of extra compensation to a man already under contract to build a house at a fixed price participates to some extent in the "formal" guaranties which justify the enforcement of exchanges. From the standpoint of the "channeling" function, for example, such a promise receives a certain canalization from being related to an existing business deal. There is not here to the same degree as in purely gratuitous promises a shadowy no-man's land in which it is impossible to distinguish between the binding promise and tentative or exploratory expressions of intention.

How far legal sanction ought to be extended to these transactions bordering on and surrounding exchanges is a legislative question which cannot be discussed here, though it may be observed that it is precisely in this field that the greatest difference between the common law and the civil law exists. Probably our own law is in need of some reform. The written promise of a surety who guarantees the performance of one party to an exchange, for example, probably ought to be made enforceable without consideration. As to offers, the problem is more difficult, and probably some distinction between kinds of offers is in order.

Unbargained-for Reliance.—An uncle promises to give his nephew one thousand dollars; in reliance on this promise the nephew incurs an indebtedness he would not otherwise have incurred. In this case we have a change of position which is not bargained for as the price of the uncle's promise. Where the element of exchange is removed from a case, the appeal to judicial intervention decreases both in terms of form and of substance. The appeal is diminished substantively because we are no longer in the field which is in modern society the most obviously appropriate field for the rule of private autonomy. From the formal standpoint, when we lose exchange, we lose the formal guaranties which go with the situation of exchange.

Section 90 of the Contracts Restatement provides in effect that a promise which has given rise to unbargained-for reliance may or may not be enforced, depending on the circumstances of the case. The section makes explicit only two criteria bearing on the question whether relief should be granted, namely, the seriousness of the promisee's reliance and its foreseeability by the promisor. On the basis of the analysis presented in this article, the following additional inquiries would be relevant: (1) Was the promise prompted wholly by generosity, or did it emerge out of a context of tacit exchange? (2) Were the desiderata underlying the use of formalities satisfied in any degree by the circumstances under which the promise was made? As bearing on the second question, we may ask whether the promise was express or implied, and whether after the promise was made the promisee declared to the promisor his intention of acting on it.

Nominal Consideration.—It has been held that a promise to make a gift may be made binding through the payment of a "nominal" consideration, such as a dollar or a cent. The proper ground for upholding these decisions would seem to be that the desiderata underlying the use of formalities are here satisfied by the fact that the parties have taken the trouble to cast their transaction in the form of an exchange. The promise supported by nominal consideration then becomes enforceable for reasons similar to those which justify the enforcement of the promise under seal.

Release of Claims.— . . . If when a creditor releases his debtor the desiderata underlying the use of formalities are satisfied by the circumstances surrounding the informal transaction, then we have an explanation for the observed relaxing of "formal" requirements in this situation. An analogy from the law of gifts will again be helpful. Ordinarily the effective gift of a chattel requires either some document of transfer or a delivery of the chattel itself. It has been held, however, that where the chattel is already in the possession of the donee, mere words of donation are sufficient. This is partly because in such a situation donative words are accompanied by a sense of present deprivation which is absent where the chattel remains in the donor's hands. The cautionary function of form is thus satisfied in this situation without the imposition of form. So, I believe, if we look at the problem now under discussion from the standpoint of the cautionary function of form it will be apparent that there is a difference between releasing a claim and creating a claim by a promise. The release of a claim, even if made orally, carries with it normally a sense of deprivation which is lacking in the case of a promise. Where words have this effect, where they tend to produce a psychological wrench on the speaker, they satisfy the desideratum of inducing deliberation as well as a writing or a seal. On the side of "substance," it may be observed that releases are normally transactions ancillary to a relationship of exchange. . . .

Moral Obligation as Consideration.—Courts have frequently enforced promises on the simple ground that the promisor was only promising to do what he ought to have done anyway. These cases have either been condemned as wanton departures from legal principle, or reluctantly accepted as involving the kind of compromise logic must inevitably make at times with sentiment. I believe that these decisions are capable of rational defense. When we say the defendant was morally obligated to do the thing he promised, we in effect assert the existence of a substantive ground for enforcing the promise. In a broad sense, a similar line of reasoning justifies the special status accorded by the law to contracts of exchange. Men *ought* to exchange goods and services; therefore when they enter contracts to that end, we enforce those contracts. On the side of form, concern for formal guaranties justifiably diminishes where the promise is backed by a moral obligation to do the thing promised. What does it matter that the promisor may have acted without great deliberation, since he is only promising to do what he should have done without a promise? For the same reason, can we not justifiably overlook some degree of evidentiary insecurity?

In refutation of the notion of "moral consideration" it is sometimes said that a moral obligation plus a mere promise to perform that obligation can no more create legal liability than zero plus zero can have any other sum than zero. But a mathematical analogy at least equally appropriate is the proposition that one-half plus one-half equals one. The court's conviction that the promisor ought to do the thing, plus the promisor's own admission of his obligation, may tilt the scales in favor of enforcement where neither standing alone would be sufficient. If it be argued that moral consideration threatens certainty, the solution would seem to lie, not in rejecting the doctrine, but in taming it by continuing the process of judicial exclusion and inclusion already begun in the cases involving infants' contracts, barred debts, and discharged bankrupts.

*Gratuitous Promises in Economics and Law**

Richard A. Posner

I. The Economics of "Gratuitous" Promises

Why would "economic man" ever make a promise without receiving in exchange something of value from the promisee, whether it be money, a promise of future performance beneficial to the promisor, or something else of value to him? It is tempting to answer this question simply by invoking "interdependent utilities." Since people may indeed derive utility or welfare from increases in the utility or welfare of family members, or for that matter of strangers,[1] interdependence may explain why (some) gifts or transfers are made. But it cannot explain why a *promise* to make a transfer in the future is made. Promises, as distinct from transfers, seem related to situations of bilateral performance, of exchange. *A* promises *B* $25,000 in exchange for *B*'s building a house for *A*. *B* will not build without a promise of payment in advance; *A* will not pay in advance without *B*'s promise to build. But if *A* wanted merely to transfer $25,000 to *B* (his favorite charity), why would he *promise* *B* to make the transfer in the future? Why not wait until he is ready to make the transfer and just do it? The purpose of a promise seems to be to induce performance of some sort by the promisee; if reciprocal performance is not desired, there seems no reason to make a promise.

The approach taken here is that a gratuitous promise, to the extent it actually commits the promisor to the promised course of action (an essential qualification), creates utility for the promisor over and above the utility to him of the promised performance. At one level this proposition is a tautology: a promise would not be made unless it conferred utility on the promisor. The interesting question is how it does so. I shall argue that it does so by increasing the present value of an uncertain future stream of transfer payments.

To illustrate, suppose *A* promises to give $1000 a year for the next 20 years to the *B* symphony orchestra. The value of the gift to *B* is the discounted present value of $1000 to be paid yearly over a 20-year period in the future. Among the factors that will be used by *B* in discounting these expected future receipts to present value is the likelihood that at some time during the 20-year period *A* will discontinue the annual payments. Depending on *B*'s estimation of *A*'s fickleness, income prospects, etc., the present value of the gift of

*Reprinted by permission, from 6 J. Legal Studies 411 (1977).

1. See Gary S. Becker, A Theory of Social Interactions, 82 J. Pol. Econ. 1063 (1974).

$1000 a year may be quite small; it may not be much more than $1000. But suppose the gift is actually worth more to *B* because *A* is certain to continue the payments throughout the entire period, though this fact is not known to *B*. If *A* can make a binding promise to continue the payments in accordance with his intention, *B* will revalue the gift at its true present worth. The size of the gift (in present-value terms) will be increased at no cost to *A*. Here is a clear case where the enforcement of a gratuitous promise would increase net social welfare.

This can be seen even more clearly by considering *A*'s alternatives if his promise is not enforceable. One possibility would be for *A* to promise a larger gift, the discounted value of which to *B* would equal the true value as known to *A*. The higher cost of the gift to *A* would be a measure of the social cost of the unenforceability of his promise. Another possibility would be for *A* to substitute for the promised series of future transfers a one-time transfer the present value of which would be the same as that of the series of enforceable future transfers. However, the fact that *A* preferred making a future gift to a present one suggests that they are not perfect substitutes; there are many reasons (including tax and liquidity considerations) why they might not be. Consequently, if *A* cannot bind himself to make a series of future gifts, he may be led to substitute a one-time transfer, the present value of which is less than that of the series of future gifts, although greater than that of a declared but unenforceable intention to make a series of future gifts. Thus, nonenforceability of gratuitous promises could tend to bias transfers excessively toward immediacy.

The above analysis rests on the assumption of asymmetry of information between promisor and promisee. Such an assumption may seem implausible: why would not the asymmetry be corrected by a simple communication from *A* to *B*, which would make both parties better off? However, because the relevant information concerns *A*'s subjective intentions, the asymmetry is both plausible and difficult to eliminate. *A* can state his true intentions to *B*, but how is he to convince *B* that the statement is correct? One way of making his statement credible is for *A* to make it costly for himself to lie; embodying the statement in a promise that is legally enforceable does this.

. . . Suppose that *A* really is fickle and *B* assesses his fickleness accurately. There is then no asymmetry in the information possessed by the parties. But *A* may still want to make a gift having a present value that is larger than it would be if *B*'s future receipts had to be discounted by the probability that *A* would actually make each payment when the time came to do so. *A* will balance the utility to him of making a larger (in present-value terms) gift now against the disutility of losing the freedom to change his mind in the future. He may decide that the utility of the larger gift now is greater, in which event it will be in his self-interest to make a promise that commits him irrevocably. Once again, enforcement of a gratuitous promise will lead to a net increase in social welfare.

The economic case for enforcing the gratuitous promise, it should be noted, is similar to that for enforcing bilateral promises. The failure to enforce bilateral promises would bias exchanges toward those that take place instantaneously, as distinct from those that are completed only over a period of time, even though the former may often be less valuable (as in our examples), or more costly, than the deferred exchange. But the symmetry between gratuitous and bilateral promises has been obscured in conventional legal analysis by a tendency to view a promise as a pure cost to the promisor, a limitation on his freedom of action and nothing more. Under this analysis, if the promisor receives nothing from the promisee in return—if, that is, the promise is unsupported by consideration in the conventional sense—the promise confers no benefit on the promisor and there is therefore no social cost in allowing him to break the promise, at least in the absence of any detrimental reliance by the promisee. For example, *A* might promise to give *B* $100 in two weeks. At the end of the two weeks, *A* changes his mind and decides to keep the $100. His change of mind makes *B* worse off but *A* better off; thus there is no basis, in the absence of detrimental reliance by *B* (e.g., *B*'s taking some time off from work in reliance on receiving the $100), for thinking that *A*'s change of mind has reduced the wealth of the society. But this analysis ignores the fact that being legally bound to make an intended transfer may enhance ex ante the value of the transfer to *A* and thereby increase the social product, just as in the case of bilateral promises. . . .

II. Optimal Rules for Enforcing "Gratuitous" Promises

. . . The design of optimal rules of substantive law must always take into account the costs of enforcement. Promises should not be enforced where the enforcement cost—to the extent not borne by the promisor—exceeds the gain from enforcement. The qualification is, of course, essential: if the promisor bore the full costs of enforcement, it would be a matter of indifference to society whether he chose to make enforceable a promise that seemed to confer on him but trivial utility relative to enforcement costs. But it is in fact unlikely—quite apart from the public subsidy of the court system—that such a promisor would bear those costs fully: if he reneged on his promise, and the promisee brought suit against him, the promisor would not be required to defray the promisee's costs of suit. Another category of enforcement costs that are not fully internalized consists of the costs of legal error. Here the focus is not on the promisor but on the mistaken or dishonest "promisee" who imposes on his "promisor" the costs of defending a groundless suit, at the same time incurring litigation costs of his own which have no social value either.

The question whether it is economical for society to recognize a promise as legally enforceable thus requires a comparison of the utility of the promise to the promisor with the social cost of enforcing the promise.[2] The utility of a "gratuitous" promise (a term I shall continue to use for the sake of convenience) would seem to depend primarily on (1) the size of the promised transfer and (2) the optimal length of the period for completing the transfer (the longer the period, the greater will be the loss of utility from having to substitute an immediate transfer if the promise is not enforceable). The social costs of enforcing the promise depend first of all on the administrative costs of enforcement. These in turn are a function in part of the size of the promised transfer, for expenditures on litigation are an investment in its outcome and therefore tend to be larger, the greater the stakes in the litigation.[3] The social costs of enforcement also depend on the likelihood of an error—e.g., of finding a promise where none in fact was made.[4]

Because the size of the promised transfer appears on both sides of the cost-benefit equation, it is difficult to specify with any confidence the effect of size on the net social gain from enforcement. . . . I conclude[5] that the effect is probably positive—i.e., that the case for legal enforcement of gratuitous promises will generally be stronger the larger the promised transfer. In any event, that assumption is employed in the balance of the article.

2. This type of approach is hinted at in Lon L. Fuller, Consideration and Form, [p. 40 supra].

3. See, for example, William M. Landes, An Economic Analysis of the Courts, 14 J. Law & Econ. 61 (1971).

4. This likelihood is in turn a *negative* function of the stakes, since a greater investment by the parties in litigation should reduce the probability of an erroneous determination. See Richard A. Posner, An Economic Approach to Legal Procedure and Judicial Administration, 2 J. Leg. Studies 399, 414-15 (1973).

5. [See Appendix, 6 J. Legal Studies at 425-426.]

III. The Approach of the Courts in the Light of Economic Analysis

A. General Rule of Nonenforceability

The general rule is that gratuitous promises are not enforceable. A good example of the rule and its economic logic would be a case where a man promised to take a woman to dinner but later reneged. The man presumably derived some utility from making the promise, and his utility might be greater if the promise were legally binding on him. But the increment in utility, if any, is probably small, both compared to that of the dinner itself and absolutely given the small size of the promised transfer. Moreover, the legal-error costs of enforcing such promises would be high because of the difficulty of distinguishing in casual social relations between a mere present intention, subject to change at will, and a promise intended to be binding on the promisor.

An additional factor reinforces the conclusion that it would be uneconomical to enforce such promises. The administrative costs of enforcement in such a case, while not high in absolute terms, are so high relative to the stakes that legal enforcement would be attempted only rarely. The man in our example would derive only a negligible increment in utility from being able to make a legally binding promise[6] because the woman would know that he knew that in the event he reneged she would not sue. The binding character of the promise would be illusory, and the benefits from its formal status as a binding promise therefore few. But the costs of enforcement would not be negligible.

A moment's reflection will suggest, however, that the analysis would not be materially altered if the dinner promise had been bilateral—if, that is, in return for the man's promise to take her out the woman had promised to accompany him. Where the utility of the promises being exchanged is small, the gains from legal enforcement are likely to be swamped by the costs of enforcement. The law recognizes this and refuses to enforce trivial social promises, especially within the family—where an additional factor, pointing in the same direction, is the existence of an inexpensive alternative to legal enforcement: refusal to engage in promissory transactions in the future. If the husband reneges on his promise, the wife will refuse in the future to perform services in exchange for his promises. Perhaps, then, the real reason for the law's generally not enforcing gratuitous promises is not a belief, which would be economically unsound, that there is a difference in kind between the gratuitous and the

6. Indeed, that utility might well be offset simply by the cost to him in reduced freedom of action that the binding character of the promise would impose.

bargained-for promise, but an empirical hunch that gratuitous promises tend both to involve small stakes and to be made in family settings where there are economically superior alternatives to legal enforcement.

B. Past Consideration

Among the exceptions to the general principle that gratuitous promises will not be enforced are several which are grouped under the rubric of "past consideration." A subsequent promise to pay a debt barred by the statute of limitations, or to pay a debt discharged in bankruptcy, or to pay a debt that is uncollectable because the debtor was a minor at the time the debt was contracted, is legally enforceable even though there is no fresh consideration for the promise. There are classes of promise in which the utility of the promise to the promisor is often great and the costs of enforcement low. First, as regards utility, it should be noted not only that the stakes are often substantial (these are formal debts after all) but that the *incremental* gain in utility from the enforceable character of the promise may be great. The legal promise conveys information (which a mere stated intention to pay would not) about the promisor's attitude toward the payment of debts barred by a technicality. The information conveyed enhances the promisor's reputation for credit-worthiness and may induce people—not necessarily the promisee himself, which is why the promise itself may not be bilateral—to extend credit to him in the future. And enforcement costs are likely to be low or at least no higher than in conventional bilateral-contract cases because the underlying obligation—the original debt—is fully bilateral. The original debt is not directly enforceable only because of a condition which in the case of the statute of limitations slightly, and in the case of discharge in bankruptcy or voidability by reason of minority not at all, increases the likelihood of error compared to what it would have been in a suit on the original bilateral contract that gave rise to the debt.

The foregoing are cases where, although the promise is not bilateral, the promisor's intent is not donative, that is, not motivated by interdependence between the promisor's and the promisee's utility functions. Another class of "past consideration" cases, however, is best understood on the premise of the law's (implicit) recognition of the existence of interdependent utility functions. These are cases involving promises to compensate rescuers or others who have rendered an unbargained but valuable service to the promisor. The existence of a promise in such a case is strongly attested by the presence of circumstances likely to induce an act of altruism by the promisor toward the promisee. *A* sees *B* about to be run down by a speeding car and pushes him out of the way. He saves him but sustains a serious injury in the process. In economic terms, *A* rescued *B* because at the moment of danger *B*'s expected utility or wealth was very low; the rescue was like a gift to a starving man. But after the rescue the wealth positions of the parties are dramatically reversed: now *A*'s wealth is low relative to *B*'s since *B* is whole and *A* is injured. Hence it is to be expected that *B* would promise to reward *A*.[7] The presence of altruistic motivation makes the promise a more plausible one—i.e., one less likely to be a figment of the promisee's imagination—than in the standard unilateral promise case. Stated otherwise, the legal-error costs of enforcing the promise are lower in the rescue case.

The facts of a leading rescue past-consideration case, Webb v. McGowin,[8] illustrate the benefits that may accrue to the promisor in such cases if the promise is legally enforceable, over and above the benefits of the transfer itself. The rescued person promised to pay his rescuer $15 every two weeks for the rest of the rescuer's life. This was a generous gift to the extent that the promise was enforceable but a much less generous one to the extent it was not. Had the promisor believed that such a promise was unenforceable, he might have decided instead to make a one-time transfer that might have had a much lower present value than that of the annuity which he in fact promised. Both parties would have been made worse off by this alternative. Hence, it is not surprising that the court held the promise to be enforceable.

Lon Fuller in a well-known article suggested a different rationale for the past-consideration doctrine.[9] Proceeding from the premise that the requirement of consideration is designed in part to prevent people from making promises on the spur of the moment—promises they do not really mean to make and therefore should not be forced to honor (the "cautionary" function of consideration)—he argues that where the promise is to do what the promisor is morally obligated to do anyway, we need not worry whether he is acting deliberately or not—he *should* have made the promise and that is all that is important.[10] This paternalistic approach is both difficult to square with the basic premises of contract law and an unnecessary embellishment to a theory of the enforcement of gratuitous promises. Fuller is aware of

7. See William M. Landes & Richard A. Posner, Salvors, Finders, Good Samaritans, and Other Rescuers: An Economic Study of Law and Altruism, 7 J. Legal Studies [83, 115-116] (1978).

8. 27 Ala. App. 82, 168 So. 196 (1935).

9. Lon L. Fuller, [p. 45 supra].

10. [41 Colum. L. Rev.] at 821.

the relevance of economic considerations in explaining the pattern of enforcement and only fails to see that economic analysis can also explain the past-consideration cases.

C. Promises Under Seal

Promises under seal are a traditional and, again, an economically appropriate exception to the requirement that an enforceable promise must be supported by consideration. The requirement of the seal eliminates the major administrative costs associated with the enforcement of unilateral promises. The formalities and written character of the promise reduce both the costs of determining the content of the promise and the probability that the promise was not made or was not intended to be binding.

The abolition by statute of the seal in many states is therefore a mysterious development from the standpoint of efficiency. The decline of this simple but reliable method of making a gratuitous promise binding has been deplored, and various proposals for a substitute method suggested. The legislative character of the abolition movement may reflect simply the difference between the courts and legislatures in the emphasis placed on efficiency. Or, less probably, it may reflect the rise of alternative methods of imparting enforceability to gratuitous promises, such as those discussed in this paper. One way of making a unilateral promise enforceable is for the promisor to exact a merely nominal consideration from the promisee, since courts normally inquire only into the existence and not into the adequacy of the consideration. But not only is this a cumbersome alternative to the promise under seal; increasingly, there is the danger that such a "contract" may be deemed unconscionably one-sided and so not enforced.

D. Charitable Pledges

There is considerable authority for relaxing the requirement of consideration (or reliance) in connection with promises of charitable donations, often to the point where the requirement seems to disappear.[11] This may be thought simply to reflect a special judicial partiality for charity (a partiality that might itself be based on an economic concern for the free-rider or public-good problems that may reduce charitable giving below optimal levels). But that is not an

11. See, for example, Allegheny College v. National Chautauqua County Bank of Jamestown, 246 N.Y. 369, 159 N.E. 173 (1927); Restatement of Contracts (Second) §90, Comment *f* (1973).

adequate explanation since one effect of enforcement is to increase the cost of making promises of charitable donations by reducing the donor's freedom of action; this could result in an actual decline in charitable giving. An alternative explanation, based on the approach of this paper, does not rely on the meritorious character of charity but instead emphasizes the large size of many charitable donations and the (related) desire of the donor to spread payment of a gift over a significant period of time, for tax, liquidity, or other reasons, as in the symphony-orchestra example discussed earlier.

E. Contract Modification

Often it is possible for a party to make a binding promise, unsupported by any fresh consideration, to modify a term of an existing contract. For example, the payor in a construction contract might agree to pay a higher price to a builder who had encountered unexpected soil conditions. The motives for such promises are various: to gain a reputation for "fair dealing" (really risk sharing), to avoid driving the promisee into bankruptcy (which might prevent his completing performance or raise the cost of his doing so), or even to be altruistic (the contingency giving rise to modification may have dramatically altered the relative wealth position of the parties). In any event, the stakes are often substantial in such cases, while the increment in utility to the promisor may also be substantial because of the length of time over which optimal performance may extend.

Consider the example of the house purchaser who promises the builder a higher than contract price because the builder has encountered some unexpected difficulty which may make it impossible[12] to complete the contract at the agreed price. If the purchaser merely declares his intention of paying the builder a higher price, but is free to renege, the builder may decide not to complete performance but instead to take his chances in bankruptcy court. Yet the promisor dare not pay him the extra price in advance in exchange for the builder's promise to continue, for if the contractor is financially shaky for other reasons, the prepayment may end up in the hands of a trustee in bankruptcy, with the purchaser relegated to the status of an unsecured creditor. This is a clear case where the enforcement of a promise not supported by fresh consideration enhances the welfare of the promisor.

The facts of a real case upholding enforceability of such a prom-

12. Yet not fall within the bounds of the contract doctrine that allows discharge on grounds of "impossibility"—on which see Richard A. Posner & Andrew M. Rosenfield, Impossibility and Related Doctrines in Contract Law: An Economic Analysis [p. 122 infra].

ise, Goebel v. Linn,[13] are rather similar to those of the last example. The defendants were brewers who had a contract with the plaintiff in the case, an ice company, to supply them with ice at a price not to exceed $2 a ton. An unusually mild winter ruined the local ice "crop" and the ice company informed the defendants that it would not continue to supply them with ice at the contract price. The defendants had a large stock of beer on hand that would spoil without refrigeration, and therefore agreed to pay the ice company $3.50 to continue the supply of ice under the contract. The defendants later repudiated the agreement and the ice company sued. In upholding the plaintiff's claim, the court observed that the defendants

> chose for reasons which they must have deemed sufficient at the time to submit to the company's demand and pay the increased price rather than rely upon their strict rights under the existing contract. . . . Suppose, for example, the defendants had satisfied themselves that the ice company under the very extraordinary circumstances of the entire failure of the local crop of ice must be ruined if their existing contracts were to be insisted upon, and must be utterly unable to respond in damages; it is plain that then, whether they chose to rely upon their contract or not, it could have been of little or no value to them. Unexpected and extraordinary circumstances had rendered the contract worthless; and they must either make a new arrangement, or, in insisting on holding the ice company to the existing contract, they would ruin the ice company and thereby at the same time ruin themselves.[14]

The result in this case has been criticized on the ground that it exposes promisees to extortion. In economic terms, the making of a contract may confer on the seller a monopoly vis-à-vis the buyer which the seller can exploit by threatening to terminate the contract unless the buyer agrees to pay a higher price than originally agreed upon. The court in *Goebel* was aware of this danger but found that the ice company's claim was not extortionate in this sense. This raises the question, however, whether extortion can be given a meaningful definition in the modification setting. To answer this question, it is helpful to distinguish three situations in which modification might be sought:

1. Nothing has changed since the contract was made, but the promisor, realizing that the remedies for breach of contract would not fully compensate the promisee, gives the promisee the unhappy choice of either paying the promisor more to complete the contract or pursuing his legal remedies.

2. Something has changed since the contract signing: the prom-

13. 47 Mich. 489, 11 N.W. 284 (1882).
14. 47 Mich. at 492-93, 11 N.W. at 285.

isee has given up alternative sources of supply or otherwise increased his dependence on the promisor. If modification is permitted the promisor can extract a monopoly rent from the promisee.

3. Something has changed since the contract signing: an unexpected event which, as in Goebel v. Linn, prevents the (willing) promisor from completing the promised performance without a modification of the contract.

The third case is the clearest for allowing modification. The inability of a willing promisor to complete performance removes the factor of strategic behavior that is present in cases one and two. No exploitation of a monopoly position or of the inadequacy of contractual remedies is involved in allowing modification in the third case. The first case might also seem one where modification should be allowed, on the basis of Holmes's "bad man" theory of contract law which has close affinities with the economic approach.[15] The legal obligation of a promisor is to perform or pay damages. If the promisee wants more—wants in effect specific performance—he must pay extra for it. That is all that *seems* to be involved in the first case but if we pause to ask why the promisee in the first case would ever agree to pay extra, we shall see that the first case is in reality a version of the second, the monopoly case. If the promisee in the first case has equally good alternative sources of supply, or at least no worse than he had when he made the original contract, he will have no incentive to pay a premium above the contract price for the promisor to perform as agreed; he will allow the promisor to breach and turn elsewhere. He will pay the premium only if his dependence on the promisor has increased since the signing of the contract, i.e., only if the contract gave the promisor a monopoly position vis-à-vis the promisee.

Alaska Packers' Ass'n v. Domenico[16] was such a case. The plaintiffs (technically "libelants") hired out as sailors and fishermen to the defendant (appellant), but soon after beginning work stopped and threatened to quit unless their wages were raised above the agreed amount. Defendant's agent agreed to pay the higher wage demanded but defendant later reneged. The court refused to enforce the modified contract, noting that

> the libelants agreed in writing, for a certain stated compensation, to render their services to the appellant in remote waters where the season for conducting fishing operations is extremely short, and in which enterprise the appellant had a large amount of money invested; and, after having entered upon the discharge of their contract, and at a time when it was impossible for the appellant to secure other men in their

15. [See Holmes, The Common Law, p. 28 supra.]
16. 117 Fed. 99 (9th Cir. 1902).

> places, the libelants, without any valid cause, absolutely refused to continue the services they were under contract to perform unless the appellant would consent to pay them more money.[17]

This seems a clear case where the motive for the modification was simply to exploit a monopoly position conferred on the promisors by the circumstances of the contract. It might seem that the promisee would have been in even worse shape if the men had quit as they threatened to do. However, since their only motive for threatening to quit was to extract a higher wage, there was probably little danger of their actually quitting. The danger would have been truly negligible had they known that they could not extract an enforceable commitment to pay them a higher wage.[18]

The court in *Alaska Packers'* criticized the earlier result in Goebel v. Linn, yet the cases are readily distinguishable, with the help of economic analysis. In *Goebel,* without a modification the promisor might well have terminated the contract, so the modification conferred a real benefit on the promisee. But in *Alaska Packers'* the likelihood of termination was much less since the threat to terminate was not a response to external conditions genuinely impairing the promisor's ability to honor the contract but merely a strategic ploy designed to exploit a monopoly position. A firm rule of nonenforceability in such cases solves the monopoly problem and thereby facilitates the making of contractual arrangements in which the promisee will be dependent on the good faith of the promisor.

One can relate this distinction back to the basic theme of this paper by noting that one effect of enforcing the kind of modification attempted in the *Alaska Packers'* case would be to reduce the benefits of contracting to people in the same situation as the plaintiffs in that case. Seamen thereafter could not expect to be promised a high wage in exchange for agreeing to work for a stated period at that wage, since the employer would know that the seamen were not obliged to honor their promise but could at any time "hold him up" for a higher wage. In a different form, this is the same problem as that of the man who derives little value from promising a future gift because the promise is not binding on him.

An intermediate case between the involuntary threat to terminate (Goebel v. Linn) and the monopolistic (Alaska Packers' Ass'n v. Domenico) is that of a promisor who threatens to terminate only because a third party has offered him a higher price for his goods.

17. Id. at 102.

18. If modifications were enforceable in these circumstances, the men might actually quit when the employer called their bluff in order to enhance the credibility of future threats. This incentive would disappear with a well-settled rule against enforceability.

Because the higher price is a genuine opportunity cost of continued compliance with the contract, the promisor should be allowed to terminate subject only to his obligation to make good the promisee's loss from the breach, and hence he should be allowed to negotiate with the promisee over a modification that will compensate the promisor for the lost opportunity. This was the result in Schwartzreich v. Bauman-Basch, Inc.[19]

*Unilateral and Implied Contracts and Restitution**

I. Unilateral Contracts

Another contract-law concept that encourages rescues notwithstanding the absence of a general common law counterpart to the maritime doctrine of salvage is that of the "unilateral contract." The owner of lost property can post a reward and anybody who, knowing of it, complies with its terms is legally entitled to it. The posting of the reward is the "offer" and performance of its conditions the "acceptance" which creates a legally binding contract. Because the potential finders of lost property will often be numerous and unidentified, there is no feasible way in which the owner could negotiate with each of them for the return of his property. The unilateral-contract approach enables voluntary transacting without actual negotiations with the potential transactors. . . .

Since the unilateral-contract doctrine enables the parties in the lost-property situation in effect to write their own contract, the law need not intervene and write a contract for them prescribing the finder's reward. [However,] in some cases the cost of communicating the terms of the offer to potential finders (who may be numerous and scattered) will be disproportionate to the value of the property lost. This is the economic basis of laws found in some states entitling the

19. 231 N.Y. 196, 131 N.E. 887 (1921). Indeed, from an economic standpoint a foregone benefit is no different from a direct cost; both are opportunity costs.

Section 2-209(1) of the Uniform Commercial Code provides that absence of consideration is not a defense in an action to enforce a modification of a contract. However, the Official Comment to this section states that the modification must be in "good faith" and implies that, under this standard, the modification in the *Alaska Packers'* case would not be enforced.

*The two excerpts comprising this selection are reprinted by permission from (1) William M. Landes & Richard A. Posner, Salvors, Finders, Good Samaritans, and Other Rescuers: An Economic Study of Law and Altruism, 7 J. Legal Studies 83, 116-118 (1978); and (2) Richard A. Posner, Economic Analysis of Law 97-98 (2d ed. 1977), and William M. Landes & Richard A. Posner, supra, at 109-110, 113-115. In the second excerpt, some footnote material has been incorporated into the text.

finder of lost property to claim a fixed reward (e.g., 10 percent of the value of the property found) from the owners, whether or not the owner has offered any reward.[1] Owners in general may benefit from such a law because knowledge of the law will activate some finders to whom the terms of an offered reward could not be communicated at reasonable cost.

. . . A highly questionable—and generally rejected[2]—use of laws compelling return of lost property has been to deny the finder the right to claim a reward offered by the owner.[3] The "reasoning" is that since the finder *had* to return the property under the compulsion of law, the return is not consideration supporting the promise of a reward and the promise is therefore unenforceable. But the owner of the property, knowing of the law and gauging its effect, will adjust the reward according to his perception of its effectiveness. If he still offers a positive reward, this suggests that the resources devoted to enforcing the law are insufficient to induce the optimal level of finding.

II. Implied Contracts and Restitution

A physician chances upon a stranger lying unconscious on the street, treats him, and later demands a fee. Has he a legal claim? The law's answer is "yes," but judges and legal scholars have had difficulty articulating the rationale for this result. The older legal terminology spoke of an "implied contract" between the physician and the stranger for medical assistance. But the notion of an implied contract in the absence of any communication, express or implied, has been attacked as a fiction, and modern writers prefer to base the physician's legal right on the principle of "unjust enrichment." This term suggests a moral basis for law (perhaps) divorced from the economic. In fact, the principal case outcomes are better explained in economic than moral terms, and it turns out that the concept of an implied contract is a useful shorthand for an economic approach which, among other things, suggests an unbroken continuity between express contracts and the questions nowadays treated under such rubrics as restitution and unjust enrichment.

In the case first put, the costs of a voluntary transaction would be prohibitive. The source of the high transaction costs in that case was

1. See, for example, Flood v. City National Bank of Clinton, 253 N.W. 509 (Ia. 1934); Annot., 95 A.L.R. 1176 (1935).

2. See, for example, Berthiaume v. Doe, 22 Cal. App. 78, 133 P. 515 (1913).

3. See Rheinhauer v. De Krieges, 188 Misc. 747, 67 N.Y.S.2d 211 (N.Y. City Ct. 1946); Note, Rewards for the Return of Lost Property: Are They Void in New York?, 24 St. John's L. Rev. 287 (1950).

incapacity; in other cases it might be time (e.g., the stranger is conscious but bleeding profusely and there is no time to discuss terms). In such cases we must consider whether, had transaction costs not been prohibitive, the parties would have come to terms and if so what (approximately) the terms would have been. If a court can be reasonably confident both that there would have been a transaction and what its essential terms would have been (that the physician use his best efforts and that the patient pay the physician's normal fee for treatment of the sort rendered), it should not, and does not, hesitate to write, after the fact, a contract between the parties.

Consider now a case in which the courts refuse to imply a contract. A man stands under my window, playing the violin—quite beautifully, let us say—and when he has finished knocks on my door and demands a fee for his efforts. Having enjoyed his playing, I nonetheless refuse. The court would deny his claim for the fee—however reasonable the fee might appear to be—on the ground that, although the violinist conferred a benefit on me (and not with the intent that it be gratuitous), he did so "officiously." Translated from legal into economic terminology, this means he conferred an unbargained-for benefit in circumstances where the costs of a voluntary bargain would have been low. In such cases, as has been emphasized repeatedly in this book, the law insists that the voluntary route be followed—and is on firm economic grounds in doing so. . . .

[The earlier discussion assumed that the physician did not intend to render treatment without compensation.] The Restatement of Restitution [establishes] a presumption that where a professional (e.g., a physician) is the rescuer he does intend to charge and is entitled to compensation equal to his usual fee for the type of service rendered to the rescued person. Conversely, the nonprofessional rescuer is presumed not to intend to charge.[4]

This distinction may have an economic rationale.[5] The physician is a professional. Both the opportunity cost of his time and the amount of time he provides in rendering medical assistance are likely to be greater than those of the passerby who, noticing a person lying injured in the street, must decide whether to summon assistance. The greater cost to the physician of effecting rescue reduces the likelihood that altruism alone would prompt him to do so. At the same time, the costs to the legal system of determining an appro-

4. The case law appears to go beyond the Restatement and make the presumption of no intent to charge irrebutable, with the result that the nonprofessional rescuer is never entitled to a monetary reward.

5. As implicitly recognized in John P. Dawson, Negotiorum Gestio: The Altruistic Intermeddler, 74 Harv. L. Rev. 817, 1073, 1085, 1126 (1961).

priate award are lower in the professional's case: the award can virtually be read off the physician's fee schedule, whereas the non-professional rescuer by definition does not sell equivalent services in a market.

One difference between common law and maritime principles is that while the maritime salvor is rewarded only if the salvage is successful, the physician (or other professional rescuer on land) is entitled to his normal fee regardless of success. However, medical treatment is more standardized than maritime salvage technique and therefore more readily evaluated. This, combined with the difficulty in many cases of evaluating the contribution of the physician's services to the patient's recovery, is no doubt why physicians generally charge for services rendered rather than the results obtained; consistently with its fundamental (economic) purpose of simulating the market, rescue law follows this pattern. . . .

A question has sometimes arisen whether the proper fee to award to the physician in a rescue case is *his* standard fee or the standard fee of physicians in his locality. The courts correctly hold that it is the former. The higher fee presumably reflects a higher quality of services rendered, but even if it does not, it would be a mistake to give the physician less for it would induce him to substitute away from providing services in emergencies.

The courts have divided over a related question—whether, if the physician regularly varies his charges according to the income of the patient (that is, price discriminates), he should be permitted to claim a higher fee in a rescue case where it turns out that the person he treated was affluent.[6] The physician in his normal practice "sizes up" the patient and charges according to an estimate of the patient's income, but he does not make a thorough investigation to find out what the income actually is. In the emergency case, where there is no regular physician-patient relationship, the physician might after the fact undertake a rather minute investigation of the patient's financial circumstances to enable him to discriminate more precisely than he normally does. This is an argument against permitting discrimination in the rescue case. The more common argument that discrimination is morally or economically objectionable is simply irrelevant in this setting since the purpose of the rescue award should be to simulate rather than reform the practices prevailing in the professional's regular market. To use rescue doctrine to change the medical fee system would be quixotic.

As a detail, we note that in common law cases where the courts

6. Compare Cotnam v. Wisdom, 83 Ark. 601, 104 S.W. 164 (1907), with Matheson v. Smiley, 40 Man. 247, (1932) 2 D.L.R. 787.

do recognize salvage rights, they have traditionally spoken of an "implied contract" between the parties. This usage has been sharply criticized as involving a fiction.[7] Modern writers prefer to view the obligation as imposed in order to avoid the "unjust enrichment" of the victim at the expense of the salvor. Yet the older term can be given a precise economic meaning: an implied contract is one the parties did not make but would have made had they had the opportunity to negotiate, because the circumstances made an exchange between them necessary to maximize value.

As a further refinement, one can distinguish between a contract "implied in fact" and one "implied in law." The former is a contractual agreement inferred from a previously existing contractual relationship between the parties, the latter an agreement fashioned by the court between parties who did not previously have such a relationship. The rule of general average illustrates the former; the right of a physician to reimbursement from the unconscious accident victim whom he finds in the street, the latter.

A difficult group of [nonaccident] cases involves situations where, although the number of parties is small, usually only two, there are pronounced elements of bilateral monopoly. Some examples are:

(1) *A* and *B* are joint tenants of a property. *A* makes improvements and seeks to charge *B* for a share of them. *B* refuses. Has *A* a legal claim against *B* for reimbursement of a share of the expense?

(2) *A* and *B* are second mortgagee and mortgagor, respectively. *A* pays the interest owed by *B* to the first mortgagee in order to avoid a foreclosure which would wipe out *A*'s, the junior creditor's, interest. Can *A* sue *B* for the discharge of *B*'s debt?

(3) *A* and *B* are adjacent landowners. Both are plagued by marshy soil conditions. *A* drains his land and in doing so unavoidably lowers the water table on *B*'s land as well, to *B*'s benefit; can *A* claim from *B* a share of the expense of drainage?[8]

Example (2) brings out the sharp difference between this group of cases and those previously discussed. *A* in the example is seeking reimbursement for discharge of another's contractual obligation, even though no emergency precluded negotiations between *A* and *B*. However, earlier we suggested an economic rationale for judicial intervention in cases where the parties are bilateral monopolists, and

7. See, for example, United Australia, Ltd. v. Barclays Bank, Ltd., [1941] A.C. 1, 23-29.

8. For a good discussion of such cases see John P. Dawson, The Self-Serving Intermeddler, 89 Harv. L. Rev. 1409 (1974).

we saw that the courts in admiralty cases do in fact intervene in such cases.[9]

How does the common law deal with the problem? In case (1), joint tenancy, the improver's claim for restitution is denied. In case (2), discharge of another's debt to protect one's own interest, restitution is allowed. And in case (3), improvement by one landowner that benefits his neighbor, restitution is again denied. Although the pattern of the cases has been called "decidedly irregular,"[10] it appears to be consistent with the economics of the problem. Since a joint tenant has a right to the partition of jointly owned property, the usual effect, and apparently the purpose, of denying restitution for a joint tenant's improvements is to induce the partition of the property.[11] This eliminates the problem of bilateral monopoly, at least in the typical case, because after partition an improvement by one of the former joint tenants will no longer confer an uncompensated benefit on the other.

In the debt case, the usual objection to the courts' writing contracts between parties who failed to agree on terms—that the courts cannot readily approximate the terms that would have been negotiated in a competitive market—is absent. The amount of the debt that is discharged, a sum certain, is a close approximation to the competitive price for the service rendered by the discharging party to the debtor. The costs of using the legal system in this case are low relative to those of a market distorted by bilateral monopoly.

The most difficult case is that of the neighboring landowners where an improvement by one must benefit the other.[12] The choice between forcing the parties to bargain under conditions of bilateral monopoly and using the legal system to measure the benefit con-

9. [The authors explain, 7 J. Legal Studies at 91: "Even where there is both mental capacity and adequate time for negotiating, the process of voluntary exchange may not work efficiently. Suppose the sinking ship is far out at sea—though in no immediate danger of sinking—and a potential rescuer comes upon it by chance or by responding to its distress signal. There is time for negotiation but little likelihood of another ship's chancing on the scene. The potential rescuer therefore has a monopoly position which he can use to try to extract the victim's promise, prior to initiation of any rescue efforts, to pay him all or most of the value of the ship and cargo. At the same time, because the rescuer has no alternative customer for his rescue services at the place where he has found the ship in distress, the 'rescuee' has a monopoly position, making the situation one of bilateral monopoly. Transaction costs under bilateral monopoly are high because there is a range of possible prices which invites haggling. The haggling may be protracted, costly, and sometimes unsuccessful in producing agreement on terms."]

10. Id. at 1418.

11. Id. at 1423-27.

12. These include, however, joint-tenancy cases in which, even after partition, an improvement by one of the former joint tenants of his now wholly owned parcel would unavoidably increase the value of the parcel owned by the other former joint tenant.

ferred on the nonagreeing landowners is a difficult one, so we are not surprised that the legal system should here opt for nonintervention.

NOTES AND QUESTIONS

1. One way of organizing your thinking about the readings in this chapter is to ask whether *all* promises should not, prima facie, be enforced. Two economic reasons come to mind as to why some promises should not be enforced. First, a nonenforceable promise may have economic utility that would be destroyed if all promises were enforceable (can you think of examples of this?). Second, sometimes the costs of enforcement outweigh the benefits, those costs including not only the direct costs of utilizing the legal system but also the costs of legal error (on which see Richard A. Posner, Economic Analysis of Law 430-433 (2d ed. 1977)).

2. Fuller argues that the half-completed exchange provides a stronger case for enforcement of a promise than a completely executory contract because the former involves an element of unjust enrichment and the latter does not. Can you restate this distinction in economic terms? Cf. the Birmingham excerpt in Chapter 2.

3. In the example put by Fuller where the uncle promises his nephew a reward for not smoking, why should the uncle not be permitted to sue if the nephew, having agreed not to smoke, reneges? Is it because the costs to the uncle of the breach are negligible? Would they be negligible in the case of a commercial contract that was breached while still completely executory? Cf. the discussion of expectation damages in Barton's article in Chapter 7, and in the Notes and Questions at the end of that chapter. Are there other economic objections to enforcement in this hypothetical?

4. One approach to the problem of legal-error costs in contract cases is simply to deny enforcement to entire classes of contracts in which those costs seem excessive in relation to the benefits of enforcement. Another is to attempt to reduce those costs through devices like the parol evidence rule, the Statute of Frauds, and the seal. Does Fuller regard the doctrine of consideration as designed in part to reduce legal-error costs? How could it do this?

5. Would you think it a good idea to require that all promises be reduced to writing in order to be legally enforceable? Would this be feasible with regard to transactions, both commercial and personal, in which time is at a premium—e.g., an investor placing an order with his stockbroker? The Statute of Frauds applies mainly to real estate transactions, where it can be argued that (a) the costs of

reducing the contract to writing are small relative to the stakes of the transaction and (b) the transaction normally proceeds at a sufficiently leisurely pace to make it possible to reduce it to writing without incurring significant costs in terms of lost opportunity.

6. Suppose that Jones tells Smith he will pay Smith $1000 if Smith weaves a rug for him. Smith begins to work, without notifying Jones that he has done so. A month passes and Jones, not having heard from Smith, arranges to purchase a rug from someone else. Smith subsequently presents Jones with a finished rug and demands payment. Would it be sensible, from an economic point of view, to allow Smith to recover? Suppose that Smith had notified Jones that he had begun work on the rug. What difference should this make? What if Jones, upon receiving notification from Smith, tells him to forget the whole thing—that he no longer has an interest in a rug made by Smith or anyone else? Is there an economic argument for *not* applying the doctrine of promissory estoppel in this situation? See Crook v. Cowan, 64 N.C. 627 (1870), and Sections 56 and 63 of the Second Restatement of Contracts.

7. Mills v. Wyman, 20 Mass. (3 Pick.) 207 (1825), involved a lawsuit against the father of a young man whom the plaintiff had cared for when the young man became ill away from home. The plaintiff's services were rendered without any thought of compensation, and were not bestowed at the request of the father. In fact, the father only learned about the plaintiff's kindness after his son had died. Influenced, in the court's words, by "a transient feeling of gratitude," the father promised in writing to pay the plaintiff for the expenses incurred in caring for his son. The father later reneged on his promise and the plaintiff sued. Although expressing moral disapproval, the Massachusetts court held the father was under no legal duty to pay.

Can this case be reconciled, on economic grounds, with Webb v. McGowin, discussed in Posner, p. 52 supra? What additional information, if any, do you need to answer this question?

8. A question that arises in unilateral-contract cases is whether the finder, in order to be entitled to the reward, must know of it before he completes performance. The majority position is that he must (e.g., Fitch v. Snedaker, 38 N.Y. 248 (1868)). This result is critized on economic grounds in Richard A. Posner, Economic Analysis of Law 72-73 (2d ed. 1977):

> The legal justification, casuistic rather than practical, for this result is that acceptance requires knowledge of the offer; the economic issue is whether the return of lost property would be encouraged or discouraged by a rule requiring actual knowledge of the offer. To analyze this question, it is necessary to distinguish between two types

> of finder: the finder who is induced to search for lost property by the knowledge that a reward has been offered for its return, and the casual finder, who will not invest in search but who will return lost property if he happens to find it, knowing that there is or may be a reward. A rule requiring actual knowledge discourages the casual finder (assuming he knows about the rule), but by the same token encourages the active searcher by reducing the likelihood that his competitor, the casual finder, will return the property if he finds it first. The question then becomes whether the increase in returns by active searchers is likely to be greater or less than the decrease in returns by casual finders. At a guess, it is likely to be less, for it would seem that active searchers are much less common than casual finders, in which event a rule that encourages the former only by discouraging the latter is likely to reduce the amount of lost property returned.[1]

Does this analysis undermine the positive economic theory of law?

9. Suppose one were to approach the question of whether to enforce promises from the standpoint of maximizing personal autonomy rather than economic efficiency. Would this lead one to favor Fuller's or Posner's view of the enforceability of gratuitous promises?

10. Suppose a promise not intended to induce costly reliance by the promisee in fact does so, the promisee reasonably believing that such reliance is within the contemplation of the promisor. In these circumstances, the promisee may be able to enforce the promise under the doctrine of promissory estoppel (Section 90 of the Restatement of Contracts). Is the rationale for enforcement in these circumstances based on tort or contract concepts? Does this or should this make a difference in terms of the measure of damages applied in such a case? In this last regard, compare the text of Section 90 in the Second Restatement with the original version in the First Restatement.

1. See William M. Landes & Richard A. Posner, The Private Enforcement of Law, 4 J. Legal Studies 1, 44-46 (1975), for a formal analysis of this problem. [Footnote in original.]

Chapter 4

Duress and Unconscionability

*Duress by Economic Pressure**

John Dalzell

It will be suggested . . . that, at least as compared with the consent to a valid contract, the consent secured by duress is in some way less genuine, more superficial, in that the latter is the product of constraint, not of a free will, being given merely to avoid a more serious evil. As Justice Holmes has said, it is characteristic of duress that the victim makes a choice, in accordance with his own self-interest, between two evils. But a similar motivation underlies the ordinary contractual transaction. We speak of a contract as being "voluntary," the result of "free will," but it is easy to forget that a will exercises its freedom only in selecting one of several possible courses of action. I agree to pay ten cents for a loaf of bread, not because I want to give the baker ten cents, but because that's the only way I can get the bread. I am choosing between alternatives, giving up the dime or doing without the bread. If my will were completely unrestrained, I should almost certainly prefer to get the bread and also keep the money. My freedom is simply the opportunity to decide whether I will give up the ten cents, or do without the bread—to choose one of two courses, neither of which is entirely satisfactory. That is, I am "free" to select the lesser of two evils; so far as the present point is concerned, that is exactly the situation I [am in if I sign a] contract at the point of a gun. The unpleasant alternative to buying the bread might conceivably be death, too; yet if I were

*Reprinted, by permission, from 20 North Carolina Law Review 237, 238-240, 255-264 (1942).

forced to surrender my last worldly possession to get food we would hesitate to call the exaction duress.

It seems more reasonable to say that a contract or payment secured by duress is defective not because of some difference in the nature of the consent, but because of the impropriety of the alternative presented; that is, of the pressure used. . . .The theory underlying this article is that, to constitute duress, the following elements are both essential and sufficient: (1) the transaction must be induced by a wrongful threat, (2) for which the law offers no adequate remedy, that is, no remedy which (by practical laymen's standards, not those of the common-law nor even of equity) is really sufficient to compensate for the wrong suffered if the threat should be carried out. While this analysis is believed appropriate for all forms of duress, its application to the field of economic or business compulsion alone is intended to be discussed here. . . .

Private individuals are . . . aware of the effectiveness in some situations of a threat to break a contract. In some contractual dealings, the two parties cannot always keep abreast of each other in performance as the work progresses. Inequalities of investment in preparation and performance, or other inequalities between the parties, create situations where one can exert considerable pressure on the other by a threat of disregard of contract obligations. A threat to break a contract is always a threat to commit a wrong (except in situations where there is a legal excuse, which are of course excluded from this discussion), and the common law allows damages for that wrong. Our courts have usually but not invariably refused to see any relievable duress in contracts or payments made under such a threat. . . .

[Consider the case of a] debtor representing a partnership who, after computing their liability from their own records for work already completed, in one sentence, admits owing $4,260 and offers a $4,000 note in full settlement, adding that the creditor can take the note or sue, just as he likes. But the creditor is faced with pressing financial obligations, which have been awaiting this payment—so pressing that any considerable delay in meeting them will mean ruin for the creditor. He, accordingly, takes the $4,000 note and gives a receipt in full; later he attacks the settlement on the ground of duress. The Michigan Supreme Court, in one of the important decisions in this field, Hackley et al. v. Headley, reversed the trial court and rejected the claim of duress, saying:

> "In what did the alleged duress consist in the present case? Merely in this: that the debtors refused to pay on demand a debt already due, though the plaintiff was in great need of the money and might be financially ruined in case he failed to obtain it. It is not pretended that

> Hackley & McGordon had done anything to bring Headley to the condition which made this money so important to him at this very time, or that they were in any manner responsible for his pecuniary embarrassment except as they failed to pay this demand. The duress, then, is to be found exclusively in their failure to meet promptly their pecuniary obligation. But this, according to the plaintiff's claim, would have constituted no duress whatever if he had not happened to be in pecuniary straits; and the validity of negotiations, according to this claim, must be determined, not by the defendants' conduct, but by the plaintiff's necessities. The same contract which would be valid if made with a man easy in his circumstances, becomes invalid when the contracting party is pressed with the necessity of immediately meeting his bank paper. But this would be a most dangerous, as well as a most unequal doctrine: and if accepted, no one could well know when he would be safe in dealing on the ordinary terms of negotiation with a party who professed to be in great need."

Inadequacy of the remedy available for a threatened wrong had little weight in that decision. The last-quoted statements seem based on the doctrine that a subjective test for duress is impracticable; this theory has been widely discarded since the above decision. The other argument by the court against duress was that the debtor did not cause the embarrassing circumstances which made his threat effective. Where the debtor consciously took advantage of those circumstances, however, the fact that he did not create them should be treated as of little importance. It is so in other cases of duress. When the employer whose funds have been embezzled secures repayment from the guilty employee's mother by reminding her of the danger of criminal prosecution of the son, there is relievable duress; but the employer's threat is effective because of the crime committed by the son, not because of any circumstances for which the employer is responsible. The debtor in the Michigan case knew of the creditor's financial embarrassment and threatened a wrong, a breach of contract, knowing that threat would be practically irresistible because of the circumstances. . . .

. . . These cases are typical of the weight of authority, but there are some decisions which have treated a refusal to pay money due under a contract as relievable duress. Where a seaman's wages, payable at the end of a voyage, were withheld until he gave a release on a disputed claim, comparatively early American decisions treated the release as of no effect. Another employee was given the same relief as against a settlement agreed to, at the end of a term of employment in Panama, as the only means of collecting out of sums due him from the employer, enough to pay passage money back home; in this case the court looked on the threat used, since it in effect was a threat to keep the employee in a distant country, as analogous to duress by imprisonment. . . .

Even these minority decisions which recognize the possibility of duress in a refusal to pay money due cannot be said to give any express approval to the idea that the true test is "threatened wrong plus inadequate legal remedy." No clear reference to inadequacy of remedy appears in any of them. Yet in all of them one essential factor in the decision is the victim's pressing need for immediate payment, either because he is far from home without passage money, or is faced with labor and material claims which demand immediate satisfaction; in all of them, then, the common law remedy, an action to enforce the contract, is insufficient because of the delay involved in its assertion. . . .

Our system of free competition or Anglo-Saxon individualism also encourages the seller to refuse delivery on his contract in order to force payment of higher prices, where the buyer is unable to supply his needs elsewhere. The payment or contract secured by these means is not the result of duress, according to practically all our decisions.

In the days when ice was a product of nature rather than of electricity, and a summer's supply depended almost entirely on the amount cut out of lakes and stored during the preceding winter, a firm of brewers had contracted for a year's supply of ice at $1.75 a ton, or $2 if scarcity developed. The brewers had chances during the spring to buy ice elsewhere, and talked to the ice company here involved about making such arrangements, but were assured that the contract would be carried out. In May, however, when it was too late to get ice elsewhere, the seller refused further deliveries at the contract price, because of failure of the winter's ice crop. Five dollars a ton was the price originally demanded by the seller, but this was finally reduced to three dollars and fifty cents. The only ice available was that of this seller, and it was shown that lack of ice for two days, or possibly even one day, would have ruined all the good beer in the making. Of course the brewers gave in, paid three dollars and fifty cents a ton for eight months, and then when sued on a note given to the seller, sought relief on the ground of duress. The decision resulting, Goebel v. Linn, is another leading authority from Michigan; the court said, of the defendant brewers' claim of duress:

> "It is to be observed of these circumstances that if we confine our attention to the very time when the arrangement for an increased price was made the defendants make out a very plausible case. They had then a very considerable stock of beer on hand, and the case they make is one in which they must have ice at any cost, or they must fail in business. If the ice company had the ability to perform their contract, but took advantage of the circumstances to extort a higher price from the necessities of the defendants, its conduct was reprehensible, and it would perhaps have been in the interest of good morals if defendants

> had temporarily submitted to the loss and brought suit against the ice company on their contract. No one disputes that at their option they might have taken that course, and that the ice company would have been responsible for all damages legally attributable to the breach of its contract."

After pointing to eight months of acquiescence by the brewers as some evidence that the new arrangement was voluntary, the decision concludes:

> "But if our attention were to be restricted to the very day when notice was given that ice would no longer be supplied at the contract price, we could not agree that the case was one of duress. It is not shown to be a case even of a hard bargain; and the price charged was probably not too much under the circumstances. But for the pre-existing contract the one now questioned would probably have been fair enough, and if made with any other party would not have been complained of. The duress is therefore to be found in the refusal to keep the previous engagements. How far this falls short of legal duress was so recently considered by us in Hackley & McGordon v. Headley, 45 Mich. 569, that further discussion now would serve no valuable purpose."

The rule which this concluding language expresses, and for which the decision is generally cited, that a threat to refuse delivery of goods according to contract necessarily falls far short of legal duress, indicates a total blindness to business realities, and sometimes works a serious injustice. The ice dealer's threat was a gun pointed at the heart of the brewer's business, and should be treated as such. The court says that if the victim, "in the interest of good morals," had refused to pay the higher price, "all damages legally attributable" to the wrong would have been recoverable. This assurance is not very satisfactory to one who learns that there may be a vast difference between the damages recoverable as "legally attributable" to the wrong, and the damages *actually resulting* from the wrong. Moreover, the remedy of damages is about as satisfactory after the business is dead, as it would be after the pistol had been discharged and the man was dead.

There are other arguments in the decision, almost certainly mere make-weights to support the conclusion already settled upon to follow the rule in Hackley v. Headley. The court talks of the fairness of the substituted agreement, or rather of the lack of evidence that it was unfair considering market prices at the time the new agreement was made. In German law, duress problems are decided by looking at the reasonableness of the transaction compelled by the duress, and even by altering the terms when necessary to make the agreement reasonable; but Anglo-American law is devoted to the theory that the courts should avoid wherever possible all consideration of the reasonableness of the terms of a contract. Although reasonableness of the terms of the contract may be indirect evidence of the absence of coercion, in measuring the reasonableness of the terms for this purpose, something other than current market prices of the product should be considered; from the viewpoint of the buyer who has a valid contract entitling him to the goods at less than market prices, the payment of market prices is not reasonable. And if society is interested in enforcing contracts, this is also the social viewpoint, "in the interest of good morals," as the Michigan decision admitted. It was also suggested that possibly the brewers agreed to the increase in price as the only means of assuring a supply of ice for themselves, because without it the ice dealer's business would collapse and he would be unable to perform on any of his contracts. If there had been evidence that this was the situation, it should have been considered; but the court's suggestion was admittedly a hypothesis in its most naked form, without a shred of evidence to cover it. The idea is intriguing in its troublesome possibilities, but should not play any part under the evidence in this case. The fact that the brewers had sufficient bargaining leverage to reduce the ice dealer's price from the originally demanded $5.00 a ton to $3.50 a ton, is substantial evidence that the brewers had some influence over the ice dealer; but the threat of the latter against the business life of the brewer was the controlling factor in the situation, and was, as a matter of plain business fact, simply irresistible.

*Institutional Change and the Quasi-Invisible Hand**

Victor P. Goldberg

. . . Consumers regularly enter into contracts with the terms specified by the producer—they are what we might call "contract term takers." When a customer parks a car in a parking lot he enters into a contract specifying liability for theft or damage and a number of other terms. Bargaining over the terms of the contract is usually not possible; neither the lot attendant nor the customer would normally be capable of preparing a valid agreement and lawyer's fees would make redrafting out of the question. The lot owner who will enter into a large number of agreements will find it in his best interest to have a lawyer "mass produce" a standard contract: this contract should reflect the owner's interests in the best possible manner. If customers could band together somehow and spread the

*Reprinted, by permission, from 17 J. Law & Econ. 461, 462, 483-490 (1974), copyright 1974 by the University of Chicago Law School.

costs they might be able to render the contract terms more favorable to themselves. There are a number of ways to effect this. One method would be to use lawsuits to obtain a judicial narrowing of the lot owner's discretion in stating contract terms (financing for the suit might come from a single martyr or an automobile association); another would be to establish legislative restrictions on the terms of the contracts; a third would be to leave adjustment of contract terms to a parking lot licensing or regulating agency. Lot owners have an incentive to avoid these solutions, maintain maximum control over contract terms, and make legal action as expensive as possible for the customer (for example, attain the right to hold the customer's car until the litigation is settled). . . .

[Many economists treat] the problem [of the form contract] by assuming it away. . . . If people voluntarily enter into contracts it is because it is in their best interest to do so. If the terms of one producer are unsatisfactory, the customer will shop around for others; if information on contract terms were costlessly available (and could be analyzed costlessly) he would continue shopping until he received precisely the desired combination of price, quantity, and other contract terms. This, implicitly, is how economists have handled the problem. Additional sophistication occasionally creeps in by the recognition of costs of attaining, processing, and evaluating information; the consumer then would engage in such information processing to the point at which the expected marginal benefits of the additional information are equated to the marginal costs of its acquisition.

Suppose, however, that rather than view the standard form contract as a voluntary agreement, we view it instead as private legislation; the legislature in effect delegates the lawmaking process to private parties. . . . We will first stipulate that we are interested here only in the "hidden" terms of the contract—those beside the basic price and quantity terms. While such terms could be tailor-made for each contract, there are substantial economies to be gained by spreading the costs of producing (and analyzing the impact of) these terms over a large number of contracts. The firm, which regularly enters into the same type of transactions, will be able to achieve these economies (either by itself or by purchasing the service from specialists—lawyers); the consumer, generally, will not. The standard form contract therefore will be legislation produced in an arena which rewards the resources held by one party—the firm. The result, in Llewellyn's words "has seemed even in such highly competitive spheres as installment sales, residence leases, investments, and commercial banking to be . . . [the] accumulation of seller-protective instead of customer-protective clauses."

We might expect competition in the market to constrain the

firm's power in this arena. After all, the firm makes its price in this arena too, and if the industry is reasonably competitive we would expect that this competition would shield the price taker from the firm's power. Why will not competition among producers protect the contract term taker as well? The answer is twofold. On the one hand the cost of acquiring and processing information on contract terms is much greater than for price; unless the firm intentionally makes the particular term an important selling point—as is sometimes the case with the length or inclusiveness of the warranty—few, if any, customers will perceive the existence of variations in terms. Any movement toward contractual equilibrium due to the aggressive bargain-seeking of a few customers will be slow indeed due to both (1) the fewness of customers who will find it worthwhile to pay the costs of acquiring information, and (2) the ease with which a producer can "contract term discriminate"—renegotiate the terms for the few aggressive customers while keeping the high information barrier for other customers virtually intact. The second answer is that the "aggressive bargain-seeking customer" is usually just a minor figure in the equilibrating process. More important, in general, is the role of new entry (or exit) of producers. If the firms in an industry are making profits because they have written standardized contract terms that are very favorable to them, they will attract new entrants into the industry. The entry will continue until excess profits are bid away. The benefits to the firms of the standardized terms will be capitalized into the firms' value. Thus, while competition between producers will in the long run yield zero profits, the firm will be able to attain a capital gain (or prevent a capital loss) by choosing the appropriate standard contract terms.

This does not necessarily mean, however, that the industry as a whole will be better off or that the industry's gains will come at the expense of the consumer. It might well be that the equilibrium terms arrived at are optimal for both producers and consumers, but there is no reason to presume this to be true. Consider, for example, the following scenario. Assume a competitive insurance industry with minimal government intervention. Firms in the industry compete by lowering their price and then compensate for this by decreasing the coverage (in as hidden a way as possible) with other firms being forced to cut also in order to remain competitive. A sort of "Gresham's Law" of bad policies driving out good would ensue. Both the quality of insurance contracts and the total sales of the industry are likely to fall.

This is not the end of the story. Both producers and consumers will have incentives to search for methods for improving upon this result. . . . Brand names and advertising might be used as indicators of product quality in general (including the terms of the contract); consumers might take price as an indicator of quality; or private producers of information might appear. While such private market solutions will, to some extent, ameliorate the Gresham's Law problem considered in the previous paragraph, there is no reason to believe that the market will negate the standard form contract problem.

If the government's role is restricted to passive enforcement of private contracts, then there will be many standard form contract terms produced which are, in effect, legislation produced by a single party. The consumer need not necessarily suffer as a result, but his protection by market forces will in many instances be weak. . . . In some instances all parties will benefit from the standard forms while in others all parties will be hurt. In many instances some consumers will benefit while others will be harmed. (For example, harsh terms will, in equilibrium, yield lower prices; those who would prefer the harsh term-low price combination will benefit at the expense of those who would have preferred an easier term-higher price combination.)

How should the courts react to the standard form contract? If they were to adopt the economist's faulty idealization of the contracting process, courts would accept the terms of the contract without question and hold the parties to them. Courts have essentially stuck to this approach although . . . they have often resorted to very liberal interpretations of the contract to reach what they regard as a fair result. A number of commentators have argued that only by divorcing themselves from the fiction that the standard form contract is no different from the idealized contract between equals will courts be able to come to grips with the problem. Slawson,[1] for example, argues that the court must decide what the consumer could reasonably have been expected to consider as part of the transaction. This alone the court should accept as the contract to which the consumer has manifested agreement. The other terms must then be judged against some reasonable standards; essentially, all goods sold with a standard form have an "implied warranty of fitness for intended purpose." Even if an express warranty is included in the standard form it will not be treated as part of the contract if the court finds it inconsistent with the implied warranty.

This is not the place for a detailed analysis of Slawson's proposal. Clearly, courts will differ substantially in determining what part of a standard form contract has been agreed to and what part must pass the reasonableness test; they will further disagree as to

1. W. David Slawson, Standard Form Contracts and Democratic Control of Law-Making Power, 84 Harv. L. Rev. 529 (1971).

what ought to determine reasonableness. The point, though, is that it is possible for judges to abandon the mythology of freedom of contract and to put limits on the ability of the firm(s) to produce private legislation in the form of standard contracts.

While the courts might in the future be induced to take a more pro-consumer stance in litigation, this will likely prove of only marginal assistance to most consumers. Lawsuits are expensive, risky affairs with the expenses frequently in excess of the expected gains to the single individual were he to win. Realizing this, firms would have little incentive to remove unenforceable terms from their contracts. (Many contracts carry unenforceable waivers of liability; a consumer when shown he had "agreed" to this provision would likely give up rather than bring the matter to a lawyer.) So, while some relief for the consumer might be possible in the judicial arena, it is doubtful that this in itself would be of much value.

One possible response to the standard form contract problem would be to provide consumers with an agent who would aid in the production of standardized terms. The government can fill the role of agent; assume initially an ideal government attempting to fill this role faithfully. The legislature could suggest terms that the parties might include in their contracts if they so agree, set terms that will hold unless the contract explicitly replaces them, prohibit the inclusion of certain terms, or set terms which cannot be altered by the parties. Alternatively the legislature might choose to delegate the task to a regulatory agency (or other nonlegislative body). This arrangement permits an ongoing review of contract terms; the agency can adjust terms in light of past experience and can bargain with the producers concerning possible innovations.

Not all consumers will benefit equally from the agent's efforts. Indeed, in most instances some consumers are likely to be worse off, receiving protection from a clause that affected them little or not at all in exchange for a higher price. Given that the agent's costs must be spread over a large number of consumers with different preferences, it is inevitable that the agent must regularly engage in making interpersonal comparisons in producing contract terms. To be sure, the same is true without government intervention where the firm (or the market) in effect plays the role of agent in producing and modifying standard form contract terms.

It should come as no surprise that the agent will be at least in part a "double agent." Producers will seek a voice in determining who plays the role of agent and will ultimately try to influence the nature of the terms produced, the penalties for noncompliance, and the extent of public enforcement. The results will be substantially less favorable to consumers than those of an "ideal government." But how might they compare to the "no government" case in which the legislature delegates the task of determining the standardized terms directly to the firm?

If we confine our analysis to the relative political power of the parties, then it is by no means clear that the consumer has less power in the governmental solution; indeed, it is quite likely that the opposite is the case. Relative power in itself says little about the nature of the outcomes. The consumer might still be better off with a private market solution in which he has no effective political power. But it is at least important to note that there is no reason to presume that moving from a laissez faire rule to a governmental arrangement leads to an increase in political power for the producer. . . .

*The Choice of the Institutional Framework: A Comment**

Ronald H. Coase

. . . Professor Goldberg produces no evidence to support his conclusion[1] that the choice of inappropriate private property rights would commonly make government regulation preferable. He relies on some general arguments which I find unconvincing. These arguments mainly relate to the standard form contract, a device which I tend to regard as a means of reducing transaction costs. Professor Goldberg argues that in these contracts, inappropriate conditions will be introduced, so that consumers would be better off if they were omitted or changed. But why should this be? If the introduction of a new clause onerous to consumers reduces the value of the service more than it reduces costs, producers will not wish to introduce the clause. And, if it reduces the value of the service less than it reduces costs, producers will introduce the clause, and, with competition, prices will fall to equal costs, output will expand, and consumers will be better off. . . .

Professor Goldberg attempts to blunt the force of this argument by introducing consumer ignorance. He says: "Assume a competitive insurance industry with minimal government intervention. Firms in the industry compete by lowering their price and then compensate for this by decreasing the coverage (in as hidden a way as possible) with other firms being forced to cut also in order to remain competitive. A sort of 'Gresham's Law' of bad policies driving out good would ensue." Apparently in this industry, as Professor Goldberg describes it, a firm is able to lower its price, simultaneously

*Reprinted, by permission, from 17 J. Law & Econ. 493, 494-496 (1974), copyright 1974 by the University of Chicago Law School.

1. [See pp. 75-77 supra.]

reducing the coverage of its policies, a change which its salesmen are able to conceal. Competitors lose business as clients shift to this firm, and the competitors' salesmen find themselves incapable of explaining that, although the other firm's price is lower, its coverage is inferior and that those who shift their business will be worse off, even though, as Professor Goldberg indicates, this is in fact true. Consumers never become aware of the deception and competitors, who have the strongest motives for informing consumers of the true state of affairs, never succeed in doing so. Professor Goldberg gives no instance of competition working in this way although, if we are to take his views seriously, it must commonly be found. Gresham's Law, to which Professor Goldberg refers, does not lend support to his position. Gresham's Law (which has often been confirmed) tells us that "bad money drives out good." This happens because people hold on to the good money they receive and pass on the bad, so that only bad money circulates. It implies, contrary to Professor Goldberg's general position, that people are able to distinguish good from bad.

But whatever may be the merits of Professor Goldberg's arguments, there have been many studies of regulated industries which make it abundantly clear that producers are able to secure restrictive arrangements with government regulation that they were not able to secure through the delimitation of property rights. Peltzman's study of banking regulation shows that this regulation reduced the number of banks below what they would have been without it. Siegan's study of non-zoning in Houston indicates that the system of private property rights which developed there has made land use more responsive to consumer demands than it normally is with zoning. . . .

It is not my contention that restrictive arrangements cannot result from the manipulation of property rights. It does seem, however, that they are more easily achieved through regulation.

*The Doctrine of Inequality of Bargaining Power**

M. J. Trebilcock

In what is likely to become a landmark case, the English House of Lords in Macaulay v. Schroeder Publishing Co. Ltd.[1] appears to

*Reprinted from M. J. Trebilcock, The Doctrine of Inequality of Bargaining Power: Post-Benthamite Economics in the House of Lords, 26 University of Toronto Law Journal 359 (1976), by permission of the author and the University of Toronto Press.

1. Macaulay v. Schroeder Publishing Co. Ltd., [1974] 1 W.L.R. 1308 (H.L.).

have espoused explicitly a general doctrine of inequality of bargaining power as a bar to contract enforcement. This article explores, from an essentially economic perspective, the ramifications of such a doctrine. . . .

The central facts in the case were these. An unknown 21-year-old popular-songwriter (hereinafter the plaintiff) entered into a contract in 1966 with a firm of music publishers (hereinafter the defendants). Under this contract (in standard form) the plaintiff assigned the copyrights to all his songwriting output for the term of the contract to the defendants in return for agreed royalties (generally 50 per cent of the net royalties received by the defendants) in the event of songs being published. The term was for five years, renewable automatically for a further five years if the plaintiff's royalties during the first term exceeded £5000. The defendants could terminate the agreement at any time on one month's notice, and were entitled to assign it, and any copyright held under it, without the consent of the plaintiff. The plaintiff had no right to terminate and could only assign the agreement with the consent of the defendants. The plaintiff received a payment of £50 against future royalties on the signing of the agreement. A unanimous court (Lords Reid, Diplock, Simon, Kilbrandon, and Viscount Dilhorne) held that the contract so far as unperformed was unenforceable, affirming a unanimous decision of the Court of Appeal (Russell and Cairns L.JJ., and Goulding J.) that the contract was contrary to public policy. In each case, the exclusive character of the contract was held to impose unreasonable restraints on the ability of the plaintiff to market his services. . . .

I. Market Power and Standard Forms

His lordship [Diplock] said that standard forms of contract are of two kinds. The first, of early origin, are wisely used in commercial transactions, are the result of extensive prior negotiations by the parties, and are adopted because "they facilitate the conduct of trade." Examples cited were bills of lading, charterparties, insurance policies, and contracts of sale in the commodity markets. Here, his lordship said, there is a strong presumption that the terms of these contracts are fair and reasonable because they are used by parties "whose bargaining power is fairly matched."

As to the second class of standard form contracts (essentially consumer type transactions) such a presumption was said not to apply. These were said to be of comparatively modern origin and are "the result of the concentration of particular kinds of business in relatively few hands." Said to exemplify this category were the ticket cases. The identifying characteristics of contracts falling into this category were described as follows:

> The terms of this kind of standard form contract have not been the subject of negotiation between the parties to it, or approved by any organization representing the interests of the weaker party. They have been dictated by that party *whose bargaining power, either exercised alone or in conjunction with others providing similar goods and services,* enables him to say: "If you want these goods or services at all, these are the only terms on which they are obtainable. Take it or leave it." To be in a position to adopt this attitude toward a party desirous of entering into a contract to obtain goods or services provides a classic instance of superior bargaining power.[2]

. . . While recognizing that the assumptions underlying this analysis of the use of standard form contracts have enjoyed considerable academic currency, it is submitted that they are fallacious. First, the proposition that the use of consumer standard-form contracts is the result of the concentration of market power is entirely without factual foundation. The reason why such contracts are used is exactly the same as for their use in the commercial context, that is to "facilitate the conduct of trade," or in economic terms, to reduce transaction costs. If an agreement had to be negotiated and drafted from scratch every time a relatively standard transaction was entered into, the costs of transacting for all parties involved would escalate dramatically. Moreover, it is a matter of common observation that standard forms are used (for this reason) in countless contexts where no significant degree of market concentration exists. Dry-cleaners have standard form dry-cleaning agreements, hotels standard registration forms, credit-grantors standard financing agreements, insurance companies standard life, fire, and automobile insurance policies, real estate agents standard sale and purchase agreements, landlords standard leases, restaurants set menu and price lists, and, for that matter, department and grocery stores set product ranges and price terms. The fact that in these cases a supplier's products are offered on a take-it-or-leave-it basis is evidence not of market power but of a recognition that neither producer- nor consumer-interests in aggregate are served by incurring the costs involved in negotiating separately every transaction. The use of standard forms is a totally spurious proxy for the existence of market power. The real measure of market power is not whether a supplier presents his terms on a take-it-or-leave-it basis but whether the consumer, if he decides to "leave it," has available to him a workably competitive range of alternative sources of supply. Whether this is or is not so simply

2. 1 W.L.R. at 1316; my italics.

cannot be derived intuitively from the fact that a particular supplier is offering non-negotiable standard-form terms. . . .

It is, of course, true that general use of common standard-form contracts throughout an industry may, on occasion, be evidence of cartelization. But here one must be discriminating. If a reasonable choice of different packages of price and non-price terms is available in the market, albeit all through the medium of different standard-form contracts, then obviously the allegation of a "fix" will not stand up. Even where all contracts are the same, in perfectly competitive markets where the product is homogeneous, commonality of terms is what one would expect to find (for example, the wheat market). Every supplier simply "takes" his price and probably other terms from the market and is powerless to vary them. In a perfectly competitive market, with many sellers and many buyers each supplying or demanding too insignificant a share of total market output to influence terms, all participants, sellers and buyers, are necessarily confronted with a take-it-or-leave-it proposition. Thus uniformity of terms, standing alone, is ambiguous as between the presence or absence of competition.

It is clear that the music publishing industry does not conform to all the criteria of a perfectly competitive market, given that the products (that is, the service packages) offered by different suppliers to composers are presumably widely differentiated. Because each package may possess a degree of uniqueness, each supplier may have a small measure of ability to adjust price and output combinations in relation to his differentiated product. But, provided that a substantial measure of substitutability is possible between one supplier's product and those of others, the market is as workably competitive as most real-world markets are likely to be. Moreover, as experience in the anti-trust context has demonstrated, an industry whose products are widely differentiated will almost never be able to sustain a stable cartel, as the possibilities for cheating on agreed price and output restrictions are extensive and largely unpoliceable. This difficulty in the way of effective cartelization is, of course, compounded if the industry comprises many firms and entry barriers are low, both features of the music publishing industry. . . .

. . . This is not to suggest that monopolization or cartelization may not in fact have been present in *Macaulay*. But not a shred of relevant evidence was adduced on this issue. . . . [And] whether in ordinary civil litigation between private parties there will normally be sufficient economic incentive for parties to invest in the complex task of producing reliable evidence on the issue of abuse of market power raises further problems. . . .

II. Procedural Unfairness

Lord Reid was much less concerned than Lord Diplock to ascertain the reasons for the perceived imbalance in the contractual incidents. Simply looking at the agreement, he found that the obligations on each side were not commensurate. However, on the question of "procedural unconscionability," that is, unconscionability in the contract formation process (as opposed to its outcome), he found no evidence, "nor does it seem probable, that this form of contract made between a publisher and an unknown composer has been moulded by any pressure of negotiation. Indeed, it appears that established composers who can bargain on equal terms can and do make their own contracts." Lord Diplock himself also picked up this latter issue in passing in his judgment. . . . Both he and Lord Reid appear to be saying no more than that good songwriters were able to obtain better contracts than bad ones (or unknown ones), which, one would have thought, was unremarkable. Indeed, if this had not been the case, good songwriters could then claim that they were being oppressed, which would mean that music-publishing firms could do nothing right.

Further, as has already been argued, the fact that there was no negotiation with this particular publisher over his terms (that is, they were offered on a take-it-or-leave-it basis) is quite beside the point, if choice from across the market of different packages of terms was possible. This possibility itself constitutes the "pressure of negotiation" vis-à-vis particular suppliers. Moreover, even the presence of dickering between parties, standing alone, is ambiguous as between the presence or absence of competition. Dickering may, for example, be merely a reflection of attempts by a monopolist to price-discriminate among customers by ascertaining and exploiting different demand elasticities. . . .

This leads into another issue which, curiously, no member of either the Court of Appeal or the House of Lords addressed. Should the defendants have known that the plaintiff was likely to be entertaining expectations about the contract with which the actual terms were in fact at substantial variance and the significance of which the defendants should have known the plaintiff did not fully appreciate? This, in the Offical Comments to article 2-302 (unconscionability) of the U.S. Uniform Commercial Code, is called the element of "unfair surprise." There may be good grounds, both legally and economically, for intervening where this is present. Where a contract is so worded or arranged that the supplier knows or should know that the other party does not understand its implications, and he knows or should know that the other party reasonably entertains other understandings as to its legal incidents, perhaps based on prevailing contractual practices elsewhere in the market, to allow him to sign the contract without correcting these misunderstandings is tantamount to misrepresentation and thus conducive to suboptimal allocative decisions. . . .

The judicial development of a rule against unfair surprise would seem a productive direction to take in resolving some of these cases. Moreover, such a rule has the advantage that its application, at least in a limited form, is mostly independent of intractable issues of market power. However, the rule needs to be fashioned with some care. In its more limited, and least controversial, form, it would deal with contractual documents which in their wording or organization are apt to mislead consumers. A useful adjunct to such a rule might be judicial abolition or confinement of the parol-evidence rule in a consumer standard-form setting so as to protect reasonable reliance by consumers on information conveyed to them in advertisements or at point-of-sale but not incorporated in the ensuing formal contract, thus creating additional incentives for suppliers to ensure the accuracy of this information.

In its more expansive, and more controversial, form a rule against unfair surprise might deal with documents which in their wording and organization are apt not so much to cause misunderstanding as to cause nonunderstanding. If resources are efficiently allocated by private exchange when both parties to the exchange are optimally informed as to its costs and benefits, then liability rules that conduce to that end may have a useful role to play. On the demand side, a consumer will be making a rational investment in information if he invests resources in search and evaluation of information to the point where the expected marginal benefits from further search and evaluation are equal to the marginal costs of further such activity. On the supply side of the market in information, a supplier will be producing for consumers of his products and services a socially optimal amount of information about them if the price which consumers are prepared to pay for the marginal benefits of this information is equal to the marginal social costs (in terms of real resources consumed) of producing it.

There seem to be good reasons for supposing that in many markets this latter condition will not hold. Consumer ignorance in such markets, even following economically rational search, may permit non-competitive price-quality dispersions to persist for reasons such as the following. Even in competitive markets, a firm offering non-competitive terms may occupy too insignificant a share of the market to attract disparagement from competitors, particularly when a competitor who engages in justified disparagement has no way of confining the gains from such disparagement to himself alone. While the marginal social costs to the non-competitive firm of disclosing information to consumers that makes clear the inferiority of its terms may be trivial, the marginal private costs to the firm of disclosure (in terms of lost sales) will induce suppression of the information even though consumers may be willing to pay the marginal social costs of its production. In this sense, market outcomes will not be allocatively efficient, in a Pareto optimal sense. This problem may be particularly severe in markets involving expensive and complex goods and services which consumers purchase infrequently and of which they have little "experience" information. Given limited innate ability to make accurate price/quality comparisons, extensive search, evaluation, self-education, or purchased expertise may be necessary to generate even modest marginal returns and would be an economically irrational investment on the part of a consumer. On the other hand, firms in the market may be able to provide the desired information at much lower marginal social cost. In other words, in this respect sellers may have a lower-cost production function for information than consumers and, provided consumers are prepared to pay for more information, should be required to provide it. Again, in markets characterized by monopolization and therefore a lack of competitive incentives to produce countervailing information about alternative contractual offerings, a firm may produce less information about its terms than is socially optimal. In addition, in markets characterized by a high level of instability, that is, a rapid turnover of buyers and sellers and therefore a high information depreciation rate, less than socially optimal amounts of information may be produced by the market.

Markets in information are probably flawed in a more general sense by another factor—the public goods characteristic of much information. Once information has been produced, it will be difficult to prevent those who do not buy a product or service (and therefore the information that accompanies it), but who nevertheless derive value from the information, from using it although they do not pay for it. This will leave consumers who do buy such products or services (and the accompanying information) facing a disproportionately large part of the costs of the information while others who also value it are able to pay nothing. Market mechanisms will therefore not accurately reveal to suppliers the true demand function of consumers for information and are likely to lead to its systematic under-production.

If this analysis is correct in theory, then the practical question that follows is how does one move the production of information on the supply side of the market closer to the socially optimal?

A number of policy expedients might be considered. In the *Macaulay* type of setting, judicially imposed liability (non-enforceability) on a supplier who fails to make his contractual provisions reasonably intelligible to the average consumer is one possibility. Legislated conspicuousness standards, as imposed in the warranty disclaimer provisions of section 2-316 of the U.S. Uniform Commerical Code, are another. Legislated disclosure provisions, as exemplified in truth-in-lending and packaging and labelling legislation, are another. "Cooling-off" provisions enabling a consumer to disaffirm a transaction within a stipulated period of entering into it, as exemplified in door-to-door sales legislation, are yet another. Ultimately the government might turn information into a more or less pure public good and provide it itself out of general revenues.

A major problem in all of these approaches lies in determining whether consumers perceive the marginal benefits of possessing more information (what kinds, how much, what form?) to be greater than the marginal social costs, including law-making and enforcement costs, entailed in providing it. Experience with mandatory disclosure requirements has generally not been encouraging. . . .

Distinct from rules against unfair surprise, another line of attack on fine-print clauses in standard form contracts, based again on perceived aberrations in the bargaining process, derives from the so-called Coase theorem.[3] This theorem asserts that, in a world of zero transaction costs, irrespective of the legal allocation of risks, the mutual interests of the parties will tend to lead them to bargain their way to the most efficient allocation of risks, that is, the risk allocation that maximizes the joint value of their respective resources, in which state, in a Pareto optimal sense, both parties are better off. If, on the other hand, transaction costs are significant, at least in relation to the stakes involved, allocative efficiency may not be achieved through voluntary exchange, and liability rules may be justified which attempt to simulate the market outcomes that would have occurred had frictionless exchange been possible.

The Coase theorem does not permit of a straightforward application to the standard form contracting setting, for, unlike many tort cases where a priori bargaining over risk allocation is impossible, in standard-form contracts some voluntary interaction, by definition, occurs. One implication from this is that in those areas of a transaction where bargaining does typically occur, one might often expect to find adjustments made which are designed to offset any legal allocations of risks in areas of the transaction where information and transaction costs arguably prevent negotiation. Thus, importantly, in

3. [See p. 6 n.6 supra.]

this context, the general balance of advantage between the parties may not be significantly affected by the law's intervention.

From broadly these premises, Goldberg has argued[4] that in the case of standard form insurance policies, the costs to the consumer of obtaining, processing, and evaluating information about the implications of "hidden," subsidiary clauses in such contracts will tend to direct competitive forces, even in workably competitive markets, away from the subject-matter of these clauses and towards broader price-quantity comparisons. The result of such a process may be harsh-term–low-price policies, whereas many consumers, in the absence of information and transaction costs, may have preferred an easier-term–higher-price combination. Thus, bargaining processes are distorted. This may be so, Goldberg argues, even though the industry is making no supra-competitive profits. Therefore, the argument goes, the industry would be made no worse off, and many consumers might be made better off, by liability rules designed to produce the mix of terms that would have been reached by the parties in a world without information or transaction costs. Unlike rules against unfair surprise, these rules would take information markets as given and simply substantively regulate the contents of contracts.

There are several difficulties with Goldberg's argument. First, even assuming that information and transaction costs relative to the stakes involved in matters dealt with in subsidiary terms (for example, the termination and assignment provisions in *Macaulay*) are as high as Goldberg asserts, how does one determine whether more or fewer consumers will be advantaged under a legal reallocation of risks which produces an easier-term–higher-price contract and displaces previous harsher-term–lower-price combinations, given that on Goldberg's hypothesis, information costs are such that consumers' true preferences can never be revealed?

If the answer to this is that in fact one must look for some kind of revealed preference on the part of the general body of affected consumers, say in the form of transactions which reallocate offered risks which a minority of consumers are left bearing (unwittingly), then one is conceding that transaction costs are not generally so high as to prevent voluntary reallocation of risks, and firms in the industry will have an incentive to reflect the generally preferred combination of terms in adjustments to their standard-form contracts, thus avoiding needless transaction costs.

A further factor unaccounted for in Goldberg's analysis, as in that of other critics of standard-form contracts who point to the

4. [See p. 74 supra.]

absence of subjective consumer consent to all contractual terms, is the price that most consumers attach to uncertainty. Making the usual assumption that most consumers are risk-averse, consumers who sign contracts containing clauses which have been drafted by the other party with his advantage obviously in mind and which they do not understand will reflect their aversion to the assumption of undetermined, but intuitively adverse, risk allocations by discounting the consideration they are prepared to offer for entering into such contracts.

Finally, if courts were to impose liability rules on parties to standard form contracts on Goldberg's rationale, then ex post, ad hoc judicial interventions cannot fairly take the form simply of invalidating "harsh" clauses. In addition, other clauses will have to be reworked to compensate the supplier for the expanded package of contractual benefits which he is now providing to the consumer. In effect, this form of judicial policing of standard-form contracts should strictly involve reformulating whole contracts. If substantive intervention is to occur, this may argue for general, ex ante, legislative intervention where "harsh" terms are invalidated and the market is permitted to take care of consequential adjustments to other terms.

Returning now to the analysis of the decision in *Macaulay*, market power arguments and considerations of procedural unfairness have disappeared as plausible explanations for the decision. This leaves only one other possible ground for invalidation to be considered, [substantive unfairness].

III. Substantive Unfairness

. . . [T]he concept of substantive unfairness, in the sense of a judicially perceived non-equivalence in the values exchanged by contracting parties, poses real conceptual difficulties following a determination of (1) no abnormal market power and (2) no aberrations in the process of contract formation. Almost by definition, the outcome of such a process cannot be unfair. Moreover, in determining whether the values exchanged are reasonably equivalent, the court has little option but to identify some significantly more satisfactory choice that was open in the market to the complaining party and use this as a benchmark. But in doing this, it will essentially be retracing steps 1 and 2, substituting itself for the plaintiff in the process of search and negotiation, and, given our assumptions of no abnormal market power and no aberrations in the contract formation process, presumably arriving at the same contractual outcome.

One way out of this logical bind might be to say that an ex facie appearance of substantial non-equivalence in the values exchanged raises a presumption of either abnormal market power or procedural unfairness which the defendant then carries the onus of rebutting. However, there are problems also with this approach in that it is hard to know how one would obtain even an initial feel for equivalences without resort to market data. But, be that as it may, this was not the approach taken by the court in *Macaulay*. In fact, it confined its entire enquiry into the issue of substantive unfairness to the parameters of the contractual document itself. Whether substantially better contracts were available to the plaintiff in the market we will never know. The one objective benchmark that would have been useful in evaluating this contract was never invoked.

Lord Reid carried the decision of the court on this issue. While he was critical of the publisher's termination and assignment rights under the contract, his central objection rested on the fact that the plaintiff's obligation to provide exclusive songwriting services to the defendants for the term of the contract was matched by no obligation whatever on the other side: "What are the [defendants] bound to do with those fruits? Under the contract nothing. . . . As has been said, they may put them in a drawer and leave them there." However, his lordship was prepared to acknowledge that this would normally be perverse: "No doubt the expectation was that, if the songs were of value, they would be published to the advantage of both parties." Indeed, making the usual profit-maximizing assumption, it is difficult to understand why the defendants would have bothered to incur the costs involved in securing the contract if they never had any intention of attempting to promote the plaintiff's songs. However, Lord Reid was able to imagine possible reasons. For example, a publisher "might think it likely to be more profitable to promote work by other composers with whom he had agreements and unwise or too expensive to try to publish and popularize the [plaintiff's] work in addition. And there is always the possibility that less legitimate reasons might influence a decision not to publish the [plaintiff's] work."

Leaving aside these last unspecified reasons, the example given of a reason for suppression of a composer's work makes no economic sense. First, it assumes that one songwriter's work is a perfect substitute for that of others, which with such widely differentiated products is quite implausible. Even if this were so, a publisher should be indifferent as between old and new songwriters' work. Second, and more important, it assumes that the hypothetical publisher is the only publisher in the market. If this is not so, then, while there may be some substitution effects between a new songwriter's songs and those of other writers under contract to the same publisher, much more substantial substitution-effects in aggregate, away from other publishers' songs, will generally occur, thus more than compensating for substitution effects within the first publisher's own, much smaller, stable of writers. . . .

In any event, it is clear from the case that the defendants had not simply put the plaintiff's songs in a drawer. Russell, L.J., in the Court of Appeal said that at the time of the contract "as a composer he was not then well-known, though we understand he now is." Given the exclusive nature of his contract with the defendants, this new fame can only have been as a result of their efforts. However, this need not be left entirely to conjecture. For example, it is again clear from Russell, L.J.'s, review of a collateral dispute over whether royalties had been fully accounted for that the plaintiff's songs had been published in Germany and Scandinavia, presumably in Britain, and possibly also in the U.S. Moreover, the contract was in its second five-year term, which meant that the condition of automatic renewal—composer's royalties in excess of £5000 during the first term—presumably had been met. . . .

However, in the House of Lords, Lord Diplock dismissed evidence of the defendants' efforts under the contract as irrelevant. . . . Pursuing Lord Reid's objections to the contract, his lordship proceeded from the assumption of one-way contractual obligations as follows:

> If no satisfactory positive undertaking by the publisher can be devised, it appears to me to be an unreasonable restraint to tie the composer for this period of years so that his work will be sterilized and he can earn nothing from his abilities as a composer if the publisher chooses not to publish. If there had been [in the contract] any provision entitling the composer to terminate the agreement in such an event the case might have had a very different appearance.[5]

First of all, the reasonableness of the length of the tie must surely be judged by starting with an examination of what was received in return for it. It has already been suggested that the plaintiff received a valuable (and indeed costly) promise of good faith evaluation and promotion of his songs, special royalty arrangements on foreign publications, and access to foreign markets which apparently domestic publishers were unable to meet, and finally, of course, royalties on domestic publications. As to the royalty arrangements, Lord Reid had early in his judgment accepted that "this was not an unreasonable basis for the remuneration of a composer unknown when the agreement was entered into." However, having said this,

5. *Macaulay*, supra note 1, at 1313-14.

Lord Reid did not bother, when considering the reasonableness of the tie, to relate the royalty arrangements to it. It is difficult to conceive how he could have made his earlier judgment on the reasonableness of the royalty arrangements without considering what the plaintiff was expected to provide in return. . . .

First, therefore, the tie has to be evaluated in relation to the price received for it. Second, and more important, the reasonableness of the relationship must then, it is submitted, be carried to the marketplace and tested against some ascertained, objective, contractual benchmark, at least where the market in question is workably competitive. The first step was not clearly taken in *Macaulay*. The second step clearly was not taken at all.

The validating condition hypothesized by Lord Reid—a right in a composer to terminate in the event of non-publication—also requires analysis. This appears to misunderstand the high-risk nature of the popular songwriting, music-publishing, and recording industries. To quote some suggestive U.S. figures, a music publisher in 1965 estimated that 30,000 songs are recorded and released on single records in the U.S. each year. 85,000 musical compositions were deposited for copyright, and "probably several hundred thousand other songs are written each year but no one apparently will invest the four dollars required to copyright them. . . . There are some publishers who consistently come up with winners . . . and others who get lucky from time to time. But, generally, there is no rainbow. Songs often produce only a pittance, and frequently a loss on which the writers earn little or nothing and the publisher doesn't recoup his direct expenses, such as cost of demonstration record, advance to writers, ads, and other promotional expenses, not to mention his daily overhead. . . ." . . .

In signing unknown songwriters, music-publishing and recording firms must therefore make risk calculations similar to those made in the insurance business. In effect, what is the actuarial probability of an unknown songwriter later proving a commercial success? If the chance, for example, is only one in ten, then the terms offered all such songwriters will have to reflect the fact that with nine writers out of ten the publisher will incur evaluation and promotional expenses that will have to be recouped from the efforts of the one writer who proves a success. Given that in advance the publisher has no way of discriminating among unknown risks, he offers all unknown writers the same terms. To allow a writer to terminate his contract when success beckons is to ignore the risk-spreading nature of the enterprise. If successful writers could withdraw (for example, on account of previous nonpublication) and take better terms elsewhere whenever prospects of entering the ranks of the "established" looked good, a publisher would be left with unrecoupable losses on his other nine contracts. Perhaps by parity with the reasoning of the court in *Macaulay*, the publisher should be able to argue that these latter contracts were retrospectively one-way streets, and unconscionable—that the composers through superior bargaining power had pushed him to the wall on them. To allow withdrawal by the successful writer would be tantamount to an insured asking for his money back after the term of a life-insurance policy had expired on the grounds that he had not died during the period of the coverage.

IV. The Effect of the Doctrine

The intent of the doctrine of inequality of bargaining power, at least as it emerges from *Macaulay*, is clearly to redistribute contractual incidents between contracting parties, for example, to make it less costly for songwriters to secure publishers' services and more costly for publishers to provide them, in other words to adjust the relative values exchanged. What will be its effect?

This is most easily considered by taking two polar market models: a perfectly competitive market and a monopolized market. By assumption, in a perfectly competitive market both for the final product and for intermediate inputs, no excess profits are being made (that is, no profits beyond a reasonable return on capital), so that any reduction in industry profits will also induce a reduction in output and thus intermediate inputs (for example, the work of unknown songwriters). The response of firms in such a market to a cost-increasing rule (for example, all contracts terminable on non-publication) will be to offset this cost increase with an appropriate reduction in the prices they are willing to pay for songwriters' services as a factor input in the production of music or records. In the music-publishing industry, the most obvious way of reducing the price paid for songwriters' services for firms [is] to cut their royalty rates. Alternatively, or in addition, because of the reduced prospect now of returns on successful composers' efforts (because of greater ease of contractual termination) publishers in their turn will presumably find it no longer rational to make the same investment in promoting unknown songwriters. Probably they will "carry" high risks for shorter periods before setting them adrift. If this is what unknown songwriters were really demanding, why had not some publishers in the market already found it in their interests to meet that demand? If, going further than regulating termination provisions, royalty rates were also frozen at their previous level by an additional rule, firms would then reduce their demand for this class of writer, perhaps partly substituting the services of more established songwriters by paying them more to produce more, or the services of "unknown" songwriters from other jurisdictions. Indeed, at the limit, music publishers may demand that composers compensate them directly for their promotional efforts on a composer's behalf, thus inducing a composer (rather than a publisher), in effect, to make an investment in human capital by securing at his own expense the services of an agent (a common arrangement in other contexts). In other words, any attempt to regulate the full wage (that is, the nominal wage plus other, non-explicit, "wage" terms of the contract which regulate returns to the recipient) payable to unknown songwriters will operate like a minimum-wage law, perhaps benefiting some writers whose services continue to be retained, and prejudicing others whose services are displaced by substitution away from them and towards other factors of production. The lesson of economics, in this context, is that legal liability rules are unlikely to be able to affect the broad balance of advantage between buyers and sellers.

If the market for the final products of songwriters' services is monopolized, little changes in the analysis. A single music-publisher acting as a monopolist in the sale of a songwriter's output is also likely to respond to a cost-increasing rule (for example, termination on non-publication) by reducing royalties or "carry" periods. He has limited ability (depending on the price elasticity of demand and supply for his product) to pass on increased costs to consumers of the final product, and thus has an incentive to minimize costs similar to firms in a competitive industry. Even assuming supra-competitive profits, further rules which proscribe reductions in royalty rates or other contract variations (that is, increase the full wage to songwriters) will generate similar economic incentives to firms in a competitive industry to make substitutions of other factors. . . .

Only in the situation where a music publisher is acting as a monopsonist (that is, sole buyer) of songwriters' factor-inputs in the production of the final products being marketed by the publisher could rules imposing an increase in the full wage payable to songwriters avoid displacement effects. But problems of identifying such a factor market and of determining the magnitude of an imposed wage increase which is possible without creating displacement effects are acute.

In short, to attempt comprehensive wage rate regulation and control over employment of factors by judicial fiat in an industry like the music publishing industry, with many firms and substantial product differentiation, would make the acknowledged problems of public-utility regulation look easy. But anything short of this is like squeezing putty.

*Unconscionability: A Critical Reappraisal**

Richard A. Epstein

The classical conception of contract at common law had as its first premise the belief that private agreements should be enforced in accordance with their terms. That premise of course was subject to important qualifications. Promises procured by fraud, duress, or undue influence were not generally enforced by the courts; and the same was true with certain exceptions of promises made by infants and incompetents. . . . Yet even after these exceptions are taken into account, there was still one ground on which the initial premise could not be challenged: the terms of private agreements could not be set aside because the court found them to be harsh, unconscionable, or unjust. . . .

This general regime of freedom of contract can be defended from two points of view. One defense is utilitarian. So long as the tort law protects the interests of strangers to the agreement, its enforcement will tend to maximize the welfare of the parties to it, and therefore the good of the society as a whole. The alternative defense is on libertarian grounds. One of the first functions of the law is to guarantee to individuals a sphere of influence in which they will be able to operate, without having to justify themselves to the state or to third parties: if one individual is entitled to do within the confines of the tort law what he pleases with what he owns, then two individuals who operate with those same constraints should have the same right with respect to their mutual affairs against the rest of the world.

Whatever its merits, however, it is fair to say that this traditional view of the law of contract has been in general retreat in recent years. That decline is reflected in part in the cool reception given to doctrines of laissez-faire, its economic counterpart, since the late nineteenth century, or at least since the New Deal. The total "hands off" policy with respect to economic matters is regarded as incorrect in most political discussions almost as a matter of course, and the same view is taken, moreover, toward a more subtle form of laissez-faire that views all government interference in economic matters as an evil until shown to be good. Instead, the opposite point of view is increasingly urged: market solutions—those which presuppose a regime of freedom of contract—are sure to be inadequate, and the only question worth debating concerns the appropriate form of public intervention. That attitude has, moreover, worked its way (as these things usually happen) into the fabric of the

*Reprinted, by permission, from 18 J. Law & Econ. 293-311 (1975), copyright 1975 by the University of Chicago Law School.

legal system, for today, more than ever, courts are willing to set aside the provisions of private agreements.

One of the major conceptual tools used by courts in their assault upon private agreements has been the doctrine of unconscionability. That doctrine has a place in contract law, but it is not the one usually assigned it by its advocates. The doctrine should not, in my view, allow courts to act as roving commissions to set aside those agreements whose substantive terms they find objectionable. Instead, it should be used only to allow courts to police the process whereby private agreements are formed, and in that connection, only to facilitate the setting aside of agreements that are as a matter of probabilities likely to be vitiated by the classical defenses of duress, fraud, or incompetence. . . .

I. Unconscionability Applied

The merits of these exceptions to the general rule in favor of contractual enforcement is one question; their proof in particular cases is quite another. The courts could place upon the defendant a burden of proving fraud, duress or incompetence, say by the preponderance of the evidence. That approach would tend to insure that each of these defenses will be established only where the facts of the case so warrant. There is, however, a cost created by putting this burden upon the defendant. Solely because he cannot meet the appropriate standard of proof, he may not be able to establish a contractual defense in a case where it in fact applies. If this last form of error results in substantial costs, then it should be appropriate to modify the rules of evidence in a manner that makes it easier for the defendant to establish fraud, duress or incompetence. It may well be that the relaxation of the standard of proof required to make out any defense will increase the number of instances where the undeserving defendant is able to defeat the plaintiff's legitimate contractual expectations. But if the costs thereby created are low, then the change in the rules of proof is justified on the grounds that it reduces the total error in enforcement, even though all error is not thereby eliminated.

The legal system has long used this rationale to justify some restrictions on the freedom of contract. The Statute of Frauds, which requires that certain kinds of agreements be put in writing, has the prevention of fraud as one of its chief objects. Yet its application necessarily insures the nonenforcement of certain untainted oral transactions. The parol evidence rule, which prohibits the use of oral evidence to vary or contradict the provisions of an "integrated" written contract, is also designed to control fraud; and it, too, frustrates the enforcement of legitimate consensual arrangements. One can attack either of these two rules on the ground that the control of fraud comes at too high a price (measured by the number of proper transactions nullified), given the alternative means of its control and prevention. But neither rule can be attacked on the ground that it is directed toward an illegitimate end.

The doctrine of unconscionability, properly conceived and applied, serves the same general end as the Statute of Frauds and the parol evidence rule. Ideally, the unconscionability doctrine protects against fraud, duress and incompetence, without demanding specific proof of any of them. Instead of looking to a writing requirement to control against these abuses, it looks both to the subject matter of the agreements and to the social positions of the persons who enter into them. The difficult question with unconscionability is not whether it works towards a legitimate end, but whether its application comes at too great a price. . . .

One of the strengths of the unconscionability doctrine is its flexibility, an attribute much needed because it is difficult to identify in advance all of the kinds of situations to which it might in principle apply. One recent case, for example, that appears to warrant the application of unconscionability rules, involves recently returned prisoners of the Vietnam war. After receipt of accumulated back pay, these men were approached by experienced salesmen who proceeded to sell them unattractive municipal bonds. These transactions should as a class be set aside at the option of the buyers. We have here a narrow class of purchasers, vulnerable by reason of their long captivity, given sudden control over substantial funds. Opposite them are salesmen who know how to exploit them. Proof of fraud is apt to be difficult in this case, even if the fraud itself is likely. Setting aside the transaction gives the shrewd buyer a chance to repudiate an arm's length deal he does not like, but it is highly unlikely that many buyers took conscious advantage of this legal benefit. It is also possible that some proper transactions will be set aside, but again those costs are apt to be small, measured against the gains derived. But the limits of the principle must be noted. The case should go the other way if, for example, these men on their own initiative went to a brokerage house to purchase these same bonds.

The limitations on the use of conscionability doctrines are as important as their application. Should, for example, the doctrine be used to protect those who are poor, unemployed, on welfare, or members of disadvantaged racial or ethnic groups? The perils of this course are great. First, it is difficult, if not impossible, to assert that the persons who fall into any or all of these classes are not in general competent to fend for themselves in most market situations. They are not infants, impressionable heirs, or gullible prisoners of war. Second, the subject matter of the transactions is for the most part standard consumer goods that are sold in generally competitive markets, and not interests in trust funds or real estate difficult to value even under the best of circumstances. The costs of setting these transactions aside, moreover, are apt to be quite great, for it will be more expensive for members of the "protected" class to contract on their own behalf within a complex web of legal rules. In addition, there will no doubt be both opportunity and incentive for many to take advantage of the rights conferred upon them by law to manipulate the system to their own advantage. The absence of protective rules will have costs, measured by the tainted transactions given full legal effect, but these costs, all things considered, are apt to be lower than those incurred by demanding proof of fraud to set the transactions aside.

In consumer transactions, therefore, it will be necessary to take great care in specifying the circumstances where protective rules should be adopted in order to prevent fraud or duress. One possible case that might warrant the use of such protective rules involves door-to-door salesmen, who often rely on both high pressure tactics and outright fraud to complete a sale. Yet I suspect that the unconscionability doctrine functions at best as a very blunt instrument in cases of this sort, and that it is better to adopt some legislative solution to control the problem. Here for example it is possible to specify a short "cooling off" period in which the buyer is allowed as a matter of positive law to disaffirm the contract of sale at his own option without a showing of fraud or duress. In this context, moreover, it might even be desirable, given the costs of such a rule upon honest merchants, for the legislature to adopt one rule for encyclopedias and quite another for beauty products, particularly if different levels of abuse are involved in the two cases. We are not faced with an elegant question of legal theory or with a moral question of great urgency. The only issue is what combination of common law doctrine and legislative enactment will work to miminize the abuses in consumer transactions.

II. Substantive Unconscionability

. . . [O]ur attention [now] shifts to the cases in which courts will strike down either whole contracts or, more frequently, particular clauses on the ground that they are, as a *substantive* matter only, unfair and unconscionable. It is difficult in the abstract to insist that no contract language invites invalidation for these reasons. But the crucial point is that most clauses that do *in fact* appear in agreements cannot be fairly challenged on those grounds. It is difficult to know what principles identify the "just term," and for the same reasons that make it so difficult to determine the "just price." And the problem with substantive unconscionability is further increased because the clauses so attacked are, at the time of formation, arguably in the interests of both parties to the agreement. . . .

A. "Add-On" Clauses

One sort of clause that has come under both judicial and statutory scrutiny is the so-called "add-on" clause used in consumer sales. These clauses govern the security interest taken back by the seller, and, in one common form, provide that all previous goods purchased by the buyer from the seller will secure the debts incurred with the current purchase. The security agreement also provides that each payment made with respect to any of the items purchased would be applied against all outstanding balances, allowing the seller in effect to retain his security interest in all the goods sold until the debts with respect to all items are discharged. A single default on a single payment could trigger the plaintiff's right to repossess all the goods subject to the comprehensive security arrangement.

Although agreements of this kind can [be] and have been attacked on unconscionability grounds, they make good sense in the cases to which they apply. One of the major risks to the seller of personal property is that the goods sold will lose value, be it through use or abuse, more rapidly than the purchase price is paid off. The buyer can, and quite often does, have a "negative" equity in the goods. The seller, therefore, who takes back a security interest only in the goods sold, runs the real risk that repossession of the single item sold will still leave him with a loss on the transaction as a whole, taking into account the costs of interest and collection. One way to handle this problem is to require the purchaser of the goods to make a larger cash down payment, but that, of course, is something which many buyers, particularly those of limited means, do not want to do. Another alternative is for the buyer to provide the seller with additional collateral; yet here the best collateral is doubtless in goods sold by the seller to the buyer. Other goods already in the possession of the buyer may be of uncertain value, and they may well be subject to prior liens. Again, they may be of a sort that the seller cannot conveniently resell in the ordinary course of his business. Even if the goods are suitable collateral for the loan, it could take a good deal of time and effort for the seller to determine that fact. The "add-on" clause allows both parties to benefit from the reduction in costs in the setting up of a security arrangement. . . .

The sense of these clauses, regardless of the particular form which they take, is demonstrated anew, moreover, once we realize that they operate within one very strong constraint, often imposed by statute, which restricts the creditor in a secured transaction to the recovery of principal, interest and costs in cases of default by the buyer. Within the framework of these limitations, the add-on clause can do no harm at all, for it only makes it more certain that the seller will be able to collect that to which on any view he is entitled.

B. *"Waiver-of-Defense" Clauses*

Unconscionability arguments have been used to attack other clauses that govern the financing of consumer sales. Thus in many cases where the goods are purchased on an installment contract, the seller's rights under the contract are then sold, usually at a discount, to a finance company, which is then entitled to collect the payments as they come due from the buyer. In order to insulate itself from the disputes between the buyer and the seller of the goods, the company often insists that the original contract of sale include a term for its benefit which requires the buyer to continue to pay his installments to it even if the seller has not made good, for example, his warranty obligations.

In spite of the enthusiasm for consumer protection, it is unwise to strike these clauses down as unconscionable. Suppose the seller sold goods under warranty for cash. The buyer then could only get the seller to honor the warranty by request or, that failing, by legal action; the withholding of payment is no longer a possible alternative. I take it, however, that no one would argue that this arrangement is unconscionable, even though it leaves the buyer at risk on the warranty. Why then should the position be different if he is at risk because he has waived his defenses against the finance company?

The same point can be made if we consider another alternative method of financing the purchase of consumer goods. Suppose the seller says to the buyer of his goods, "If you wish to buy them on time, you must take out a bank loan for credit." Under that arrangement, the buyer remains unconditionally liable on his note to the bank even if his seller is in breach of his warranty obligation. If that arrangement is not unconscionable, why should it be unconscionable for the buyer to have no remedy against the lender because he happens to be chosen by the seller instead of the buyer?

There are also strong economic reasons that indicate that it is [in] no one's interest, ex ante, to prohibit finance companies from disassociating themselves from the disputes between buyer and seller. The main advantage of seller financing over buyer financing is that it allows the parties to reduce the transaction costs of putting the credit arrangement together when security interests are necessary. Yet if that arrangement is incumbered by involving the finance company in disputes in which it wants no part, then there will be a shift to less desirable modes of financing. If it is argued that the finance companies should be held liable because they are better able to supervise the general activities of sellers, the quick answer is that if that is the case, then they will agree to do so as a matter of course for a fee. The fact that they do not is a strong suggestion that they have neither time nor skill to get involved in the narrow disputes which are apt to arise in consumer cases. What knowledge does the finance company have on the question of whether the buyer tampered with goods or used them in accordance with instructions? If buyers want protection against having to pay the price where there is a defect in the goods in question, then they should deal with sellers who carry their own contracts. Whether that arrangement is preferable as an economic matter to one that contemplates third party financing is *not* the question that should be asked by the legal system. So long as both have their uses, as is likely the case, there is no principled justification for the judicial or legislative prohibition of either of them.

C. Exclusion of Liability for Consequential Damages

A close examination of still other clauses that have been incorporated into standard form contracts reveals that they too should be able to escape from the taint of unconscionability. In Collins v. Uniroyal Inc.,[1] a case of quite recent vintage, the defendant tire company sold a tire under a contract of sale which contained the following guarantee.

> ROAD HAZARD—In addition, every such U.S. Royal Master tire, when used in normal passenger car service, is guaranteed during the life of the original tread against blowouts, cuts, bruises, and similar injury rendering the tire unserviceable. Tires which are punctured or abused, by being run flat, improperly aligned, balanced, or inflated, cut by chains or obstructions on vehicle, damaged by fire, collision or vandalism, or by other means, and "seconds" are not subject to the road hazard provision of this Guarantee.
>
> ---
>
> *This Guarantee does not cover consequential damage, and the liability of the manufacturer is limited to repairing or replacing the tire in accordance with the stipulations contained in this Guarantee. No other guarantee or warranty, express or implied, is made.*

The purchaser of the tire was killed when the car he was driving went out of control after the tire blew out. The weight of the evidence established that no defect whatsoever in the tire caused the accident, ruling out recovery on any tort theory of products liability. The New Jersey Supreme Court held, however, that the limitation in the war-

1. 64 N.J. 260, 315 A.2d 16 (1974).

ranty against the recovery of consequential damages was unconscionable under the Uniform Commercial Code, and that the defendant accordingly was liable on a contract theory for the death of the decedent.

The Court's argument in support of that conclusion is, I believe, erroneous. Under the New Jersey law, the defendant was required by statute to sell the tire with only a warranty of merchantability, under which its liability is triggered only if the tire is defective. The defendant here gave the buyer an extra measure of protection under its supplemental warranty, without which the plaintiff concededly could have recovered nothing. What is achieved by holding the defendant liable because it gave the plaintiff protection not required by statute when the effect of the decision may well be to *reduce* the protection that sellers will give their purchasers? Is it in the general interest of consumers that Uniroyal *not* include warranties of the sort provided in this case?

Thus far we have assumed that there is justification for a rule that treats all limitations against recovery for consequential damages for personal injury as prima facie unconscionable. Yet even that restriction itself is not beyond criticism. In typical actions for breach of the warranty of merchantability, the plaintiff must show something beyond his own injury in the use of the goods in order to recover consequential damages. Indeed the very restrictions about proper use and maintenance incorporated into the warranty in *Collins* apply with equal force to the straightforward warranty of merchantability. It might well be wise for a seller to tell his buyers that it is too difficult for him to determine whether a particular injury is attributable to his own manufacture, to the plaintiff's conduct, or to some external cause. The best solution might be to offer the tire at a lower price, leaving the buyer, if he chooses, to purchase insurance elsewhere against this particular risk. In this manner, market mechanisms could work to bring about the best distribution of risks between the parties, superior to that ordained by statute.

*Form and Substance in Private Law Adjudication**

Duncan Kennedy

I. The Content of the Ideal of Individualism

The essence of individualism is the making of a sharp distinction between one's interests and those of others, combined with the

*Reprinted from 89 Harv. L. Rev. 1685, 1713-1721, 1746-1751, 1777-1778 (1976),

belief that a preference in conduct for one's own interests is legitimate, but that one should be willing to respect the rules that make it possible to coexist with others similarly self-interested. The form of conduct associated with individualism is self-reliance. This means an insistence on defining and achieving objectives without help from others (i.e., without being dependent on them or asking sacrifices of them). It means accepting that they will neither share their gains nor one's own losses. And it means a firm conviction that I am entitled to enjoy the benefits of my efforts without an obligation to share or sacrifice them to the interests of others.

It is important to be clear from the outset that individualism is sharply distinct from pure egotism, or the view that it is impossible and undesirable to set any limits at all to the pursuit of self-interest. The notion of self-reliance has a strong affirmative moral content, the demand for respect for the rights of others. This means that the individualist ethic is as demanding in its way as the counterethic of altruism. It involves the renunciation of the use of both private and public force in the struggle for satisfaction, and acquiescence in the refusal of others to behave in a communal fashion.

Individualism provides a justification for the fundamental legal institutions of criminal law, property, tort, and contract. The function of law is the definition and enforcement of rights, of those limits on the pursuit of self-interest that distinguish an individualist from a purely egotistical regime. The great preoccupation of individualist legal philosophy is to justify these restrictions, in the face of appetites that are both boundless and postulated to be legitimate. . . .

II. The Content of the Ideal of Altruism

The rhetoric of individualism so thoroughly dominates legal discourse at present that it is difficult even to identify a counterethic. Nonetheless, I think there is a coherent, pervasive notion that constantly competes with individualism, and I will call it altruism. The essence of altruism is the belief that one ought *not* to indulge a sharp preference for one's own interest over those of others. Altruism enjoins us to make sacrifices, to share, and to be merciful. It has roots in culture, in religion, ethics and art, that are as deep as those of individualism. (Love thy neighbor as thyself.)

The simplest of the practices that represent altruism are sharing and sacrifice. Sharing is a static concept, suggesting an existing distribution of goods which the sharers rearrange. It means giving up to another gains or wealth that one has produced oneself or that have come to one through some good fortune. It is motivated by a sense of duty or by a sense that the other's satisfaction is a reward at least comparable to the satisfaction one might have derived from consuming the thing oneself. Sharing may also involve participation in another's losses: a spontaneous decision to shift to oneself a part of the ill fortune, deserved or fortuitous, that has befallen someone else. Sacrifice is the dynamic notion of taking action that will change an ongoing course of events, at some expense to oneself, to minimize another's loss or maximize his gain.

The polar opposite concept for sharing and sacrifice is exchange (a crucial individualist notion). The difference is that sharing and sacrifice involve a vulnerability to non-reciprocity. Further, this vulnerability is undergone out of a sense of solidarity: with the hope of a return but with a willingness to accept the possibility that there will be none. Exchange, on the contrary, signifies a transfer of resources in which equivalents are defined, and the structure of the situation, legal or social, is designed in order to make it unlikely that either party will disappoint the other. If there is some chance of disappointment, then this is experienced as a risk one must run, a cost that is unavoidable if one is to obtain what one wants from the other. The difference is one of degree, and it is easy to imagine arrangements that are such a thorough mixture, or so ambiguous, that they defy characterization one way or the other. . . .

. . . [T]he "social function of maintaining the market" or the interests of dominant groups are, as tools, simply too crude to explain the detailed content of, say, the law of contracts. The vast majority of issues that arouse sharp conflict within contract law are either irrelevant to these larger considerations or of totally problematic import. Take the question of the "good faith" duties of a buyer in a requirements contract when there is a sudden price increase. The buyer may be able to bankrupt the seller and make a large profit by sharply increasing his requirements, supposing that the item in question accounts for much of his own cost of manufacture, or that he can resell it without using it at all.

The buyers and sellers in these situations do not seem to line up in terms of any familiar categories of political or economic power, and the effects on "the market" of deciding one way or another are highly problematic. Yet there is clearly something important at stake. The possible solutions range from a minimal buyer's duty not to "speculate" against the seller's interests to a good faith duty to absorb some loss in order to avoid a larger loss to one's contractual partner. The notion of altruism captures the court's dilemma far better than either class struggle or the needs of a market economy. . . .

III. Rules as an Aspect of Classical Laissez-Faire . . .

A. Laissez-Faire

It is not easy to reconstruct the Classical individualist economic vision, especially if we want to understand it from the inside as plausible, rather than absurd or obviously evil. While there were several strands of argumentation, the most important seems to have been the idea that the outcome of economic activity within a common law framework of contract and tort rules mechanically applied would be a natural allocation of resources and distribution of income.

The outcome was natural because it was a reflection of the real bargaining power of the parties, given the supply and demand conditions in the market in question. No legal intervention could change it except in the direction of making everyone worse off, unless the reformer was willing to establish full collectivism. It was simply an implication of the immutable laws of economics that piecemeal reform must be self-defeating or counterproductive.

The refusal to enforce contracts or contract terms because of disapproval of the abuse of bargaining power is a case in point. Each party was willing to exchange on the designated terms; each therefore thought he would profit. Refusal to enforce deprives each of that profit. It does *not,* however, modify their bargaining power. If we refuse to enforce a particular term, they will readjust the rest of the bargain, and the stronger will exact in the form of a higher price, or whatever, the advantage that can no longer express itself in an allocation of a risk. The net result will be to drive some of the buyers out of the market, because they cannot afford to pay the higher price imposed by regulation. The victims of exclusion from the market are likely to be precisely those poorer buyers the regulator was trying to help.

If we respond by trying to fix the price directly, the result will be an imbalance of supply and demand, since the prices we are trying to change were those necessary to clear the market. If we want to prevent the disappointment of sellers or buyers, we will have to establish rationing or compulsory contracts. These cannot be enforced without a degree of supervision of individual businesses that amounts to socialism de facto, if not de jure.

The assertion of the "naturalness" of economic interaction under property and contract rules is not plausible for us. Its plausibility in 1900 was based on the combination of the belief that the substantive content of the common law rules was an embodiment of the idea of freedom with the belief that official intervention to enforce the rules was nondiscretionary. The basis of the first belief . . . was conceptualism. The second notion expressed itself through a complex of doctrines, including stare decisis, the nondelegation doctrine, the void for vagueness doctrine, objectivism in contracts, the reasonable person standard in torts, the distinction between questions of law and questions of fact, and the general idea that law tended to develop toward formally realizable general rules.

If one could believe that the common law rules were logically derived from the idea of freedom and that there was no discretionary element in their application, it made sense to describe the legal order itself as at least neutral, nonpolitical if not really "natural." The economy was regulated, if one compared it to the state of nature, but it was regulated in the interests of its own freedom. What happened to economic actors when they exercised that freedom had almost as much claim to being natural as what would have happened if there was no state at all.

B. The Altruist Attack on Laissez-Faire

The altruist attack on laissez-faire denied the neutrality of the outcomes of bargaining within the background rules. The altruists began from the proposition that outcomes are heavily conditioned by the legal order in effect at any given moment. Those who enforce that legal order must accept responsibility for the allocation of resources and distribution of income it produces. In particular, bargaining power is a function of the legal order. All the individualist rules restrain or liberate that power. Changes in the rules alter its pattern. The outcome of bargaining will therefore be radically different according to whether we allow a state of nature, enforce a much more regulatory individualist regime, or a still more regulatory altruist one. All the outcomes are equally "natural." The question is which one is best.

The persuasiveness of the altruist attack depended heavily on discrediting both conceptualism and the claim that the legal order is composed of rules judges merely apply. As long as one believed in these two ideas, one could distinguish easily enough between an individualist regime and either the state of nature or a more altruist welfare state. Only the individualist regime was based on freedom. Under that regime, economic actors were never subjected to political restraints or to interference based on altruism. The rules that governed conduct depended neither on legislative consensus nor on a utopian morality, but on deduction from first principles acceptable to everyone. They were applied without the exercise of discretion by judges who had no power to inject their own politics or morals into the process.

The altruists attempted to show that neither conceptualism nor the idea of law as rules had any reality at all as a basis for defining a truly individualist legal order. . . . [T]he charge against conceptualism was that it was a mystification: there simply was no deductive process by which one could derive the "right" legal answer from abstractions like freedom or property. The attack on the claimed objectivity of the law-applying process covered the whole complex of doctrines that supposedly eliminated the discretionary element from official intervention. The aim was to show that as a matter of fact most rules were standards. The legal order, in this view, was shot through with discretion masquerading as the rule of law.

If the judges had neither derived the common law rules from the concepts nor applied them mechanically to the facts, then what *had* they been doing? The altruist answer was that they had been legislating and then enforcing their economic *biases*. The legal order represented not a coherent individualist philosophy, but concrete individualist economic interests dressed up in gibberish. This once recognized, the next target was the argument that interference with the "free market" (market regulated by conceptually derived groundrules mechanically applied) would necessarily make everyone worse off.

The altruists demonstrated that no single general analysis could predict the effects of legal intervention in the economy. Everything depended on the structure of the particular market, which in turn depended on the legal system. It was quite true that attempts to regulate the exercise of economic power by interfering with particular terms of bargains *might* be self-defeating, if the market was perfectly competitive (so that price was equal to cost), or if the stronger party could shift his exactions from one term to another. But this was not *always* the case. Compulsory standardized terms in insurance policies might reduce the bargaining power of the sellers by increasing the buyers' understanding of the transaction.

Even supposing that the result of intervention is to force most people to transact on the new set of terms at a higher price while driving the rest out of the market, this might be justified on paternalist grounds. According to the new, post-conceptual mode of analysis, the common law was already full of paternalism, that is, of rules like those of capacity, which could no longer be rationalized through the will theory. The extension of the protective policy to, say, disclaimer of warranties to consumers would not represent any radical break with common law tradition.

It was also possible to relativize the argument about direct price regulation: its impact was a function of the whole situation, rather than of any general maxim about supply and demand. For example, where sellers cannot easily withdraw from the market, a compulsory price reduction may not reduce supply, except over the long, long run. A monopolist who is forced to reduce his price may *increase* supply in order to maintain the highest possible level of profit.

Finally, there were many ways to influence economic outcomes in an altruist direction without directly regulating outcomes, and there was no reason at all to believe that these would reduce welfare. The optimizing tendencies of the market will work, within the lee-ways we choose to leave for them, no matter how we make the initial definition and allocation of property rights. For example, we can limit the tactics employers can use in bargaining with employees. This changes the balance of power that existed under the old rules about what people could do with their property. But it does not "impede the functioning of the market" any more or less than we impeded it by imposing the rules of property and contract in the first place.

This line of altruist argument applies with exactly equal force to changes in form and to changes in substance. For example, a working class automobile buyer may be highly skilled at price bargaining but have neither the time nor the education to argue successfully about warranties. Competition may not force the seller to translate his self-interested warranty terms into lower price, because there may be no competition.

The normal rule that parties are bound to their contracts whether or not they read and understand them has obvious advantages in many situations, but here it will allow the seller to dictate to the buyer. The judge may reduce the seller's bargaining power if he adopts a more flexible approach based on a "reasonable under-standing of a prudent lay buyer in all the circumstances." The result may be that there is a net increase in protection for buyers, a change whose cost is absorbed by the seller out of his monopoly profits.

It *may* be that the judge can counteract the ill effects of the normal rule about intent through substantive doctrines about duress, fraud, unconscionability or whatever. But there will be formal prob-lems with these doctrines as well. They may be underinclusive in ways that are desirable in general but deprive them of efficacy in this situation (e.g., failure to explain the boilerplate is not fraud because there has been no false statement of fact). A series of highly par-ticularized applications of a general standard of "reasonable under-standing" may be the only effective way to deal with the problem, short of the more intrusive approach of judicially constructed compulsory terms.

The choice between the old "strict" rule, a standard of "reasonable understanding," and compulsory terms cannot be made in a neutral fashion. Each choice affects the balance of economic power, to the advantage of one side and the disadvantage of the other. Since these effects are directly attributable to the legal order, the judge must take responsibility for choosing among them. He is an "interventionist" no matter what he does.

. . . [But] [t]here is a strong argument that the altruist judges who have created the modern law of unconscionability and promissory estoppel have diverted resources available for the reform of the overall substantive structure into a dead end. . . .

Nonetheless, I believe that there is value as well as an element of real nobility in the judicial decision to throw out, every time the opportunity arises, consumer contracts designed to perpetuate the exploitation of the poorest class of buyers on credit. Real people are involved, even if there are not very many whose lives the decision can affect. The altruist judge can view himself as a resource whose effectiveness in the cause of substantive justice is to be maximized, but to adopt this attitude is to abandon the crucial proposition that altruistic duty is owed by one individual to another, without the interposition of the general category of humanity.

Further, judges like Skelly Wright are important actors in a symbolic representation of the conflict of commitments. Given the present inability of altruism to transform society, it is only a dramatic production, ancillary to a hypothetical conflict that would be revolutionary. As such, the judge is a cultural figure engaged in the task of persuading adversaries, in spite of the arbitrariness of values. More, he is at work on the indispensable task of imagining an altruistic order. Contract law may be an ideal context for this labor, precisely because it presents problems of daily life, immediate and inescapable, yet deeply resistant to political understanding. It seems to me that we should be grateful for this much, and wish the enterprise what success is possible short of the overcoming of its contradictions.

NOTES AND QUESTIONS

1. Goebel v. Linn, discussed by Dalzell, is also discussed in Posner, Gratuitous Promises in Economics and Law, pp. 54-57 supra,

who concludes, contrary to Dalzell, that the decision *is* correct. What is the source of the disagreement between Dalzell and Posner? Do they interpret the facts of the case differently? Does it make a difference whether the problem presented by the case is doctrinally pigeonholed in one way (modification) or another (duress)?

Posner describes three different situations in which a promisee might agree to a modification of the terms of his contract, and argues that an economic justification for enforcing the modification exists in only one of the situations. Which of Posner's three situations describes the facts in Hackley v. Headley, also discussed by Dalzell? The facts of the case are more complicated than Dalzell's statement of them suggests. Consider the following extract from the court's opinion (45 Mich. 569 at 573-574):

> Headley's account of the circumstances under which this receipt was given is in substance as follows: On August 3, 1875, he went to Muskegon, the place of business of Hackley & McGordon, from his home in Kent county, for the purpose of collecting the balance which he claimed was due him under the contract. The amount he claimed was upwards of $6200, estimating the logs by the Scribner scale. He had an interview with Hackley in the morning, who insisted that the estimate should be according to the Doyle scale, and who also claimed that he had made payments to others amounting to some $1400 which Headley should allow. Headley did not admit these payments, and denied his liability for them if they had been made. Hackley told Headley to come in again in the afternoon, and when he did so Hackley said to him: "My figures show there is 4260 and odd dollars in round numbers your due, and I will just give you $4000. I will give you our note for $4000." To this Headley replied: "I cannot take that; it is not right, and you know it. There is over $2000 besides that belongs to me, and you know it." Hackley replied:"That is the best I will do with you." Headley said: "I cannot take that, Mr. Hackley," and Hackley replied, "You do the next best thing you are a mind to. You can sue me if you please." Headley then said: "I cannot afford to sue you, because I have got to have the money, and I cannot wait for it . . ."

In light of this fuller statement of the facts in the case, which of Posner's three prototypical situations is applicable? Does the more detailed statement of facts in the opinion indicate a weakness in Dalzell's analysis? Can the case be explained as involving a separate bilateral agreement between the parties to surrender a legal claim in exchange for a reduction in the contract price?

2. In a well-known law review article, Contracts of Adhesion—Some Thoughts About Freedom of Contract, 43 Colum. L. Rev. 629 (1943), Friedrich Kessler describes the growing use of standard form contracts as part of a larger process of legal and economic rationalization:

> The development of large scale enterprise with its mass produc-

> tion and mass distribution made a new type of contract inevitable—the standardized mass contract. A standardized contract, once its contents have been formulated by a business firm, is used in every bargain with the same product or service. The individuality of the parties which so frequently gave color to the old type contract has disappeared. The stereotyped contract of today reflects the impersonality of the market. It has reached its greatest perfection in the different types of contracts used on the various exchanges. Once the usefulness of these contracts was discovered and perfected in the transportation, insurance, and banking business, their use spread into all other fields of large scale enterprise, into international as well as national trade, and into labor relations. It is to be noted that uniformity of terms of contracts typically recurring in a business enterprise is an important factor in the exact calculation of risks. Risks which are difficult to calculate can be excluded altogether. Unforseeable contingencies affecting performance, such as strikes, fire, and transportation difficulties can be taken care of. The standard clauses in insurance policies are the most striking illustrations of successful attempts on the part of business enterprises to select and control risks assumed under a contract. The insurance business probably deserves credit also for having first realized the full importance of the so-called "juridical risk," the danger that a court or jury may be swayed by "irrational factors" to decide against a powerful defendant. [Id. at 631.][1]

Kessler argues that many standard form contracts are likely to be biased in favor of the businessmen who create them. In some cases, however, standardized terms are imposed upon the parties to a contract by legislative fiat—and where this is the case, the terms are often skewed in the interest of the weaker party or at least designed to insure a roughly balanced bargain. The modern insurance contract is, in fact, one of the most striking examples of standardization by legislation. See Edwin Patterson, Compulsory Contracts in the Crystal Ball, 43 Colum. L. Rev. 731, 735-736 (1943).

According to Kessler, the standard form contract has also played an important role in what he calls the "decline of the free enterprise system" (43 Colum. L. Rev. at 640-641).

> The individualism of our rules of contract law, of which freedom of contract is the most powerful symbol, is closely tied up with the ethics of free enterprise capitalism and the ideals of justice of a mobile society of small enterprisers, individual merchants and independent craftsmen. This society believed that individual and cooperative action left unrestrained in family, church and market would not lessen the freedom and dignity of man but would secure the highest possible social justice. It was firmly convinced of a natural law according to which the individual serving his own interest was also serving the interest of the community. Profits can be earned only by supplying consumable commodities. Freedom of competition will prevent profits from rising unduly. The play of the market if left to itself must there-

1. Reprinted by permission.

> fore maximize net satisfactions. Justice within this framework has a very definite meaning. It means freedom of property and of contract, of profit making and of trade. Freedom of contract thus receives its moral justification. The "prestabilized harmony" of a social system based on freedom of enterprise and perfect competition sees to it that the "private autonomy" of contracting parties will be kept within bounds and will work out to the benefit of the whole.
>
> With the decline of the free enterprise system due to the innate trend of competitive capitalism towards monopoly, the meaning of contract has changed radically. Society, when granting freedom of contract, does not guarantee that all members of the community will be able to make use of it to the same extent. On the contrary, the law, by protecting the unequal distribution of property, does nothing to prevent freedom of contract from becoming a one-sided privilege. Society, by proclaiming freedom of contract, guarantees that it will not interfere with the exercise of power by contract. Freedom of contract enables enterprises to legislate by contract and, what is even more important, to legislate in a substantially authoritarian manner without using the appearance of authoritarian forms. Standard contracts in particular could thus become effective instruments in the hands of powerful industrial and commercial overlords enabling them to impose a new feudal order of their own making upon a vast host of vassals. This spectacle is all the more fascinating since not more than a hundred years ago contract ideology had been successfully used to break down the last vestiges of a patriarchal and benevolent feudal order in the field of master and servant (Priestley v. Fowler). Thus the return back from contract to status which we experience today was greatly facilitated by the fact that the belief in freedom of contract has remained one of the firmest axioms in the whole fabric of the social philosophy of our culture.[2]

What evidence is there to support Kessler's contention that competitive capitalism exhibits an "innate trend" towards monopoly? Does Kessler regard the "one-sidedness" of freedom of contract as a cause or consequence of this trend? Compare Max Weber's remarks on freedom of contract in Chapter 7.

3. Goldberg, like Kessler, regards the standard form contract as a kind of "private legislation." Is the comparison with legislative enactment an apt one? The central question posed in the Goldberg article is whether, generally speaking, one class of contractors (large firms) has the power unilaterally to impose disadvantageous terms on another class of contractors (individual consumers). Goldberg doubts that competition significantly constrains the power of large firms to impose terms on "contract term takers." Coase disagrees. What is the source of their disagreement? Does Goldberg's argument rest, as Coase suggests it does, on the assumption of "consumer ignorance"?

2. Reprinted by permission.

Goldberg states that the power of firms to dictate contract terms is in part due to the fact that few customers "will find it worthwhile to pay the costs of acquiring information" concerning the terms offered by competing firms. Coase, on the other hand, argues that individual firms will have a strong incentive to bring the disadvantages of the terms offered by their competitors to the attention of consumers. Does Trebilcock agree with Coase? Is there a "free rider" problem in disparaging (however truthfully) a competitor? See Richard A. Posner, Economic Analysis of Law 82 (2d ed. 1977).

4. Epstein contends that the doctrine of unconscionability "should be used only to facilitate the setting aside of agreements that are as a matter of probabilities likely to be vitiated by the classical defenses of duress, fraud, or incompetence." Later in his article Epstein asserts that "one of the strengths of the unconscionability doctrine is its flexibility, an attribute much needed because it is difficult to identify in advance all of the kinds of situations in which it might in principle apply." Are these statements consistent?

Despite appearances, do Kennedy and Epstein perhaps share a common view of how the unconscionability doctrine should be employed? Doesn't Epstein's discussion of the "vulnerable veteran" case imply that courts should adopt a flexible approach of the sort advocated by Kennedy? What then explains their different views regarding the use of the unconscionability doctrine to protect the poor? Epstein states that the "perils" of using the doctrine in this way are "great." Kennedy finds "an element of real nobility in the judicial decision to throw out, every time the opportunity arises, consumer contracts designed to perpetuate the exploitation of the poorest class of buyers on credit." Does their disagreement on this question reflect more fundamental disagreement on the appropriateness of using the legal system as an instrument of distributive justice? For a fuller consideration of this issue, see Chapter 7.

5. Should the doctrine of unconscionability be used to protect the poor? Consider the views of Alan Schwartz, A Reexamination of Nonsubstantive Unconscionability, 63 Va. L. Rev. 1053, 1056-1059 (1977):

> A contracting party's poverty is commonly thought to militate in four ways against enforcing an agreement. First, poverty may impede the buyer's efforts to purchase a "fair" contract. The cost of a contract reflects, among other things, the agreement's allocation of risk between buyer and seller. For example, a contract disclaiming product warranties usually is cheaper than a contract providing such warranties. Although an affluent buyer often can pay the premium necessary to induce a seller to assume significant risks under a contract, a poor buyer may experience great difficulty in trying to buy away disfavored terms.

Second, poverty is thought to correlate strongly with a buyer's lack of commercial sophistication. A poor consumer, therefore, is often said to be at a disadvantage relative to more affluent parties in understanding and negotiating contracts. Third, poverty may restrict the flow of commercial information to poor consumers. If sellers provide less information in ghetto markets than in other markets, even a poor consumer skilled in bargaining may be unable to evaluate the terms of a proposed agreement. Fourth, poverty may exacerbate the consequences of certain contract clauses. An acceleration clause, for example, may bear more harshly upon a poor consumer than upon an affluent consumer. . . .

Prohibiting a contract clause because a poor buyer finds it difficult to purchase more favorable terms yields a nonoptimal result. Assume, for example, that a retailer is offering two contracts that are identical except for one clause: the first contract, which costs $100, includes a warranty against product defects, while the second contract, which costs $90, includes a disclaimer of the warranty. The hypothetical retailer has customers for both contracts, but the state, by statute or judicial opinion, later bans the warranty disclaimer. Under these circumstances, the prohibition against warranty disclaimers neither helps nor hurts those customers who would have purchased warranty coverage. The prohibition, however, harms the customers who would have purchased a contract disclaiming all warranties. These consumers apparently value the insurance against product defects provided by a warranty less than they value other uses for their $10. Therefore, the prohibition against disclaimers yields a nonoptimal result: some buyers regard themselves as worse off than before the ban, and no buyers regard themselves as better off.

This result is particularly undesirable because banning warranty disclaimers is likely to affect the poor more adversely than the affluent. A poor person spends a large percentage of his income on goods for which his demand is income-inelastic,[3] e.g., food, shelter, and clothing. As his income rises, he will begin to purchase goods for which his demand is more income-elastic. Analysis indicates that a poor person's demand for warranty protection is probably more income-elastic than that for "necessities." Many of the contract clauses that are now of concern, such as warranty disclaimers, shift purchase risks to buyers. Poor people generally are more risk averse than rich people because they cannot withstand large losses.[4] The poor, however, may lose relatively less than the middle class when purchase risks materialize because, in the circumstances discussed here, the poor have less at stake. For example, middle class buyers who default may lose valuable property, while poor buyers have much less property to lose. Also, accidents may cause middle class buyers to lose wages, while poor buyers on welfare may lose no income at all. Because a poor person, thus, is probably more anxious than a rich person to forego the insurance a warranty affords, prohibiting warranty disclaimers or other

3. Income elasticity measures the responsiveness of demand for a certain good to changes in income. More specifically, it is defined as the percentage change in income quantity divided by the percentage change in income. [Citations omitted.]

4. H. Raiffa, Decision Analysis: Introductory Lectures on Choice under Uncertainty 91-94 (1970).

> contract clauses will bear more harshly upon the poor than upon the affluent. Therefore, a contracting party's poverty, other things being equal, should militate in favor of, rather than against, enforcing a contract clause. . . .[5]

6. On the economics of consumer fraud see Michael R. Darby & Edi Karni, Free Competition and the Optimal Amount of Fraud, 16 J. Law & Econ. 67 (1973); Richard A. Posner, Economic Analysis of Law 80-84, 271-276 (2d ed. 1977).

5. Reprinted by permission.

Chapter 5

Mistake and Impossibility

*Mistake, Disclosure, Information, and the Law of Contracts**

Anthony T. Kronman

I. Mistake and the Allocation of Risk

Every contractual agreement is predicated upon a number of factual assumptions about the world. Some of these assumptions are shared by the parties to the contract and some are not. It is always possible that a particular factual assumption is mistaken. From an economic point of view, the risk of such a mistake (whether it be the mistake of only one party or both) represents a cost. It is a cost to the contracting parties themselves and to society as a whole since the actual occurrence of a mistake always (potentially) increases the resources which must be devoted to the process of allocating goods to their highest-valuing users. . . .

Information is the antidote to mistake. Although information is costly to produce, one individual may be able to obtain relevant information more cheaply than another. If the parties to a contract are acting rationally, they will minimize the joint costs of a potential mistake by assigning the risk of its occurrence to the party who is the better (cheaper) information-gatherer. Where the parties have actually assigned the risk—whether explicitly, or implicitly through their adherence to trade custom and past patterns of dealing—their own allocation must be respected. Where they have not—and there is a

*Reprinted, by permission, from 7 J. Legal Studies 1 (1978).

resulting gap in the contract—a court concerned with economic efficiency should impose the risk on the better information-gatherer. This is so for familiar reasons: by allocating the risk in this way, an efficiency-minded court reduces the transaction costs of the contracting process itself.

The most important doctrinal distinction in the law of mistake is the one drawn between "mutual" and "unilateral" mistakes. Traditionally, courts have been more reluctant to excuse a mistaken promisor where he alone is mistaken than where the other party is mistaken as to the same fact. Although relief for unilateral mistake has been liberalized during the last half-century (to the point where some commentators have questioned the utility of the distinction between unilateral and mutual mistake and a few have even urged its abolition) it is still "black-letter" law that a promisor whose mistake is not shared by the other party is less likely to be relieved of his duty to perform than a promisor whose mistake happens to be mutual.

Viewed broadly, the distinction between mutual and unilateral mistake makes sense from an economic point of view. Where both parties to a contract are mistaken about the same fact or state of affairs, deciding which of them would have been better able to prevent the mistake may well require a detailed inquiry regarding the nature of the mistake and the (economic) role or position of each of the parties involved. But where only one party is mistaken, it is reasonable to assume that he is in a better position than the other party to prevent his own error. . . .

. . . One well-established exception protects the unilaterally mistaken promisor whose error is known or reasonably should be known to the other party. Relief has long been available in this case despite the fact that the promisor's mistake is not shared by the other party to the contract.

For example, if a bidder submits a bid containing a clerical error or miscalculation, and the mistake is either evident on the face of the bid, or may reasonably be inferred from a discrepancy between it and other bids, the bidder will typically be permitted to withdraw the bid without having to pay damages (even after the bid has been accepted and in some cases relied upon by the other party). . . .

A rule of this sort is a sensible one. While it is true that . . . the mistaken party is likely to be the one best able to prevent the mistake from occurring in the first place . . . , the other party may be able to rectify the mistake more cheaply in the interim between its occurrence and the formation of the contract. At one moment in time the mistaken party is the better mistake-preventer (information-gatherer). At some subsequent moment, however, the other party may be the better preventer because of his superior access to relevant information that will disclose the mistake and thus allow its correction. This may be so, for example, if he has other bids to compare with the mistaken one since this will provide him with information which the bidder himself lacks. . . .

The cases in which relief is granted to a unilaterally mistaken promisor on the grounds that his mistake was known or reasonably knowable by the other party appear . . . to conflict sharply with another line of cases. These cases deal with the related problems of fraud and disclosure: if one party to a contract knows that the other is mistaken as to some material fact, is it fraud for the party with knowledge to fail to disclose the error and may the mistaken party avoid the contract on the theory that he was owed a duty of disclosure? This question is not always answered in the same way. In some cases courts typically find a duty to disclose and in others they do not. It is the latter group of cases—those not requiring disclosure—which appear to conflict with the rule that a unilateral mistake will excuse if the other party knows or has reason to know of its existence.

In the cases not requiring disclosure, one party is mistaken and the other party knows or has reason to know it. Can these cases be reconciled with those which stand for the proposition that a unilateral mistake plus knowledge or reason to know will excuse the mistaken party? More particularly, can the apparent divergence between these two lines of cases be explained on economic grounds? . . .

II. The Production of Information and the Duty to Disclose

It is appropriate to begin a discussion of fraud and nondisclosure in contract law with the celebrated case of Laidlaw v. Organ.[1] Organ was a New Orleans commission merchant engaged in the purchase and sale of tobacco. Early on the morning of February 19, 1815, he was informed . . . that a peace treaty had been signed at Ghent by American and British officers, formally ending the War of 1812. . . .

Knowledge of the treaty was made public in a handbill circulated around eight o'clock on the morning of the nineteenth. However, before the treaty's existence had been publicized . . ., Organ . . . called on a representative of the Laidlaw firm and entered into a contract for the purchase of 111 hogsheads of tobacco. Before agreeing to sell the tobacco, the Laidlaw representative "asked if there was any news which was calculated to enhance the price or value of the article about to be purchased." It is unclear what response, if any, Organ made to this inquiry.

1. 15 U.S. (2 Wheat.) 178 (1817).

As a result of the news of the treaty—which signalled an end to the naval blockade of New Orleans—the market price of tobacco quickly rose by 30 to 50 percent. Laidlaw delivered the tobacco as promised, and then apparently regained possession. Organ brought suit to recover damages and to block Laidlaw from otherwise disposing of the goods in controversy. Although the report of the case is unclear, it appears that the trial judge directed a verdict in Organ's favor. The case was appealed to the United States Supreme Court which in an opinion by Chief Justice Marshall remanded with directions for a new trial. . . . Marshall's opinion is more famous, however, for its dictum than for its holding:

> The question in this case is, whether the intelligence of extrinsic circumstances, which might influence the price of the commodity, and which was exclusively within the knowledge of the vendee, ought to have been communicated by him to the vendor? The court is of opinion that he was not bound to communicate it. It would be difficult to circumscribe the contrary doctrine within proper limits, where the means of intelligence are equally accessible to both parties. But at the same time, each party must take care not to say or do anything tending to impose upon the other. . . .

News of the treaty of Ghent affected the price of tobacco in New Orleans. Price measures the relative value of commodities: information regarding the treaty revealed a new state of affairs in which the value of tobacco—relative to other goods and to tobacco-substitutes in particular—had altered. An alteration of this sort is almost certain to affect the allocation of social resources. If the price of tobacco to suppliers rises, for example, farmers will be encouraged to plant more tobacco and tobacco merchants may be prepared to pay more to get their goods to and from market. In this way, the proportion of society's (limited) resources devoted to the production and transportation of tobacco will be increased. . . .

From a social point of view, it is desirable that information which reveals a change in circumstances affecting the relative value of commodities reach the market as quickly as possible (or put differently, that the time between the change itself and its comprehension and assessment be minimized). If a farmer who would have planted tobacco had he known of the change plants peanuts instead, he will have to choose between either uprooting one crop and substituting another (which may be prohibitively expensive and will in any case be costly), or devoting his land to a nonoptimal use. In either case, both the individual farmer and society as a whole will be worse off than if he had planted tobacco to begin with. . . .

Allocative efficiency is promoted by getting information of changed circumstances to the market as quickly as possible. Of course, the information doesn't just "get" there. Like everything else, it is supplied by individuals (either directly, by being publicized, or indirectly, when it is signalled by an individual's market behavior).

In some cases, the individuals who supply information have obtained it by a deliberate search; in other cases, their information has been acquired casually. A securities analyst, for example, acquires information about a particular corporation in a deliberate fashion—by carefully studying evidence of its economic performance. In contrast, a businessman who acquires a valuable piece of information when he accidentally overhears a conversation on a bus acquires the information casually.

As it is used here, the term "deliberately acquired information" means information whose acquisition entails cost which would not have been incurred but for the likelihood, however great, that the information in question would actually be produced. These costs may include, of course, not only direct search costs (the cost of examining the corporation's annual statement) but the costs of developing an initial expertise as well (for example, the cost of attending business school). If the costs incurred in acquiring the information (the cost of the bus ticket in the second example) would have been incurred in any case—that is, whether or not the information was forthcoming—the information may be said to have been casually acquired. The distinction between deliberately and casually acquired information is a shorthand way of expressing this economic difference. . . .

If information has been deliberately acquired (in the sense defined above), and its possessor is denied the benefits of having and using it, he will have an incentive to reduce (or curtail entirely) his production of such information in the future. This is in fact merely a consequence of defining deliberately acquired information in the way that I have, since one who acquires information of this sort will by definition have incurred costs which he would have avoided had it not been for the prospect of the benefits he has now been denied. By being denied the same benefits, one who has casually acquired information will not be discouraged from doing what—for independent reasons—he would have done in any case.

It might be claimed that whenever the benefits of possessing any kind of information are either increased or decreased, one would expect to find *some* overall adjustment in the level of investment in the production of such information. If he is not permitted to benefit from the information he acquires, even the bus rider will in the future pay less attention to the conversations going on around him (although it would certainly be strange if he stopped riding buses altogether). But while it is true that in reality every adjustment (upwards or downwards) in the benefits of possessing a particular kind of information will have an incentive effect of some sort, the effect may vary in magnitude—it may be greater or lesser. Strictly speaking, casually acquired information (as I have used the term up to this point) represents the ideal limit of a continuum—the case in which the change in magnitude that results from eliminating one of the benefits of possessing certain information is zero. In any real case there will be incentive effects which fall somewhere along the continuum. However, where the decline in the production of a certain kind of information which is caused by denying its possessor the right to appropriate the information for his own benefit is small, it is likely to be more than offset by the corresponding social gain which results from the avoidance of mistakes. . . .

One effective way of insuring that an individual will benefit from the possession of information (or anything else for that matter) is to assign him a property right in the information itself—a right or entitlement to invoke the coercive machinery of the state in order to exclude others from its use and enjoyment. . . . The assignment of property rights in information is a familiar feature of our legal system. The legal protection accorded patented inventions and certain trade secrets are two obvious examples.

One (seldom noticed) way in which the legal system can establish property rights in information is by permitting an informed party to enter—and enforce—contracts which his information suggests are profitable, without disclosing the information to the other party. Imposing a duty to disclose upon the knowledgeable party deprives him of a private advantage which the information would otherwise afford. A duty to disclose is tantamount to a requirement that the benefit of the information be publicly shared and is thus antithetical to the notion of a property right which—whatever else it may entail—always requires the legal protection of private appropriation. . . .

It is unclear, from the report of the case, whether the buyer in *Laidlaw* casually acquired his information or made a deliberate investment in seeking it out (for example, by cultivating a network of valuable commercial "friendships"). If we assume the buyer casually acquired his knowledge of the treaty, requiring him to disclose the information to his seller (that is, denying him a property right in the information) will have no significant effect on his future behavior. Since one who casually acquires information makes no investment in its acquisition, subjecting him to a duty to disclose is not likely to reduce the amount of socially useful information which he actually generates. Of course, if the buyer in *Laidlaw* acquired his knowledge of the treaty as the result of a deliberate and costly search, a disclosure requirement will deprive him of any private benefit which he might otherwise realize from possession of the information and should discourage him from making similar investments in the future.

In addition, since it would enable the seller to appropriate the buyer's information without cost and would eliminate the danger of his being lured unwittingly into a losing contract by one possessing superior knowledge, a disclosure requirement will also reduce the seller's incentive to search. Denying the buyer a property right in deliberately acquired information will therefore discourage both buyers and sellers from investing in the development of expertise and in the actual search for information. The assignment of such a right will not only protect the investment of the party possessing the special knowledge,—it will also impose an opportunity cost on the other party and thus give him an incentive to undertake a (cost-justified) search of his own.

If we assume that courts can easily discriminate between those who have acquired information casually and those who have acquired it deliberately, plausible economic considerations might well justify imposing a duty to disclose on a case-by-case basis (imposing it where the information has been casually acquired, refusing to impose it where the information is the fruit of a deliberate search). A party who has casually acquired information is, at the time of the transaction, likely to be a better (cheaper) mistake-preventer than the mistaken party with whom he deals—regardless of the fact that both parties initially had equal access to the information in question. One who has deliberately acquired information is also in a position to prevent the other party's error. But in determining the cost to the knowledgeable party of preventing the mistake (by disclosure), we must include whatever investment he has made in acquiring the information in the first place. This investment will represent a loss to him if the other party can avoid the contract on the grounds that the party with the information owes him a duty of disclosure. . . .

A rule which calls for case-by-case application of a disclosure requirement is likely, however, to involve factual issues that will be difficult (and expensive) to resolve. *Laidlaw* itself illustrates this point nicely. On the facts of the case, as we have them, it is impossible to determine whether the buyer actually made a deliberate investment in acquiring information regarding the treaty. The cost of administering a disclosure requirement on a case-by-case basis is likely to be substantial.

As an alternative, one might uniformly apply a blanket rule (of disclosure or nondisclosure) across each class of cases involving the same sort of information (for example, information about market conditions or about defects in property held for sale). In determining the appropriate blanket rule for a particular class of cases, it would first be necessary to decide whether the kind of information involved is (on the whole) more likely to be generated by chance or by deliberate searching. The greater the likelihood that such information will be deliberately produced rather than casually discovered, the more plausible the assumption becomes that a blanket rule permitting nondisclosure will have benefits that outweigh its costs.

In *Laidlaw,* for example, the information involved concerned changing market conditions. The results in that case may be justified (from the more general perspective just described) on the grounds that information regarding the state of the market is typically (although not in every case) the product of a deliberate search. The large number of individuals who are actually engaged in the production of such information lends some empirical support to this proposition. . . .

III. Unilateral Mistake and the Duty to Disclose

. . . [By contrast, in the mistaken bid case] the special knowledge of the non-mistaken party (his knowledge of the other party's error) is unlikely to be the fruit of a deliberate search. Put differently, a rule requiring him to disclose what he knows will not cause him to alter his behavior in such a way that the production of information of this sort will be reduced.

A contractor receiving a mistaken bid, for example, usually becomes aware of the mistake (if he does at all) by comparing the mistaken bid with others that have been submitted, or by noting an error which is evident on the face of the bid itself. In either case, his knowledge of the mistake arises in the course of a routine examination of the bids which he would undertake in any event. The party receiving the bid has an independent incentive to scrutinize carefully each of the bids which are submitted to him: the profitability of his own enterprise requires that he do so. It is of course true that the recipient's expertise may make it easier for him to identify certain sorts of errors in bids that have been submitted. But the detection of clerical mistakes and errors in calculation is not likely to be one of the principal reasons for his becoming an expert in the first place. A rule requiring the disclosure of mistakes of this kind is almost certain not to discourage investment in developing the sort of general expertise which facilitates the detection of such mistakes. . . .

*Impossibility and Related Doctrines in Contract Law: An Economic Analysis**

Richard A. Posner & Andrew M. Rosenfield

Ordinarily the failure of one party to a contract to fulfill the performance required of him constitutes a breach of contract for which he is liable in damages to the other party. But sometimes the failure to perform is excused and the contract is said to be discharged rather than breached. This study uses economic theory to investigate three closely related doctrines in the law of contracts that operate to discharge a contract: "impossibility," "impracticability," and "frustration." . . .

I. The Economics of Impossibility

The typical case in which impossibility or some related doctrine is invoked is one where, by reason of an unforeseen or at least unprovided-for event, performance by one of the parties of his obligations under the contract has become so much more costly than he foresaw at the time the contract was made as to be uneconomical (that is, the costs of performance would be greater than the benefits). The performance promised may have been delivery of a particular cargo by a specified delivery date—but the ship is trapped in the Suez Canal because of a war between Israel and Egypt. Or it may have been a piano recital by Gina Bachauer—and she dies between the signing of the contract and the date of the recital. The law could in each case treat the failure to perform as a breach of contract, thereby in effect assigning to the promisor the risk that war, or death, would prevent performance (or render it uneconomical). Alternatively, invoking impossibility or some related notion, the law could treat the failure to perform as excusable and discharge the contract, thereby in effect assigning the risk to the promisee.

From the standpoint of economics—and disregarding, but only momentarily, administrative costs—discharge should be allowed where the promisee is the superior risk bearer; if the promisor is the superior risk bearer, nonperformance should be treated as a breach of contract. "Superior risk bearer" is to be understood here as the party that is the more efficient bearer of the particular risk in question, in the particular circumstances of the transaction. Of course, if the parties have expressly assigned the risk to one of them, there is

*Reprinted, by permission, from 6 J. Legal Studies 83 (1977).

no occasion to inquire which is the superior risk bearer. The inquiry is merely an aid to interpretation.

A party can be a superior risk bearer for one of two reasons. First, he may be in a better position to prevent the risk from materializing. This resembles the economic criterion for assigning liability in tort cases. It is an important criterion in many contract settings, too, but not in this one. Discharge would be inefficient in any case where the promisor could prevent the risk from materializing at a lower cost than the expected cost of the risky event. In such a case efficiency would require that the promisor bear the loss resulting from the occurrence of the event, and hence that occurrence should be treated as precipitating a breach of contract.

But the converse is not necessarily true. It does not necessarily follow from the fact that the promisor could not at any reasonable cost have prevented the risk from materializing that he should be discharged from his contractual obligations. Prevention is only one way of dealing with risk; the other is insurance. The promisor may be the superior insurer. If so, his inability to prevent the risk from materializing should not operate to discharge him from the contract, any more than an insurance company's inability to prevent a fire on the premises of the insured should excuse it from its liability to make good the damage caused by the fire.

To understand how it is that one party to a contract may be the superior (more efficient) risk bearer even though he cannot prevent the risk from materializing, it is necessary to understand the fundamental concept of risk aversion. . . .[1]

. . . The prevalence of insurance is powerful evidence that risk aversion is extremely common, for insurance is simply trading an uncertain for a certain cost. Because of the administrative expenses of insurance, the certain cost (that is, the insurance premium) is always higher, often much higher, than the uncertain cost that it avoids—the expected cost of the fire, of the automobile accident, or whatever. Only a risk-averse individual would pay more to avoid bearing risk than the expected cost of the risk.

The fact that people are willing to pay to avoid risk shows that risk is a cost. Accordingly, insurance is a method (alternative to prevention) of reducing the costs associated with the risk that performance of a contract may be more costly than anticipated. It is a particularly important method of cost avoidance in the impossibility context because the risks with which that doctrine is concerned are generally not preventable by the party charged with nonperformance. As mentioned, if they were, that would normally afford a

1. [See pp. 35-37 supra.]

compelling reason for treating nonperformance as a breach of contract. (Stated otherwise, a "moral hazard" problem would be created if the promisor were insured against a hazard that he could have prevented at reasonable cost.)

The factors relevant to determining which party to the contract is the cheaper insurer are (1) risk-appraisal costs and (2) transaction costs.[2] The former comprise the costs of determining (a) the probability that the risk will materialize and (b) the magnitude of the loss if it does materialize. The amount of risk is the product of the probability of loss and of the magnitude of the loss if it occurs. Both elements—probability and magnitude—must be known in order for the insurer to know how much to ask from the other party to the contract as compensation for bearing the risk in question.

The relevant transaction costs are the costs involved in eliminating or minimizing the risk through pooling it with other uncertain events, that is, diversifying away the risk. This can be done either through self-insurance or through the purchase of an insurance policy (market insurance). To illustrate, a corporation's shareholders might eliminate the risk associated with some contract the corporation had made by holding a portfolio of securities in which their shares in the corporation were combined with shares in many other corporations whose earnings would not be (adversely) affected if this particular corporation were to default on the contract. This would be an example of self-insurance. Alternatively, the corporation might purchase business-loss or some other form of insurance that would protect it (and, more important, its shareholders) from the consequences of a default on the contract; this would be an example of market insurance. Where good opportunities for diversification exist, self-insurance will often be cheaper than market insurance.[3]

The foregoing discussion indicates the factors that courts and legislatures might consider in devising efficient rules for the discharge of contracts. An easy case for discharge would be one where (1) the promisor asking to be discharged could not reasonably have prevented the event rendering his performance uneconomical, and (2) the promisee could have insured against the occurrence of the event at lower cost than the promisor because the promisee (a) was in a better position to estimate both (i) the probability of the event's occurrence and (ii) the magnitude of the loss if it did occur, and (b) could have self-insured, whereas the promiser would have had to

2. The appraisal costs are really part of the transaction costs, but to facilitate exposition we exclude them from the latter concept.

3. A life-insurance company, for example, self-insures by pooling the death risks of its (many) policy-holders; it holds a diversified portfolio of life expectancies. The individual could not self-insure the risk of his death.

buy more costly market insurance. As we shall see, not all cases are this easy. . . .

II. Application of the Economic Approach . . .

A. Typical Cases

In this subpart we consider the major recurring issues in the discharge case law. As one would expect, there are some inconsistent holdings among the multiple jurisdictions that have considered these issues. It is not our purpose to explain or even identify every inconsistent outcome. We are content to explain the typical outcomes in the major classes of case.

1. *Contracts for personal services.* Discharge of contracts for personal services is often sought when an employee has died unexpectedly. In Cutler v. United Shoe Mach. Corp.,[4] a machinery company had an employment contract with an inventor. When the inventor died, the court, in a suit by the inventor's estate, held the contract discharged. This outcome—typical in employee cases—is consistent with the economic approach. The employee (1) is in at least as good a position as his employer to estimate his life expectancy, (2) has better knowledge of the value of the contract to him compared to that of any alternative employment and (3) can readily purchase life insurance.

If the employer were seeking damages as a result of the employee's death, alleging that death had caused a breach of the employee's obligations under the contract, the contract should also be discharged. Estimating life expectancy is in general no more (if no less) difficult for the employer than for the employee (if the employee knew of a condition reducing his life expectancy below the actuarial level for people of his age, sex, etc., discharge would presumably not be allowed). And the employer is better able to estimate the cost to him (in firm-specific human capital, replacement costs, etc.) if the employee dies, and can usually self-insure against such an eventuality.

The discharge doctrine may also be invoked in personal-services cases when an unexpected contingency prevents the completion of the promised service without physically disabling the promisor, as in Hein v. Fox.[5] Fox had agreed to drill a well on Hein's land. In two separate drilling attempts a boulder or layer of rock was struck, once at a depth of 250 feet and again at a depth of 350 feet, preventing completion of the well, and due to wartime regulations the special

4. 274 Mass. 341, 174 N.E. 507 (1931).
5. 126 Mont. 514, 254 P.2d 1076 (1953).

casing needed to penetrate the rock was unavailable. The court properly refused discharge. Fox, a driller, was better able than his customer to estimate the probability of encountering rock deep below the surface of the earth, the costs of alternative drilling techniques, the likelihood of failing to obtain a particular input (pipe casing), and the costs of a substitute input. And Fox could have spread the risk of these contingencies among all of his customers in his price for drilling, thereby providing effective and inexpensive self-insurance.

2. *The effects of supervening illegality on teachers' contracts and on leases.* In Phelps v. School District,[6] the state board of health had ordered a school closed for two months during its regular term because of a flu epidemic and the school district had laid off the teachers at that school. The district argued that its contract with the teachers was discharged because it was legally prevented from performing it. The court properly refused discharge. Although neither party could have prevented the epidemic, the school district was the superior risk bearer. It could spread the risk among all of its schools and hence among all of the teachers; it had a "diversified portfolio" of schools. If market insurance had been desired, the district could have insured all of its employees in one transaction, thereby eliminating the need for each individual to incur transaction costs.

Although the outcome in *Phelps* is the usual one in a case of this sort,[7] an Indiana decision held on similar facts that the teachers' contract was discharged by the school closing.[8] Our analysis suggests that this result is inefficient, a conclusion supported (weakly)[9] by the subsequent action of the Indiana legislature in enacting a statute assigning to the school boards the risks created by school closings.[10]

The issue of supervening illegality as a ground for discharge also arises when a leasehold is radically modified by operation of law. But here the economic analysis must remain tentative because it may not be possible to determine a priori which party is the superior risk bearer. In Stratford v. Seattle Brewing & Malting Co., a party leased

6. 302 Ill. 193, 134 N.E. 312 (1922).

7. See, for example, Elsemore v. Inhabitants of Hancock, 137 Me. 248, 18 A.2d 692 (1941). . . .

8. Gregg School Township v. Hinshaw, 76 Ind. App. 503, 132 N.E. 586 (1921).

9. There is no presumption that legislation seeks to enhance efficiency. See, for example, George J. Stigler, The Theory of Economic Regulation, 2 Bell J. Econ. & Management Sci. 3 (1971).

10. Ind. Code Ann. §20-6-8-2 (1971) provided: "If, during the term of a teacher's contract the school or schools are closed by order of the school corporation, or by order of the health authorities, or if, through no fault of the teacher, school cannot be held, such teacher shall receive regular payments during such time the school or schools are closed." This statute has been superseded by a similar one. See id. §20-6.1-5-8 (Supp. 1976).

premises to be used "for saloon purposes."[11] The lease was subsequently modified to allow other related uses. When as the result of a referendum the lessee lost the liquor license necessary to continue saloon operations, the contract was held discharged. The effect was to assign the risk of the law change to the lessor. But in another group of cases, leases of automobile showrooms were held not to be discharged by federal restrictions on the sale of automobiles during World War II.[12] Here the lessees were assigned the risk.

In the liquor-license case, the referendum reduced the value of the property by disallowing its most profitable use. The loss in value was equal to the difference between the original rental value and the rental value after the referendum. And similarly in the automobile-showroom cases the loss was the difference between the original rental value and the rental value after the passage of the regulations restricting automobile production. It would seem that in both cases the lessor would be better able than the lessee to estimate the opportunity value of the premises in its next best use. But the lessee should be in a better position to estimate the other key parameter, the probability that the loss will occur. One would expect automobile dealers, for example, to be more knowledgeable with respect to the possibility of a limit on new-car production than the average commercial land owner.

When the two key parameters of the economic analysis point in opposite directions, the analysis is indeterminate on a general level and must proceed to an estimation of their relative empirical importance. The lessor in *Stratford* was a brewer,[13] and was therefore probably as competent as the lessee to estimate the likelihood of the loss of the liquor license. In the typical automobile case, the courts have found that the next best use of the leased showroom was as a showroom for the sale of second-hand automobiles or as an auto repair facility. Hence the typical lessee in the automobile cases may well have been as capable as the typical lessor of estimating the magnitude of the loss. We conclude that both the liquor-license and the automobile-showroom cases may have been correctly decided from an economic standpoint. . . .

3. *Transportation contracts.* Another common issue in the impossibility area is the effect of wars or other unexpected events on transportation contracts. To illustrate the relative abilities of the parties to bear risk in cases of this sort, consider the effect on

11. 94 Wash. 125, 162 P. 31 (1916).

12. See, for example, Lloyd v. Murphy, 25 Cal. 2d 48, 153 P.2d 47 (1944); Leonard v. Autocar Sales & Service Co., 392 Ill. 182, 64 N.E.2d 477 (1945).

13. The lease in fact required the lessee to purchase all of its beer requirements from the lessor's brewery.

shipping contracts of the closing of the Suez Canal by the Egyptian government in 1956. The closing required ships passing between Atlantic ports and ports in the Middle East to sail around Africa, a longer and more expensive voyage, and gave rise to voluminous litigation. The general result was the enforcement of the shipping contracts.[14] For example, in Transatlantic Financing Corp. v. United States,[15] a shipowner argued that its contract with the United States to transport wheat from the U.S. to Iran was discharged by the closing of the Suez Canal. The issue was framed by Judge Wright as follows:

> First, a contingency—something unexpected—must have occurred. Second, the risk of the unexpected occurrence must not have been allocated either by agreement or by custom. Finally, occurrence of the contingency must have rendered performance commercially impracticable.[16]

The court found that the closing of the canal was unexpected and that the risk of its occurrence had not been expressly allocated between the parties. It then addressed the ultimate question: was the closing grounds for discharge?

To answer the question, Judge Wright sought to determine which party—the owner of the ship or the government—was the superior risk bearer. His answer addressed itself to the precise elements of our economic framework:

> Transatlantic was no less able than the United States to purchase insurance to cover the contingency's occurrence. If anything, it is more reasonable to expect owner-operators of vessels to insure against the hazards of war. They are in the best position to calculate the cost of performance by alternative routes (and therefore to estimate the amount of insurance required), and are undoubtedly sensitive to international troubles which uniquely affect the demand for and cost of their services.[17]

This passage makes the decision on whether to discharge the contract turn on an examination of the key economic parameters that we have identified. The shipowner is the superior risk bearer because he is better able to estimate the magnitude of the loss (a function of delay, and of the value and nature of the cargo, which are also known to the shipowner) and the probability of the unexpected event. Further-

14. See, for example, American Trading and Prod. Corp. v. Shell Int'l Marine Ltd., 453 F.2d 939 (2d Cir. 1972); Transatlantic Financing Corp. v. United States, 363 F.2d 313 (D.C. Cir. 1966); Glidden Co. v. Hellenic Lines, Ltd., 275 F.2d 253 (2d Cir. 1960); Ocean Tramp Tankers Corp. v. V/O Sovfracht (The Eugenia), [1964] 2 Q.B. 226; and Tsakiroglou & Co. v. Noblee Thorl G.m.b.H., [1960] 2 Q.B. 348.

15. 363 F.2d 312 (D.C. Cir. 1966).

16. Id. at 315.

17. Id. at 319.

more, shipowners who own several ships and are engaged in shipping along several different routes can spread the risks of delay on any particular route without purchasing market insurance or forcing their shareholders to diversify their common-stock portfolios. And the shipping company could, if it desired, purchase in a single transaction market insurance covering multiple voyages. Of course, the shipper in the particular case—the United States Government—was well diversified too, but decision should (and here did) turn on the characteristics of shippers as a class, if an unduly particularistic analysis is to be avoided.

It might appear that the owner of the shipment would have a better idea than the shipowner of the consequences of delayed arrival. But consequential damages of this type are not relevant to the discharge question, because the rule of Hadley v. Baxendale[18] places liability for such damages (in the absence of express agreement to the contrary) on the shipper rather than on the carrier—and properly so from the standpoint of economics.[19] The question of discharge thus arises only with respect to that portion of the damages that the carrier can estimate without knowing the details of the shipper's business.

Parris v. Stratton Cripple Creek Mining & Dev. Co.[20] illustrates the application of the discharge doctrine in another transportation setting. A trucker contracted with a mining company to haul gold ore from the Cripple Creek mining field in Colorado to a nearby mill. The contract between the mining company and the milling company entitled the mill to suspend operations on 60 days notice. When the mill closed and was adjudged bankrupt, the mining company argued that the trucking contract should be discharged. The court agreed. The mining company was probably in a better position to estimate the probability that the mill would close, but the trucker was better able to ascertain the magnitude of the loss—being the difference between the contract price and the opportunity value of his service—and he could spread the risk by contracting to supply hauling services to customers who were engaged in other businesses and hence were unlikely to be affected by the mill closing.

4. *Contracts for the manufacture or supply of specialized equipment.* In Siegel v. Eaton & Prince Co.[21] a firm contracted to "furnish and erect" an elevator in the Siegel Cooper department store. The contract was held to be discharged when the store was destroyed by fire without fault on the part of Siegel Cooper. In a similar case decided a year later, Huyett & Smith Mfg. Co. v. Chicago Edison Co.,[22] the

18. 9 Ex. 341, 156 Eng. Rep. 145 (1854).
19. [See p. 164 infra.]
20. 116 F.2d 207 (10th Cir. 1940).
21. 165 Ill. 550, 46 N.E. 449 (1896).
22. 167 Ill. 223, 47 N.E. 384 (1897).

Edison Company, which had agreed to provide equipment to supply electric lighting and power in the First Regiment Armory Building during the Columbian Exposition (the Chicago World's Fair), subcontracted with Huyett to manufacture special fans and to install them in a ventilating system in the building. The Armory Building was destroyed by fire. The subcontract was held discharged, thereby placing the risk of loss on Huyett, the supplier of the specialized equipment.

The cases . . . seem correctly decided when evaluated from the standpoint of economics. A supplier of specialized equipment is better able than a purchaser to evaluate the degree to which a given piece of equipment is specialized and to estimate the costs of converting it into something usable by other prospective purchasers; and in neither case was the purchaser better able to estimate the probability of the particular casualty. The supplier could spread the risk among all purchasers by discounting the expected value of these contingencies in his contract price, thus eliminating the need for each purchaser to insure; and if explicit market insurance was desired the supplier could have covered all of his sales in a single transaction.

The analysis is not limited to suppliers of equipment. In Gouled v. Holwitz, a supplier leased a team of horses which were to be returned by the lessee "in as good condition as they are at present."[23] One of the horses was later found to have spinal meningitis and was shot to death—against the express wishes of the lessee—by an agent of the Society for the Prevention of Cruelty to Animals. The agreement to return the horse was held to have been discharged. The result was to place the risk of death by disease on the horse's owner, and this seems correct. The owner was better able to estimate both the probability of disease and the magnitude of the loss. A horse is a wasting capital asset whose value is animal-specific, depending on particular characteristics of the horse that are likely to be better known to its owner than to a lessee. Furthermore, an owner of several horses greatly reduces the risk of animal death due to disease through the portfolio effect of his multiple ownership.

5. *Contracts for the supply of agricultural products.* The next group of cases we consider concerns contracts to supply agricultural products, and illustrates how the courts can arrive at an economically efficient result yet disguise it as an apparently meaningless semantic distinction. The cases have similar facts. A supplier contracts to deliver a particular quantity and quality of an agricultural product; an unexpected event such as a flood or an exceptionally severe

23. 95 N.J.L. 277, 113 A. 323 (1921).

drought prevents delivery; the buyer seeks damages.[24] The courts generally discharge the contract where the supplier is a grower,[25] but enforce it where the supplier is a wholesaler or large dealer.[26] The result is both consistent and efficient; it places the risk of extreme weather conditions on the superior risk bearer. The purchaser from the grower can reduce the risk of adverse weather by diversifying his purchases geographically; there is empirical evidence to suggest that in some climatic regions geographical separation of only a few miles can dramatically reduce the risk of a large loss. When the seller is a wholesaler or large dealer there is no reason to allow discharge since he can diversify his purchases and thereby eliminate the risk of adverse weather.

Here as elsewhere the courts have not explicitly characterized the problem as one of identifying the superior risk bearer. They usually state that discharge will be allowed when the contract contemplates a single crop to be grown on a specific tract of land. Similarly, a comment to the relevant section of the Uniform Commercial Code allows discharge if and only if the contract refers to crops grown on land designated explicitly in the agreement.[27] This factor is irrelevant save as a reasonable instrumental variable that distinguishes cases in which the seller is a grower from those where he is a wholesaler. However, consistently with our analysis, one observes a tendency in both the pre-Code and later cases to mitigate the mechanical operation of this rule by either expansive construction of the contract or equitable reformation of its terms.[28]

6. *Grazing contracts*. In Berg v. Erickson,[29] a cattle owner from Texas (Berg) contracted to pasture his cattle on Erickson's Kansas ranch. Erickson agreed to "furnish plenty of good grass, water, and salt during the grazing season of 1913."[30] There was no rain that

24. See Pearce-Young-Angel Co. v. Charles R. Allen, Inc., 213 S.C. 578, 50 S.E.2d 698 (1948); and Squillante v. California Lands, Inc., 5 Cal. App. 2d 89, 42 P.2d 81 (1935).

25. See, for example, Matousek v. Galligan, 104 Neb. 731, 178 N.W. 510 (1920); and Pearce-Young-Angel Co. v. Charles R. Allen, Inc., 213 S.C. 578, 50 S.E.2d 698 (1948).

26. See, for example, United States Co. v. Curtis Peanut Co., 302 S.W.2d 763 (Tex. Civ. App. 1957).

27. U.C.C. §2-615, Comment 9.

28. An example of a pre-Code case is Snipes Mountain Co. v. Benz Bros. & Co., 162 Wash. 334, 298 P. 714 (1931), in which the court allowed an equitable action to reform the contract so that specific land was mentioned, thus allowing discharge. See also Matousek v. Galligan, 104 Neb. 731, 178 N.W. 510 (1920). A case decided under the Code and holding that factors outside the writing may show that the parties contracted with reference to a particular parcel of land is Paymaster Oil Mill Co. v. Mitchell, 319 So. 2d 652 (1975).

29. 234 F. 817 (8th Cir. 1916).

30. Id. at 818.

summer and although the cattle survived they failed to reach normal weight. The court enforced the contract and thus awarded damages to Berg. This result seems correct but on a rather particularistic analysis. A cattle owner would in general be better able than a landowner to estimate the magnitude of the loss in cattle value because of inadequate water and could reduce the risk by pasturing his cattle in different ranches, but this method of self-insurance might involve considerable transaction costs. Moreover, *this* landowner—a rancher—was presumably knowledgeable about cattle. The other key parameter of our analysis—the ability to estimate the probability of the drought—suggests placing the risk on the rancher (depending, however, on the particular cattle owner's prior experience in the region), especially since

> It was common knowledge that droughts were not unusual in Kansas. It was common knowledge that they decreased the growth of grass. It was common knowledge that one could not tell by the examination of pastures in Kansas, of which he [Berg] had no previous knowledge, in the spring of the year before the 13th of April, whether or not they would produce sufficient grass for 1,000 cattle throughout the coming summer. Berg knew nothing of their productive capacity; Erickson knew all about it.[31]

Like the lease cases discussed earlier, *Berg* is difficult to analyze because the two key parameters seem to point in opposite directions. To reach a correct result, a thorough investigation of the facts is necessary. The court's result reached was (as in most of the cases we have examined) probably correct, in view of the superior knowledge believed by the court to be possessed by Erickson, the rancher. The question remains whether it might not be better to decide all grazing cases the same way. . . .

B. Doubtful Cases

In many individual, and perhaps some classes of, cases economic analysis—at least of the casual sort employed by the judges and lawyers in contract cases—will fail to yield a definite answer, or even a guess, as to which party is the superior risk bearer. A good example is provided by the coronation cases. Neither party was in a superior position to foresee the event (the illness of Edward VII) that prevented completion of the contract. To be sure, the building owner had a superior ability to compute the loss, which depended on his ability to rerent the rooms on short notice, and could in principle have bought a single insurance policy on Edward's health at lower

31. Id. at 824.

cost than the renters could have insured. However, the renters may well have been superior self-insurers: enforcing the contracts would have spread the loss among a relatively large number of renters rather than concentrate it on a relatively few building owners. It is not surprising that the courts divided on whether discharge should be allowed.[32]

The choice in doubtful cases between treating nonperformance as breach or as discharge is similar to the choice in tort law between strict liability and no liability for unavoidable accidents.[33] Pending definitive empirical study, we are inclined to consider the strict-liability solution better in the contract context, though in the tort context the choice must be considered indeterminate on the basis of present knowledge.[34]

The performing party to a contract is generally the superior risk bearer. Typically, though not invariably, he is better able both to prevent the occurrence of the event rendering performance uneconomical and, if it cannot be prevented at reasonable cost, to estimate the probability of its occurrence. Often, too, he is at least as able as the payor to estimate the magnitude of the loss if the event occurs. True, the payor (that is, the buyer) will have better knowledge of the consequences of nonperformance for his business, but the rule of Hadley v. Baxendale properly assigns the risk of consequential injury to the payor in any event. Finally, the performer can often self-insure at low cost simply by diversifying the risk across the full range of his contractual obligations.

The performer is not always the superior risk bearer; otherwise there would be no place in contract law for impossibility and related doctrines. But as long as the performer is *generally* the superior risk bearer, assigning the risk to him in cases of doubt—that is, refusing discharge in those cases—can be expected to yield correct results more often than the contrary rule. Accordingly, one is not surprised

32. Compare Krell v. Henry, [1903] 2 K.B. 740 (C.A.), with Chandler v. Webster, [1904] 1 K.B. 493 (L.R.), and Herne Bay S.S. Co. v. Hutton, [1903] 2 K.B. 683 (C.A.). . . . While the coronation cases on their peculiar facts could have gone either way on an economic analysis—which may explain the division in the courts—the case against discharge is much stronger in the related but more common case where, for example, a skier books a room at a ski lodge and, having paid his deposit, seeks a refund because of poor ski conditions. Skiers as a class are superior self-insurers against poor ski conditions compared to ski lodges; the skier can find adequate conditions somewhere but the lodge cannot diversify away the risk of poor conditions (save by merger with lodges in other ski areas); market insurance may also be unavailable. . . .

[For those readers not familiar with the coronation cases, those cases involved contracts to rent rooms overlooking the planned route of the coronation procession of Edward VII. Edward became ill and the coronation was cancelled.]

33. See Richard A. Posner, Strict Liability: A Comment, 2 J. Leg. Studies 205 (1973).

34. [Ibid.]

to find that the courts indeed treat discharge as an excuse, so that nonperformance is a breach of contract unless the case fits one of the exceptions to liability carved out by the impossibility or some other excuse doctrine.

This discussion raises the broader question why in general notions of strict liability seem much more important in contract than in tort law. The concept of breach of contract is one of strict liability rather than of negligence. The difference in this regard between tort and contract law appears to be related to the fact that tort cases typically involve interactive activities and contract cases typically do not. An automobile accident, for example, is produced by a collision between two automobiles or between an automobile and a pedestrian, and there is no presumption that the injurer could have avoided the accident more cheaply than the victim. But in the typical contract case the only relevant actors are performer and payor and the productive activity under the contract is controlled and conducted entirely by the former. There is a strong presumption therefore that he is better able than the payor to prevent a mishap that will render performance uneconomical. The presumption is not absolute but it is sufficient to make strict liability the appropriate general rule defining breach of contract.

III. Remedial Consequences of Discharge . . .

A. The General Case

. . . Suppose that without negligence on anyone's part a house is destroyed by fire while under repair, and the repair contractor sues for breach. Unless there is a specific contractual provision assigning the risk to the homeowner, the courts hold that the repair contract is discharged.[35] The result appears to be sound when analyzed in an economic framework. The relevant loss is the sum of the expenses incurred (the reliance loss) and the opportunity value of the contractor's services (approximately equal to the expectation loss).[36] The magnitude of loss is presumably better known to the contractor. He has superior knowledge both of the value of the reliance loss (which depends critically on his cost schedule as a function of the stages of repair and the costs of the various inputs) and of the opportunity

35. See, for example, Young v. City of Chicopee, 186 Mass. 518, 72 N.E. 63 (1904); and Carroll v. Bowersock, 100 Kan. 270, 164 P. 143 (1917). . . .

36. The relationship between opportunity costs and the expectation interest varies over time; the two concepts are approximately equal when performance is nearly complete. See John H. Barton, The Economic Basis of Damages for Breach of Contract, [p. 154 infra].

value of his services. Although the ability to estimate the probability of the loss will depend to some extent on the specific event giving rise to discharge, in the typical repair situation neither party has a superior ability to estimate that probability. The owner of the premises has custody, of course, but the contractor may know a good deal more about fire and other hazards that might prevent performance.

As for the remedial consequences of discharge, the contractor is entitled to no part of his lost expectation interest—this distinguishes discharge from breach. Nor can he recover his reliance losses. He would be entitled to recover in a restitution action the value of any actual benefits conferred upon the owner but these may be slight, depending on the completeness of the destruction.

Many legal commentators are distressed by this outcome because it places the entire loss on the contractor. Their failure to understand the efficiency basis of the discharge doctrine leads them to view the remedy issue as separable from that of liability and to argue that it is "only fair" to apportion reliance losses. . . .

The proposals to change the remedial outcome to one where reliance losses are shared result from a misplaced emphasis on ex post loss distribution rather than ex ante risk bearing. Viewed from the risk-bearing perspective the refusal to apportion reliance losses is well founded; it creates an incentive for the one efficient risk bearer to adopt cost-justified risk-avoidance or risk-minimization techniques (diversification, market insurance, or whatever). The existing rule whereby discharge results in zero damages (save where restitution is appropriate) is analogous to the approach of the tort law. There too the focus is on determining which party, the plaintiff or defendant, is the lower-cost avoider of the event in question, and it is clearly not proper to approach the question by attempting to ascertain which party is in a better position ex post to bear the loss.

The ex post approach to risk assignment is in fact circular. Often the party who ex post is the superior risk bearer is the party who purchased an insurance policy covering the risk in question. But if this were the criterion of liability, it would give parties an incentive not to insure, for by not insuring they would increase the possibility that the court would assign the risk to the other party to the contract. So neither party might insure; or, fearing this possibility, both parties might insure. Neither result would be optimal.

The 50-50 loss-sharing approach favored by the commentators is at least superficially appealing in the case where it is difficult for the court to determine which of the parties is the superior risk bearer. If the parties are equally good (or bad) risk bearers, and each is risk averse, then each will prefer ex ante a solution that reduces the variance of the expected outcome of the contract. Splitting the loss does this, so long as each party estimates the same probability that the court will assign him the risk.[37] For in that case instead of each party facing some probability of bearing all of the costs of nonperformance each has a certainty of bearing 50 percent of those costs. Of course, if neither party is risk averse, there is no gain from such a rule. And if one party is a superior risk bearer, the *entire* loss should be placed on him in order to encourage future parties similarly situated to insure or take other measures to minimize the economic consequences of nonperformance.

Whether carving out a class of indeterminate risk allocations and applying a rule of 50-50 loss sharing to them can be justified in terms of the administrative costs of seeking in each case (or class of cases) to determine the superior risk bearer may be doubted. It is easy to exaggerate those costs. The costs of deciding a question in a lawsuit ought properly to be apportioned over all future transactions that will be controlled by the rule declared in the suit. Even if it is very expensive to decide in the first case how to assign the risk of some event that renders contract performance uneconomical, once the question is decided and a rule declared, the rule will be available to guide the behavior of future contracting parties and will thus reduce the costs of future contract negotiations. To define a class of cases where the proper assignment of risk is treated as indeterminate could stifle the evolution of rules of risk allocation designed to enhance the efficiency of the contract process.

While 50-50 loss sharing seems an unappealing alternative to the law's solution of placing the loss entirely on one party or the other, in a world where the costs of using the legal system to fill in contract terms were very low a principle of *flexible* loss sharing might be superior to either approach. Loss sharing is a common characteristic of contractual arrangements: one thinks of deductibles and coinsurance in formal insurance contracts, and of joint ventures of all sorts, including sharecropping. Sometimes loss sharing is designed to deal with the moral-hazard problem in insurance; sometimes it is itself the method of insurance, as in sharecropping. But it seems hardly feasible to design a legal rule that will imitate voluntary transacting in all its variety yet be administrable at reasonable cost. . . .

B. *Partial Performance*

. . . If there has been part payment prior to delivery and delivery is prevented by some catastrophe, the question may arise whether

37. If the parties do not estimate equal probabilities, then 50-50 loss-sharing can be presumed efficient only if the parties are assumed to have identical utility functions. See Alan Schwartz, Sales Law and Inflations, 50 S. Cal. L. Rev. 1, 8 n.20 (1976).

the payee should be required to return all or part of the payment. The answer ought to depend, in an economic analysis, on whether the purpose of the prepayment was to compensate the payee for bearing the risk that something might happen to prevent him from making delivery, or whether the prepayment was unrelated. Suppose in our hypothetical repair case that the homeowner had advanced the repair contractor part of the payment before the latter completed the repairs. If the purpose of the advance was to compensate the repairer for bearing the risk that fire or some other event would prevent him from completing the repairs, then clearly he is entitled to keep the advance—it is his insurance premium. But the advance may be completely unrelated to such risks. It could be intended to finance the purchase of supplies by the contractor (the homeowner may be the cheapest source of the necessary capital) or to protect the contractor against the risk that the homeowner might be insolvent or otherwise difficult to collect the contract price from. It could be intended simply to avoid, for tax or other financial reasons, a large, lumpy payment at the completion of construction. Given the number of plausible reasons for prepayment that are unrelated to the provision of insurance against an event that may prevent completion of performance, there can be no presumption that prepayment is intended to compensate the performing party for the risk of such an event. Accordingly, in the absence of other evidence that the payor is the superior risk bearer, his prepayments should be returned to him. This is the generally prevailing legal rule.[38]

Where it is the performing party to the contract who has partially completed performance, rather than the paying party, there will often be a valid claim for restitution (for example, where a contract to deliver 10,000 widgets is terminated after 1,000 have been delivered), even if the performer is deemed the superior risk bearer. But where there is no basis for restitution—no value conferred on the other party to the contract by partial performance—neither is there any good economic argument for redistributing the loss between the parties. The loss should then fall entirely on the superior risk bearer.

A concept related to restitution which courts have also used in these cases is that [of] the "divisible contract." If an event giving rise to discharge prevents the completion of a performance that has

38. Perhaps the *Chandler* case, note [32] supra, can be distinguished from those coronation cases allowing discharge on the ground that the contract in *Chandler* required full payment in advance. The unusual character of the payment term arguably justified the court in concluding that the cancellation of the procession was not intended by the parties to discharge the payor's obligation. In our terms, the absence of any other apparent reason for requiring full payment in advance permitted the inference that the purpose was to insure the payee against the risk of an event that would make performance uneconomical.

begun, payment of the completed portion of the performance will be held to be due if that portion is deemed divisible, and the recovery may include a pro rata portion of the performing party's expectation interest as well as its reliance loss. For example, in one well-known case a steamship company had contracted to supply a given number of trips at a fixed rate per trip to be paid monthly. When the steamship was destroyed by fire, the contract was held to be discharged but the steamship company was allowed to recover the agreed-upon rate for each of the trips that had already been supplied.[39] The basic rationale in such cases seems restitutionary, and appears to make good sense. But it would be cleaner to drop the fiction of divisibility and simply to view the contract as discharged, and then decide what compensation is due the performing party for having conferred benefits on the other party to the contract before the event giving rise to the discharge occurred. . . .

*Sales Law and Inflations**

Alan Schwartz

This article initially set out to consider how unanticipated causes of price rises, of which inflation is a paradigm example, affected the enforceability of sales contracts. In fact, these causes traditionally have had no effect on the enforceability of sales contracts; courts required defaulting promisors to pay damages. Recent commentators, however, have argued that to impose on sellers all costs attributable to unanticipated events is unacceptably harsh. They are supported in this view by a comment to section 2-615 of the Uniform Commercial Code (Code), which suggests that extraordinary, unforeseeable cost increases should excuse sellers. Moreover, a few cases decided under the Code have excused sellers when unanticipated events unexpectedly made performance more costly. The question of the effect unanticipated events should have on the enforceability of sales contracts is therefore open. It is also an important question because the most important such cause is inflation, and this country apparently has failed to achieve domestic price stability. . . .

*Reprinted by permission from 50 S. Cal. L. Rev. 1-2, 16-18, 21-22 (1976).

39. Pasquotank & N.R. Steamboat Co. v. Eastern Carolina Trans. Co., 166 N.C 582, 82 S.E. 956 (1914).

I. The Desert Case and Contract Stability

. . . The desert case for excuse assumes that the seller has not agreed to bear the risk of a serious inflation. A causation problem exists because actual price rises are often the result of several causes, the risks of some of which sellers *do* usually agree to bear. Thus, a court cannot excuse without isolating and evaluating inflation's contribution to the price rise at issue. In this section it is shown that: (1) price rises do have multiple causes; (2) a case for excuse ordinarily exists only when inflation produced more than 50 percent of the price rise at issue; (3) it will be extraordinarily difficult for courts to isolate inflation's contribution; so that (4) were courts to use the desert case, the parties would often be unable to predict the judicial outcome on the causation issue.

Inflation occurs when nominal aggregate demand exceeds the economy's productive capacity. Output cannot expand quickly enough to satisfy the increased demand, with the result that resources become scarce and therefore more expensive. Individual prices, however, do not necessarily rise at the same rate as the general price level because inflation does not affect the causes of changes in relative prices. For example, assume that product *A* originally costs less than product *B*. *Without inflation*, consumer tastes changed so that more people want *A* and less want *B*. The price of *A* will rise; the price of *B* will drop. An inflation would then increase the prices of both products. With respect to a manufacturer of *A* who has made a contract for future delivery at the original price, the market increase—and hence the seller's loss from compliance with the contract—may be substantial, but only a small fraction of this loss may result from inflation.

However, the case for excuse can only be made when (1) the price rise more than doubled the expected high; and (2) inflation caused more than 50 percent of the rise. This is so because, were inflation's contribution to be less than one-half, *excuse* would maximize *undeserved* gains and losses. To illustrate this, assume that the parties foresaw no inflation, that the contract price was $5, and that the expected price range up was $2, but the actual advance more than doubled this, being $4.20. Let inflation cause $2.05 of this rise; normal foreseeable supply factors, $2.15. Excuse saves *S* $4.20, the difference between the contract price ($5) and the market price ($9.20). Of this sum, $2.15 is an undeserved gain to *S* and an undeserved loss to *B*, as *S* was paid to forego losses caused by normal, foreseeable events. Enforcement would cause *S* a loss of $4.20 (*B*'s damages) of which only $2.05 is undeserved (and an undeserved gain to *B*), being the result of an unforeseeable inflation. Thus, *enforcement* minimizes undeserved gains and losses, and always will when inflation causes less than one-half of the price rise at issue. Courts must therefore find which portion of the rise was attributable to inflation.

If the other operative cause was a change in consumer tastes, as in the illustration above, ascertaining inflation's contribution seems terribly difficult. Sellers very roughly know their own demand curves and ultimately recognize shifts in them. Yet how much of a particular shift is attributable to a change in tastes and how much to a general increase in aggregate demand seems very hard to know without market surveys. Yet these surveys are costly—too costly to be done for many lawsuits. Moreover, surveys may be inconclusive. A buyer himself might not know whether he bought the hat because hats had become fashionable, or because his income went up, or for both reasons.

In addition, a product may increase in price because of (1) a rise in the price of demand-related goods: if the price of butter goes up, more buyers will switch to margarine, its principal substitute, the price of which will then rise; or (2) a drop in the price of supply related goods: if the price of wool drops, less will be produced, thereby reducing the supply and increasing the price of mutton. Let product *A* rise in price. If the increase was caused by the price rise of a substitute which itself was not a function of inflation, or a drop in price of a supply-related product, the *A* seller's contract should be enforced; conversely, if the *A* price rise was the result of the inflationary price increase of an important substitute, the *A* seller should be excused. This makes germane, in an action against a breaching seller, the price movements of supply and demand related goods, the causes of *these* movements, and their contribution to the price rise at issue. The lawsuit would be quite complex.

Price rises also are a function of supply elasticity. When faced with an inflationary demand increase, an industry with slack capacity—where supply is relatively elastic—will expand output; prices will not rise by much. An industry already at full capacity, however, will in the short run ration output by price. In the latter case, inflation *and* supply inelasticity *both* contributed to the price rise. Such short-run supply inelasticity in an industry seems sufficiently important and knowable that the risk of its adverse impact on prices can be classed as ordinary. Therefore, since sellers bear ordinary price-affecting supply risks, a court must distinguish the effects of inflation from those of supply elasticity, which again seems quite difficult.

Finally, when multiple factors cause a price rise, relative causation is extraordinarily difficult to establish. A particular rise may be a function of taste changes, substitute price changes, supply inelasticity, government regulation and increases in aggregate demand. Economic analysis can tell us with relative convenience which potential causes contributed to the price rise at issue; but it cannot isolate (even approximately) the contribution of each factor without a large, complex econometric model of the industry, specifying accurately the supply and demand sides of the market. The model would then require a great deal of data for its operation. The costs of doing this would seem almost always to outweigh the gains either party could derive from a lawsuit. Yet without such a model, the desert case would be nondirective in multiple cause cases. It would require a finding which absent the model could not be made, that an unanticipated inflation caused more than 50 percent of the price rise at bar. Any decision to excuse would therefore be arbitrary. . . .

II. Macroeconomic Considerations

. . . Enforcement maximizes the use of escalator clauses, which are anti-inflationary. Every sale for future delivery is attended with the risk that a subsequent inflation may adversely affect a party's costs. If sellers are excused, buyers bear this "inflation risk"; if contracts are enforced, sellers bear it. Escalator clauses, which permit a seller to adjust the contract price to reflect subsequent cost changes, minimize the seller's inflation risk. The magnitude of this risk is partly a function of supply elasticity; prices rise more in industries operating close to capacity before the demand increase. A seller who deals directly with manufacturers or suppliers has a better opportunity to know supply conditions than his buyers and is therefore more likely to predict accurately the effect an inflation would have on his industry. Thus, assigning the inflation risk to sellers, i.e., enforcing, yields more escalator clauses than would the contrary risk allocation.

It may be responded that, were buyers to bear the risk (i.e., were sellers to be excused), knowledgeable sellers would offer escalator clauses so as to reduce buyer risks, and thus buyer costs. This objection ignores the parties' unequal access to information and their incentives. The buyers' inflation risk is the risk that his seller will breach and be excused, so that the buyer would incur the expense of making two purchases and lose his expected speculative profit. The value of this risk is partly a function of the likelihood of the seller breaching—of, that is, there occurring an inflation of the requisite extent. If a buyer, because he lacks supply information, incorrectly believes that a serious inflationary price rise is unlikely, he also subjectively believes that the value of the inflation risk is less than it actually is. Thus he perceives an artificially low purchase cost. A seller would have no incentive to dispel this erroneous belief. Initially, as sellers in this legal regime are excused in the event of a serious inflation, they have little need for escalator clauses. Also, these clauses may reduce the chance of sellers escaping the deal. Finally, the fact of a seller offering an escalator clause may inform the buyer that he was undervaluing the inflation risk, and thus had an artificially low cost perception. Since more goods are purchased at lower prices, the awareness that costs are higher than they seem is one sellers do not want buyers to have. Therefore, were the inflation risk assigned to buyers, fewer escalator clauses would be used than now are.

The "macro" benefit of maximizing the use of these clauses is that they produce price reductions when demand drops, and thus assist government measures to fight inflation. This occurs because escalator clauses reduce the unpleasant side effects of anti-inflationary actions, making it more likely that they will be undertaken. For example, a restrictive monetary policy reduces aggregate demand. Manufacturers initially faced with decreased demand reduce output rather than price, because they do not know whether the decrease will continue. Reducing output produces unemployment. Since unemployment is politically unpopular, there is pressure against the government reducing the money supply. A reduction, however, would cause relatively prompt price declines in some markets sensitive to economic trends, such as commodities and raw materials. These declines, which are reflected in standard indices, trigger escalation clauses, causing sellers to reduce prices rather than output. This maintains employment. Thus, escalator clauses reduce the pressure on government not to reduce the money supply, thereby aiding it to fight inflation. Other things being equal, courts should then adopt rules encouraging the use of these clauses. To be sure, as inflations are sometimes hard to anticipate and as the supply effect may be limited, imposing the risk of inflation on sellers may not yield many more escalator clauses than would the opposite risk allocation. Also, as theories of what actually motivates government decisionmakers are quite primitive, the anti-inflationary impact of these clauses is speculative. However, some macro gains may flow from maximizing their use and none seem to flow from their absence. . . .

*Commercial Impossibility, The Uranium Market and the Westinghouse Case**

Paul L. Joskow

I. Introduction

On September 8, 1975, Westinghouse Electric Corporation, a major vendor of nuclear reactors and a major contractor for uranium fuel, announced that it would not honor fixed price contracts to deliver about 70 million pounds of uranium. Westinghouse claimed that it was not legally bound to honor these contracts by appealing to §2-615 of the Uniform Commercial Code (U.C.C.) which allows excuse from the performance of contractual obligations for reasons of "commercial impracticability." In particular, it claimed that for "unforeseeable" reasons uranium prices had risen to several times the price at which Westinghouse had agreed to deliver uranium to utilities and that performance on such contracts, with a potential loss of as much as $2.0 billion, was "commercially impracticable." Subsequent to this announcement 27 utilities in 14 separate actions brought suit against Westinghouse to either fulfill its contractual commitments or pay damages. . . .

II. Westinghouse's Behavior in the [Uranium] Market

During the late 1960's and early 1970's Westinghouse offered to supply fuel for light water reactors in the U.S. and abroad. In general, Westinghouse offered a complete nuclear fuel system, including the reactor and steam generating system, initial fuel core and a variable number of reloads. Westinghouse also agreed to supply fuel reloads to several reactors supplied by other vendors. Westinghouse generally offered uranium fuel at a fixed base price plus some escalation. The escalation factor apparently reflected changes only in certain labor and materials cost indices, however, and was not directly geared to the market price of uranium oxide. The base prices at which uranium was sold were in the range of $8 to $10 per pound. As of January 1, 1975, Westinghouse signed uranium contracts with 23 U.S. utilities and three foreign utilities involving 49 reactors, of which 11 were reactors supplied by other vendors. As of January 1, 1975, it is estimated that Westinghouse had uranium oxide commit-

*Reprinted, by permission, from 6 J. Legal Studies 119, 143-146, 171-174 (1976).

ments of approximately 60,000 tons for the period 1975-1988 and contracts to purchase only 14,000 tons during that period plus an inventory of 6,000 to 7,000 tons. This leaves a "short" position of about 40,000 tons (see Table [1]), of which about 5,000 tons are associated with contracts which have full cost pass-through provisions. In summary, as of January 1, 1975, Westinghouse had commitments to supply 60,000 tons of uranium but had only 20,000 tons available, either in hand or contracted for. This was a short position which Westinghouse refused to acknowledge until July 14, 1975. The deficit was a rather large shock to a market which in 1975 was producing about 13,000 tons per year, and including facilities then under construction had a capacity to produce between 18,000 and 20,000 tons per year.

It is fairly easy to understand why Westinghouse would have found it advantageous to act as a uranium agent for utilities buying its reactors as well as for others willing to buy fuel fabrication services. Nuclear energy was a new technology to the vast majority of the nation's utilities in the early 1970's. Since a commercial market for uranium really did not begin to develop until 1969 or 1970, there were very few individuals who had any expertise as uranium fuel buyers. the utilities themselves certainly had no expertise, and there was probably very little around to be bought. It was only natural, therefore, for Westinghouse, interested in marketing its reactor system, to act as a buying agent for utilities. By acting as an agent for several firms Westinghouse presumably could accumulate some expertise in dealing with suppliers, be able to make intelligent analyses of the market, and pool risks associated with uncertainties over exactly when particular reactors would be operating. Utilities which

Table [1]

Westinghouse Position in Uranium Market [1]
as of January 1, 1975

Westinghouse Commitments 1975-1988:	60,084 tons U_3O_8
Westinghouse Inventory Jan. 1, 1975:	5,896 tons U_3O_8
Westinghouse Purchase Agreements 1975-1978:	14,075 tons U_3O_8
Westinghouse Short 1975-1988:	40,113 tons U_3O_8

In addition General Electric is short 5,000 tons for the period 1982-1984.

[1] Kidder, Peabody & Co., Westinghouse Electric Corporation, Commercial Nuclear Power and Uranium 8 (September 25, 1975).

might have been hesitant to employ nuclear technology because of ignorance of the uranium market and future prices might now be encouraged to do so once Westinghouse was willing to guarantee supply at a fixed price. So it made good commercial sense for Westinghouse to set itself up as an uranium buying agent. It might also have been a more efficient buying arrangement than having each utility develop fuel expertise on its own. The fact that utilities found the fixed price contracts to be attractive is also not surprising since it eliminated uncertainty at a relatively small premium and saved the utility the expense of searching and contracting for uranium.

But why Westinghouse would sign fixed price contracts without *also* securing associated uranium supplies through forward contracting or development of its own uranium reserves is difficult to understand. There does not appear to have been very much room for speculative profit in the uranium industry. It was generally acknowledged as early as 1971 that the direction of prices was upward and given that the industry in the 1970-1972 period still remained slack with prices just covering extraction costs, there could not have been any real possibility of Westinghouse profiting from a price break by going short. Yet by going short on fixed price contracts, Westinghouse opened itself up to the possibility of fantastic losses if uranium prices rose. So it appears that by going short Westinghouse exposed itself to the possibility of large losses with no possibility of speculative profits. At least at first glance, Westinghouse's policy of going short appears to be irrational. Westinghouse's chief competitor, General Electric, engaged in relatively little actual uranium contracting in its fuel fabrication agreements and does not find itself in a position as serious as that of Westinghouse.

Assuming that Westinghouse's "short" policy was a conscious, rationally thought out policy, there are a number of factors that might account for its development. Westinghouse might have hoped that the AEC would indeed release its stockpile of uranium to the market at $8 per pound, providing sufficient supply at low prices for several years. Alternatively, Westinghouse might have hoped that once import restrictions were eliminated, cheap uranium could be obtained from foreign sources. Finally, it is possible that Westinghouse hoped to fill its remaining requirements from its own reserves. If Westinghouse's policy turned on these considerations, it was indeed a high risk policy. The traditional AEC concern for protecting the domestic mining and milling industry combined with vigorous opposition by the industry to the AEC's marketing its uranium stockpile made such an occurrence extremely unlikely. In any case this possibility was eliminated by December 1972. Similarly, a very rapid elimination of import controls was unlikely because of opposition from the domestic uranium industry. But perhaps more importantly, the assumption that foreign uranium would be either easily available or cheap is questionable. During this period of time Westinghouse was engaged in vigorous activity to sell its reactors in a number of foreign countries. Germany, Japan, Great Britain, France and other countries had fairly substantial nuclear programs under way by 1972, most of which would require uranium from foreign sources. In addition . . . a careful examination of the prices that the AEC had to pay during the First Expansionary Phase to encourage entry should alone have raised questions about the full economic cost of additional uranium mining and milling capacity. If Westinghouse' policy of signing fixed price contracts while remaining short was a conscious policy, it was a risky one with little prospect of large gains. . . .

III. Westinghouse and U.C.C. §2-615

. . . Under U.C.C. §2-615 Westinghouse must . . . show that the failure [to honor its contracts to supply uranium to purchasers of its reactors] was "unforeseeable" at the time the contract was signed. Since the "OPEC argument" does not appear to satisfy the "failure" requirement, I will not try to argue whether it was foreseen or should have been foreseen. In any case, in a recent federal court opinion the court held that the events in the Middle East, at least as of 1972, were sufficiently "foreseeable" that sophisticated agents should have included the possibilities of increased prices and supply interruptions in the terms of their contracts.

Under the circumstances let us allow a broader interpretation and ask whether a rise in uranium prices, given prevailing expectations prior to 1973, was either foreseen or should have been foreseen by a buying agent *like Westinghouse*. I have already argued that an examination of the demand projections and the commitments the supply sector was making for future capacity were obviously inconsistent with one another in 1972 and 1973 for the period beginning around 1979 and 1980, given the lead times required to bring on additional mining and milling capacity, unless one believed both that the AEC would dump its stockpile on the market and that all import restrictions would be completely and rapidly eliminated and substantial amounts of low cost uranium made available from foreign sources. This inconsistency was apparently recognized by many in the industry. Numerous people familiar with the uranium industry indicated that the supply picture and the demand picture would only be brought into balance if prices rose and government policy regarding the disposition of the AEC U_3O_8 stock and imports was cleared up. Some people predicted a price rise while others just spoke about tight markets developing throughout the 1972-1973 period. Since we cannot assume that all of the commentators were well trained in economics, it is not at all strange that some planners spoke of the tight market in terms of an emerging gap between quantities required and supply capabilities at prevailing prices without translating this into the need for a price increase. The question of actual price estimation required a detailed understanding of the costs of bringing on new supply and the timing of that supply, both of which were highly uncertain. That something had to give, whether it was price or demand, was, I think very clear by the beginning of 1973 and perhaps earlier from an examination of the inconsistencies between demand projections and plans for additional capacity. But a careful examination of the price data for uranium transactions gives us even more reason to believe that well informed entrepreneurs should have expected prices to rise once the industry moved out of an excess capacity situation.

In the discussion above we indicated that prior to July 1975 real prices of uranium were generally below the prices prevailing in the 1950's, when there was substantial entry into the industry. That prices would have to rise to such levels once again to encourage entry into the industry would only be surprising if one believed that the AEC paid prices far above what was really necessary to encourage entry or that that there had been important cost-reducing technological change. There does not appear to be any evidence for either proposition and, if anything, tightening mining criteria and reserve depletion have probably raised the real costs of uranium extraction. A buyer could, of course, have easily been fooled if he only looked at prevailing market prices and AEC "cost" estimates in making his price expectations. Uranium prices were indeed low for many years, reflecting the excess capacity in the uranium industry. The forward cost system did give misleading information about possible future uranium prices unless used correctly. Westinghouse was willing to supply all comers at prices between $8 and $10 per pound. But a large buyer in the market, like Westinghouse, should have been more than a naive price taker and would have done a more sophisticated analysis of price formation in the uranium market. After all, Westinghouse did commit itself to deliver about 140 million pounds of uranium. Westinghouse had an additional advantage; it knew that a large part of this commitment had not been contracted for and that Westinghouse itself represented a huge hidden future demand on the market. A price rise of some size was foreseen by many in the industry and should reasonably have been foreseeable by perhaps the largest agent in the market, Westinghouse. I have been able to find no evidence indicating that Westinghouse had, prior to 1973, performed an extensive analysis of uranium price behavior over the life of its contracts, as would have been economically appropriate given the large volume of uranium contracted for and the risk associated with a "short" selling policy. Perhaps if it had conducted such analyses, Westinghouse would have at least included an escalation clause tied more closely with the price of uranium itself rather than tying it to variables reflecting only primarily the general rate of inflation.

All things considered, it does not appear that Westinghouse satisfied the "foreseeability" requirement either. To hold otherwise would encourage suboptimal use of available information and the introduction of incorrect price information into the process of exchange.

Under U.C.C. §2-615 Westinghouse must also show that the risk of failure must not have been assumed either directly or indirectly by the party seeking excuse. Recall that Comment 8 to U.C.C. §2-615 indicates that the allocation of risk to the party seeking excuse may be found in the circumstances surrounding the contract as well as in the terms of the contract. But the reason for many of the contracts was to convince utilities to buy reactors from Westinghouse by performing a role as uranium buying agent insuring them against fluctuations in the price of uranium. Why would somebody buy a long-term fixed price contract other than to insure against fluctuations in the price of uranium? The general commercial reasons for signing long-term fixed price commodity contracts seems to preclude excuse under U.C.C. §2-615 simply because the nature of this kind of commodity contract implies the assumption of the risk of price fluctuations on the seller. The inherent uncertainties within the uranium market itself associated with enrichment, reprocessing and recycling, foreign imports, etc., were the reasons why utilities were attracted by the fixed price contracts. To hold that the risks of such uncertainties were not implicitly or explicitly to be borne by the seller from the viewpoint of buyers seems to be inconsistent with the intent and good sense of this requirement under U.C.C. §2-615.

Even assuming that Westinghouse satisfied all of the foregoing requirements, its case based on "impracticability" due to the rise in costs is still unclear. The three- to fourfold increase in uranium prices is larger than the doubling, which clearly is not sufficient, and smaller than the ten- to twelvefold increase that has been mentioned as being clearly enough in previous interpretations of impracticability. But to complicate the matter even more, many of Westinghouse's uranium contracts were written in conjunction with reactor contracts. If we were to consider the total value of the contract, including perhaps hundreds of millions of dollars for the nuclear steam supply system and other components, the increase in the cost of uranium would add a much smaller proportionate cost to the total contract. Whether Westinghouse satisfies even the impracticability test is at best questionable.

Westinghouse must also show that it did everything possible to insure itself of an adequate source of supply. Westinghouse's problem arises from the fact that it was short over 67 percent of its uranium commitments. It could have covered these shorts in a timely fashion by purchasing U_3O_8 forward when it signed the sales contracts or by developing its own reserves more quickly. Westinghouse gambled that its requirements could alternatively be obtained from the market at a favorable price. It gambled (either consciously or unconsciously) and lost. Westinghouse could have covered its requirements by obtaining long-term supply commitments as it made sales of uranium. In fact, if it had engaged in more timely contracting, market prices would have begun to rise more quickly as the market moved to a long-run equilibrium. Westinghouse would probably have realized sooner that the fixed price contracts it was signing would be unprofitable. The common law cases underlying U.C.C. §2-615 and subsequent cases under it cited above quite clearly indicate that under these circumstances a discharge will not be granted and that for reasons of economic efficiency such behavior should not be encouraged by the contract law itself.

Finally, to qualify for excuse, the seller must not by his own actions create the event causing the impracticability of performance. It was argued above that Westinghouse's own behavior in the market had important effects on both the time pattern of prices and the levels to which prices have now risen. More timely contracting on Westinghouse's part would have led to an earlier supply response and ameliorated supply bottlenecks around 1980. By keeping its requirements secret for so long and not "revealing" them to the market by contracting for supplies, Westinghouse was a major contributor to the failure of standard feedback mechanisms to signal the movement into a new expansionary phase for the uranium supply sector. Westinghouse certainly fails to meet this sensible requirement also. . . .

NOTES AND QUESTIONS

1. The analysis used in the papers in this chapter to explain the doctrine of impossibility has also been used to explain the law's treatment of mutual mistake—often, indeed, called "antecedent impossibility":

In the famous case of the sale of the cow "Rose 2d of Aberlone,"[1] both seller and buyer believed that the cow was barren, and the price was set accordingly. In fact the cow was pregnant and worth about ten times as much as the selling price. The mistake was discovered before the cow was delivered to the buyer, and the seller promptly canceled the sale. The court upheld the cancellation. If we accept the version of the facts presented in the majority opinion, the result may appear consistent with efficiency, for there was no basis for presuming the cow more valuable in the buyer's possession than in the seller's—its true worth being an order of magnitude different from what the parties had thought—and the seller had not been careless in thinking the cow barren.

However, the case can be approached somewhat differently, and perhaps more fruitfully, by observing that it was a case where an unforeseen contingency occurred and by asking how the parties would have allocated the risk of this occurrence between them had they foreseen it. This approach decomposes the contract into two distinct agreements: an agreement respecting the basic performance (the transfer of the cow) and an agreement respecting a risk associated with the transfer (that the cow will turn out to be different from what the parties believed). In fact there was some evidence that Rose's sale price included her value if pregnant, discounted (very drastically of course) by the probability of that happy eventuality. This evidence, if believed, would have justified the court in concluding that the parties had intended to transfer the risk of the cow's turning out to be pregnant to the buyer, in which event delivery should have been enforced. Even in the absence of any such evidence, there would be an argument for placing on the seller the risk that the cow is not what it seems. In general, if not in every particular case, the owner will have superior access to information concerning the actual or probable characteristics of his property. This is the theory on which the seller of a house is liable to the buyer for any latent (as distinct from obvious) defects; a similar principle could be used to decide cases of mutual mistake.[2]

2. In the celebrated case of the ship *Peerless* (Raffles v. Wichelhaus, 2 Hurl. & C. 906, 159 Eng. Rep. 375 (Ex. 1864)), plaintiff agreed to sell defendants 125 bales of cotton "to arrive ex *Peerless* from Bombay." A ship called *Peerless* sailed from Bombay in December with the cotton on board, but when it arrived at Liverpool the defendants refused to accept delivery, on the ground that they had intended that the cotton be sent by another ship named *Peerless* which had sailed from Bombay in October. The Court of Exchequer gave judgment for the defendants. The court was apparently persuaded by their argument that if the buyer meant one *Peerless* and the seller another, there was no meeting of minds and hence no binding contract.

1. Sherwood v. Walker, 66 Mich. 568, 33 N.W. 919 (1887). [Footnote in original.]
2. Richard A. Posner, Economic Analysis of Law 73-74 (2d ed. 1977).

This result is correct under the "subjective" theory of contract, is it not? But should that end the analysis? Using the materials in this chapter, formulate the question of enforcement in economic terms. What factors are relevant, on an economic view, to the question whether the contract should be enforced? If the defendants were newcomers to the India-England cotton trade, how might that fact be relevant to the economic analysis?

3. Suppose that *A*, a shrewd bargainer, enters into a contract with *B* from which *A* stands to make a much larger profit than *B* suspected when he agreed to the deal. If *B* breaches and *A* sues *B* for his lost profit, should *B* be permitted to limit his damages to those reasonably foreseeable by him at the time he entered into the contract? Does the rule of Hadley v. Baxendale (see p. 164 infra) require this result?

4. Both the Kronman and the Posner-Rosenfield articles argue that the law of contracts makes good economic sense. What kind of evidence would constitute a persuasive refutation of their argument?

5. Schwartz suggests that if the price of butter rises, the price of margarine, its substitute, will rise also. The higher price of butter will make margarine more attractive than before, so a greater quantity of margarine will be demanded. But why should the increase in output drive up the price, assuming sellers of margarine are competitive and so sell at a price equal to their cost (including a reasonable profit)? The answer is that the margarine industry may face a rising supply curve. That is, the cost of its inputs may rise with the amount of margarine produced, either because an expansion of production forces the producers to pay higher prices for inputs in order to bid them away from other demanders, or because the cheapest inputs for producing margarine are scarce so that an increase in demand must be met by using more costly inputs.

The effects of quantity on unit cost, as in the above example, can be quite important in measuring the damages from breach of contract. The Speidel-Clay article and the Case Western student note, together with the editors' comments on these pieces, in Chapter 6, deal with this issue further.

6. Suppose it is true, as Schwartz suggests, that buyers, relative to sellers, systematically underestimate the future inflation rate because of inferior knowledge. Under the Posner-Rosenfield analysis this would suggest that sellers are probably superior bearers of the risk of an unanticipated change in the inflation rate than are buyers. If so, would one expect the law to excuse performance by reason of an inflationary increase in the seller's costs or the parties to include escalator clauses by express agreement? If the parties have *equal*

knowledge (or ignorance) concerning future changes in the price level, what factors would determine whether they included an escalator clause?

7. Schwartz's article is unusual in that he attempts to relate contract law to macroeconomic policy, which involves such economic aggregates as employment, the money supply, and the price level. A course in contract law is not a very suitable vehicle for teaching macroeconomics, so we will content ourselves with raising a few questions concerning the plausibility of Schwartz's discussion. First, is it really likely that an increase in the price level (inflation) will increase demand and hence employment? The theory of a positive correlation between inflation and employment is summarized in the famous "Phillips curve," but there is increasing doubt, both theoretical and empirical, regarding the validity of the theory. The heart of the theory is the idea that an increase in the dollar receipts of a seller will cause him to expand his output until he restores equality between the price he receives and the marginal costs he incurs. However, this process will occur only if the prices he is paying for his inputs are not inflating at the same rate as the prices he is receiving for his output; if they are, as in general one expects they would be, inflation will have no effect on his output and hence on the quantity of labor (and other) inputs that he hires. Recognizing this difficulty, proponents of the Phillips curve argue that suppliers of labor inputs (i.e., workers), especially when their wages are fixed for years at a time under collective bargaining agreements, do not raise their wages as fast as their employer can raise the price of his output. But, if so, this is surely a short-run phenomenon. The unions will soon learn to include escalator clauses in their contracts to avoid being exploited in this fashion.

For lucid expositions of this argument see Milton Friedman, Price Theory ch. 12 (1976), and his Nobel lecture, Inflation and Unemployment, 85 J. Pol. Econ. 451 (1977).

A simpler reason than Schwartz's why escalator clauses reduce inflation appears in the literature on "indexation," i.e., including an escalator clause in every contract in the economy. See, e.g., Milton Friedman, Monetary Correction, in Essays on Inflation and Indexation 25 (Am. Enterprise Inst. 1974). Indexation reduces the likelihood of inflation by reducing its utility to the government. When government pays for goods or services by printing money rather than by collecting explicit taxes, it is in effect taxing holders of cash balances and other holders of claims (e.g., to an income fixed in dollar terms) who cannot adjust instantaneously and completely to a reduction in the value of the dollar. If complete indexation eliminated all such claims and made everyone perfectly hedged against inflation, the tax effect of inflation would be nullified and inflation would have no more effect on public revenues than would changing the name of the currency.

8. What is the appropriate use by the legal system of the sort of evidence collected by Joskow on the background of the Westinghouse litigation? Should it be usable as evidence in the litigation itself? As evidence pro or con a general rule of excusing sellers for unanticipated increases in the cost of performance?

9. Is Joskow's analysis congruent with Schwartz's? Is Joskow's view of the Uniform Commercial Code congruent with the Posner-Rosenfield view of the common law?

10. Would there be merit in a rule that excused the seller from having to honor his contract if the cost of performance had doubled since the contract was signed? What if it had increased 10 times or 100 times? Is there any place for arbitrary multiples in the design of optimal legal policy in this area?

11. *Developments in the Westinghouse Litigation.* Some twenty-seven utilities which had contracts with Westinghouse to purchase uranium from it brought suit to enforce their contracts. Westinghouse has settled with three of these complainants for cash, equipment, and services worth a total of $11.5 million (and with a fourth for an undisclosed amount). Suits by seventeen utilities were consolidated for trial in the United States District Court in Richmond, Virginia. At this writing (June 1978) trial has just concluded and the case is awaiting decision. The trial judge continues to urge the parties to settle, however. It has been estimated that if Westinghouse were to settle along the lines of its previous settlements, the total cost to Westinghouse would be between $600 million and $1.1 billion—and, if it were forced to honor all of the contracts in suit, that its total costs would rise above $2 billion. See Business Week, Sept. 26, 1977, at 125. Westinghouse has not only defended the contract suits on the ground that the price rise which led it to terminate the contracts was the result of unforeseeable circumstances including an international uranium cartel, but has brought a treble-damage suit in the United States District Court in Chicago against a number of the alleged participants in the cartel.

Chapter 6

Remedies

*The Economic Basis of Damages for Breach of Contract**

John H. Barton

I. The Market Transaction

The paradigm that might have been chosen for this paper, had it been written in the formative years of contract law, is a market contract: a contract to sell a specified quantity of a commodity at a specified date in the future, under conditions in which all damages can be determined by hypothetical or actual purchase or liquidation of the commodity in a market that is always available. The contract is then essentially a bet against the future course of the market. Each party enters the contract in the hope that he is guessing the market more accurately than the other, or, if the parties differ in their willingness to bear risks, in the judgment that the certain price set by the contract is more desirable than the uncertainty of the market price.

There are two goals that might guide the determination of damages for breach of such a contract: *expectation protection* (the plaintiff should be put in as good a position as if the promise had been honored), and *incentive maintenance* (the defendant should honor his promises). It is appropriate to begin with the goal of expectation protection, since that is the one usually expressed by common law courts. The goal is to give the offended party a sum of money damages that places him in as good a position as he would have been in had the contract been honored. Thus, suppose a contract is made to sell grain at price p on a specified date. In fact, grain turns out to be

*Reprinted, by permission, from 1 J. Legal Studies 277, 277-279, 280-282, 287-300 (1972).

selling at market price s on the specified date. Assuming for the moment that $s > p$, the buyer will want to enforce the contract against the seller, and the seller will want to avoid the contract. If the seller breaches, the buyer must purchase the grain on the open market at price s, so he should obtain an additional payment d sufficient to compensate him for not obtaining the grain at price p. Clearly, one is led to the damage measure $d \geqslant s - p$.

The incentive-maintenance analysis leads to the same results. Aside from financial incapacity—in which event a rather different body of law may be brought into play—the primary reason a party to a market-oriented contract might fail to keep the contract is that the other party's prediction of future price was better than his. If parties are to be prevented from dishonoring contracts on this ground, the law must impose a penalty that is as great as the cost of compliance.[1] Assuming that the case is one of seller's breach (so that $s > p$) the problem is to define a penalty d that makes it more desirable for the seller to honor the contract than to dishonor it. If he honors the contract he gains p; if he violates it, as by selling the grain on the market, he gains s, but loses the penalty d. The condition for making the penalty effective is then

$$p \geqslant s - d \text{ or } d \geqslant s - p.$$

These equivalent results are the classical measures of contract recovery in an economy of organized markets, and are telescoped in the term "expectation damages." The distinction between the two possible supporting theories must be noted, however. One seeks to penalize the potential contract violator in such a way that he normally prefers not to violate, and is thus defined by the alternatives he faces in carrying out the contract or not. Common law courts are seldom explicit about this policy of preventing default. Yet they are concerned that the damage doctrines not *encourage* default. Moreover, to the extent that contract law's ordinary role is as a threat to prevent breach, the incentive maintenance policy is implicit. The other theory seeks to place the innocent party in as good a position as he would have been in had the contract been carried out, and is thus defined by his expectations in receiving the desired performance. . . .

II. The Non-Market Transaction

Although the model described above may have been the norm at the time when contract law began its development, and may still

1. I am ignoring the litigation costs.

account for a large proportion of actual transactions, it does not exhibit the characteristic problems of contemporary contract law. To expose those problems requires only a slight increase in complexity. Our example will be that of a contract of purchase and sale of a product manufactured to order. It will be assumed that there is no market in which the product could be readily bought or sold and that the buyer expects to use the purchased product in his business in the hope of making a profit. These assumptions correspond to those underlying many actual contracts in the world of business today.

The problems immediately raised are: (a) there is no market by which a measure of damages can be defined or by which the injured party can protect himself; (b) the costs and benefits to the parties do not provide an unequivocal basis for estimation of damages, since the cost incurred by the injured party is generally different from the benefit bestowed on the breaching party; and (c), less obviously, completion of the transaction can no longer be assumed desirable, since the overall benefit to the parties may be less than the overall costs to them.

The character of these difficulties can be elucidated by considering the details of the transaction. The buyer negotiates to obtain a custom-made good from the seller. If the transaction is completed without difficulty, the seller will normally receive a profit above his costs, since he would not otherwise enter the contract. Similarly, the buyer will expect to conduct further operations on the goods or combine them with other goods and sell the whole at a profit, here called an enterprise expectation. If the transaction fails during performance, each party may be stuck with unrecoverable costs. The seller's partly completed goods may be valueless except as scrap.[2] This possible loss is seller's reliance, or, in Fuller's vocabulary, essential reliance.[3] Similarly, the buyer may have incurred expenditures—such as printing of packages—that become losses now that the contract has failed. These are buyer's reliance, or, in Fuller's vocabulary, incidental reliance.

2. A complete definition of the sunk costs would consider the alternative markets for the material on hand, e.g., sale for scrap or (possibly) completion of the contract, etc., and evaluate for each of these possible uses or markets the difference between the additional necessary cost to prepare the materials for that market and the price available in that market. If there is no market such that there would be a positive return on such additional expenditures, then the costs already expended represent the sunk cost or reliance. Otherwise, these costs should be adjusted by an amount equal to the return from preparing the materials for the alternative market offering the greatest return. In fact, this is the definition adopted by the courts, although allowance is made for the problems of uncertainty and error in choosing the alternate performance. See, e.g., Uniform Commercial Code §2-704(2). Throughout this article, it will be assumed for simplicity's sake that there is no such economically desirable alternative performance.

3. Lon L. Fuller and William R. Perdue, Jr., The Reliance Interest in Contract Damages, 46 Yale L.J. 52, 78 (1936).

		Seller/Manufacturer	
		Honor	Dishonor
Buyer/ Entrepreneur	Honor	(buyer's profit or enterprise expectation, seller's profit)	(—buyer's or incidental reliance, 0)
	Dishonor	(0,—seller's or essential reliance)	(0, 0)

[Figure 9]

This description leads to the . . . game pattern [shown in Figure 9] for the non-market transaction (in the absence of any legal remedies). A complete model would have to consider various alternative strategies of partial performance. Nevertheless, the model is qualitatively correct, and it does display the problems already mentioned. First, the expectations are not explicit in the contract and cannot be estimated easily from a market. Thus, losses become difficult to evaluate, and normal bookkeeping data often may not be very helpful. Moreover, some of the expectations may be relatively subjective; for example, the parties may have been interested in obtaining gainful employment (or institutional stability) as well as in obtaining the entrepreneurial profits associated with the transaction. Second, since the gains and losses to each party are now quite different, the policies of incentive maintenance and of expectation protection diverge.

The third point is somewhat more difficult, and requires consideration of the character of the equilibrium solution of the game as shown above. This is a non-zero sum game, whose normal equilibrium solution is the honor-honor point. It follows that in the ordinary course of business, businessmen will feel no need for contract law. The cases in which default is likely are those in which, through some casualty or change of circumstances, expected profit is converted into an expected loss. In the situation of changed circumstances, it may well be economically inefficient to complete the transaction. The changes may make the total costs of the transaction greater than the total benefits. Consequently one is properly chary about requiring the enforcement of what I have called the "non-market" contract, through injunction or through damages of a form that always induces performance. This is the point hidden in Justice Holmes' aphorism that the obligation imposed by a contract is not to comply, but either to comply or to pay damages.[4] . . .

4. O. W. Holmes, The Path of the Law, 10 Harv. L. Rev. 457, 462 (1897).

III. Contracting in the Presence of Market Uncertainty (Buyer's Breach)

The fact that a negotiated allocation will, under appropriate bargaining conditions, be optimal does not mean that the contract institution may not be misallocative due to its frictional effect in the presence of changing conditions. Under certain conditions, an integrated firm confronted with a time-varying demand curve may find it appropriate to begin work on a certain number of units and then to discontinue efforts and write off the loss on some of these units if the market changes unfavorably. Since this behavior maximizes profits in a competitive market, it must be assumed optimal. If, however, the production effort is contracted out and, because of the method by which damages are computed, the contractual arrangement effectively prevents cancellation under appropriate conditions, performance is continued—a nonoptimal result.

This result can be examined with a simple model. Suppose that production, in this model the cultivation of an agricultural commodity, requires one growing season, can be started only in May, and once started cannot be stopped. Raw materials, or seeds, costing b per unit of output, can be bought only in March. They are perishable, and can be used only in the one season. The crop is always sold in September, and, also being perishable, cannot be held over. Finally, the September price is learned in April, too late to affect the decision to purchase seeds, but early enough to affect the decision to commit land, plant, and cultivate. For simplicity, the price per unit of the crop will be assumed to be either s, with a probability π, or zero, the bottom dropping out of the market $(1 - \pi)$ proportion of the seasons. Although grossly simplified, this model does permit analysis of the problems arising when improved price information becomes available at a time when some costs are already incurred but others can still be avoided.

The critical allocation decision is then to define the production level (here, perhaps in the form of a choice of the number of acres of land to plant). The profit function for an integrated entrepreneur or farmer is

$$P = \pi\,[ns - c_t(n)] - bn,$$

where $c_t(n)$ is the total cost curve for the production process. He has to pay for n units of raw material each season, but incurs production costs and gains sales for only a proportion π of the seasons. The remaining seasons he avoids production costs and realizes no sales. Using standard techniques to establish the optimum n

$$\frac{\partial P}{\partial n} = \pi s - b - \pi \frac{\partial c_t(n)}{\partial n} \text{ or } \frac{\partial c_t(n)}{\partial n} = s - \frac{b}{\pi}$$

it can be shown that $n = u\,(s - \frac{b}{\pi})$. The good-season market price must, in effect, be discounted to allow for the loss in bad seasons.

Suppose now that the production is carried out by a separate supplier who contracts to buy seed, plant and cultivate the land, and sell the crop to an agricultural entrepreneur at a pre-negotiated price. In this case, simple contract enforcement would be non-optimal if it required the buyer to honor the contract even after the market falls. The profit functions of the entrepreneur buyer (P_e) and the manufacturer or cultivator-seller (P_m) are then as follows:

$$P_e = \pi\, sn - pn;$$
$$P_m = pn - c_t(n) - bn.$$

Assuming as before that the contract curve is the line $P_e + P_m = \max$, the parties will negotiate to maximize

$$P = P_e + P_m = \pi\, sn - c_t(n) - bn,$$

again a function of *n* alone. Since

$$\frac{\partial P}{\partial n} = \pi\, s - b - \frac{\partial c_t(n)}{\partial n} = 0,$$

it appears that $n = u(\pi s - b) = u[\pi(s - \frac{b}{\pi})]$. The fact that the entrepreneur buyer must honor the contract, even when it is a losing contract, cuts back acreage to that corresponding to a price π times the actual price. This is the way the parties react to being "locked-in" to complete performance once the contract is signed.[5]

Fortunately, contract law does not go this far. Unless the buyer has negotiated a special clause permitting termination of the contract when the market drops, he indeed cannot cancel without being in

5. The extreme version of this effect is exemplified by an entrepreneur who enters into a long-term contract to buy stated quantities from a supplier. To the extent that the supplier insists on a fixed quantity per year, the buyer will negotiate to keep that quantity low, out of fear of bad years.

The requirements contract, in which the volume is flexible, avoids this problem, but, because it fixes prices for the future, may produce a different form of misallocation, by limiting the extent to which production reacts to price changes. The effect may be in either direction, depending on whether prices rise or fall. Whether or not the effect is thoroughly random depends on whether those market situations most likely to produce requirements contracts are also associated with a probable secular trend in prices. Moreover, this problem of lag in responsiveness may be minor compared with the intimate relationship between market structure and the use of requirements contracts and with the possibility that requirements contracts are a response to differential ability to bear risk.

breach of contract. (Unprofitability of performance is not adequate grounds for rescission, and, as a ground for breach, may lead the court to view the offender with some disfavor.) Consequently, the buyer in this case is subject to damages. But the damages are limited to seller's expectation as of the time of cancellation, usually his expected profit, here $pn - c_t(n) - bn$, plus the costs *already* incurred, here bn. In that case, assuming that each party has complete knowledge of the risks, the profit functions can be written

$$P_e = \pi \, sn - \pi \, pn - (1 - \pi) \, [pn - c_t(n)];$$
$$P_m = \pi[pn - c_t(n)] + (1 - \pi) \, [pn - c_t(n)] - bn.$$

Through the same calculation as before,

$$P = P_e + P_m = \pi \, sn - \pi \, c_t(n) - bn$$

$$\frac{\partial P}{\partial n} = \pi \, s - b - \pi \frac{\partial c_t(n)}{\partial n} = 0;$$

it appears that $n = u(s - \frac{b}{\pi})$. Production is now at the correct level.

This definition of seller's expectation, which seems to correct for the rigidity of automatic contract performance, is based on a principle that contract law will not reward the seller for unwanted performance. The principle is illustrated by Clark v. Marsiglia.[6] Plaintiff had a contract to clean and repair paintings. Half-way through, defendant told him to stop. Plaintiff continued performance and sought the entire contract price. Defendant argued that he should be liable for only the portion of the price corresponding to the work done at the time of the stop-order. Hence the question posed was: under color of the contract-enforcement policy, could the seller continue work on the contract, thus forcing the buyer to pay for additional work which he did not desire?

The conventional judicial answer, which is no, can be justified in either of two ways. A first way is to make the choice between the incentive maintenance and the expectation protection policies in favor of the latter. The seller can achieve his expectation interest by recovering an amount equal to the reliance together with an amount equal to the "profit" expected from the contract. This is normally a cost to the buyer lower than that which would be incurred if the seller were to complete the contract. It would be unduly harmful to defendant to allow plaintiff to build up damages without conferring any benefit. Alternatively, if the buyer no longer wants the product, perhaps because *his* sales volume has fallen, it would be wasteful to

6. 1 Denio 317, 43 Am. Dec. 670 (N.Y. Sup. Ct. 1845).

require the seller to finish the unwanted performance. It is socially better that he not waste his resources on an unnecessary activity.

It is clear that the seller should recover his sunk costs and need recover no more costs. What about his profits? They are typically given, if not too speculative, often under a formulation of the damage measure as "contract price less cost to complete." This can mean that full profits are due, even if the contract is cancelled the day it is made and there is no reliance whatever. Such a result is unsatisfying, and can lead to rather formalistic disputes over whether or not a contract was ever made. The problem is slight in the market transaction, where the market will usually change slowly so damages for early breach are quite small, but acute in the non-market transaction.

In fact, all that is necessary to permit optimality, when both parties have complete and accurate information, is to allow termination upon the market's drop with a pre-established settlement payment to be made at that time. The parties can either negotiate a special clause providing for damages or price adjustments or rely on a judicially defined measure of damages. (In practice, specific clauses will be found in only the most sophisticated contracts, although extra-legal business custom often permits termination under the necessary circumstances, achieving the same result as if the clause were included.) If such a payment is established to allow termination after purchase of the raw materials in the event that the price drops, the profit functions become

$$P_e = \pi \, sn - p\pi n - d(1 - \pi)\, n, \text{ and}$$
$$P_m = p \, \pi n + d(1 - \pi)\, n - \pi \, c_t(n) - nb,$$

where the assumption is made that the entrepreneur pays p for completed items and d for items on which production is stopped. On adding these profits, it can be seen that the joint profit maximum is indeed achieved at the optimum production start level. No matter how the parties split their profits by negotiating over p and d, they will still negotiate to the optimum production levels. This is possible at any predictable level, and the damage measure chosen can be that which the courts will use. Its predictability (not at all clear) must be assumed along with that of the risk, and the parties must both have this information. . . .

IV. Behavioral Sources of Contract Law

The above analysis shows that, when parties with equal bargaining power negotiate about an equally understood risk or uncertainty, the court can do no better from an economic viewpoint than to enforce their understanding, much the way it enforced the contract where damages could be ascertained automatically by reference to an organized market. The typical problem in what I have called "non-market" contract law, however, is that the parties often have not negotiated such a way to handle the risk, but the risk still materializes. They either did not consider the risk at all or, while considering it, negotiated on the basis of different understandings as to its magnitude or who would assume it.

The practical problem of contract damages is thus conceptually reducible to that of mistake or misunderstanding. When the judicial system imposes damages, it can, for economic purposes, be said to be adding an unstated term to the contract. The court is saying: "You parties didn't negotiate about this risk or didn't reach any understanding about it. Now the risk has materialized, and I have to figure out what terms should be implied to cover the risk." The role for economics, then, in the law of damages is to make the additional terms consistent insofar as possible with (a) the allocation assumptions likely to have been implicitly negotiated into the contract and (b) the economic desirability or undesirability of continued performance. Goal (a) is most closely related to misunderstanding about the meaning of the negotiation while goal (b) is most closely related to failure to predict future contingencies (e.g., contract frustration). And the law should meet these goals in a way that minimizes transaction costs, the element of cost that is ultimately at stake when the parties can, by special negotiations, undo most general damage rules.

Goal (b), the incentive to continue performance, might appeal to courts more than goal (a) (allocative efficiency) because it does not require the court to make an allocation of risks. Unfortunately, it turns out that pursuit of this goal often leads to a measure of damages inconsistent with that defined on allocation grounds. For the reasons developed in the preceding section, this goal would normally seem less important than the allocative goal, and, except for the proof of inconsistency, will be ignored here.

With respect to goal (a), there is a reciprocal dependence between the judicial system and the contract-makers in defining who should bear the risk. Insofar as the judicial system consistently places an undiscussed risk on a particular party, that party will, if responsive to the system, tend to protect himself against the risk by either shifting it explicitly to the other party by negotiation or making his allocational decisions as if he faced the risk. Likewise, if commercial practice makes "normal" assumptions as to the location of the risk parties will accept these assumptions when they make their allocational decisions and the judicial system will achieve proper allocation by accepting them too.

Nevertheless, courts will sometimes have to allocate the risk without having any form of practice to rely upon. Unless transaction costs are considered, economics has nothing to say to this question, at least so long as there can be bargaining about the risk. (There may, of course, be risk-spreading or social policy reasons for one party to bear the risk, even if the other can be induced to accept it.) An answer may be definable directly in terms of transaction costs.[7] If, for example, it would be very unusual for the buyer to bear a particular risk, then, unless the parties explicitly agreed otherwise, the seller should bear it.[8] There are also reasons that can be related only to a sense of bargaining justice—this is particularly the case with questions like "did *A*'s statement mean that he was taking the risk?" No general analysis of these problems will be presented here.

What will be attempted is a more general task, based on the locations of information about the risks and about possible countermeasures. In the real-world case, contracting parties are not in symmetrical positions. There may be one party who is abler to appreciate the magnitude of the risk or to negotiate about it. There may also be a party, not necessarily the same one, who is abler to understand the effects of the law and to take in response those corrective actions that will establish optimal allocation. The problem for the law of damages is then to encourage the party able to appreciate the risk to conduct his negotiations toward optimality even though the other party negotiates in naive ignorance of the risk. The costs of exchanging full knowledge of the risk can then be avoided. If this is to be successful, the details must vary somewhat from contract type to contract type, since the typical expectations (or indifference functions) of the parties will vary also. This variance may be one of the reasons why the unity of contract law is breaking down. In this paper, two examples will be considered, one in which the party appreciating the risk magnitude and the party better situated to effect an optimal allocation are different and one in which they are the same. It will appear that the mathematics, and indeed the existing law, are drastically different in the two cases.

7. See Steven N. S. Cheung, Transaction Cost, Risk Aversion and the Choice of Contractual Arrangement, 12 J. Law & Econ. 23 (1969).

8. Note that the way risks are allocated in the case of a silent contract will often affect negotiated allocations. A party on whom a risk will fall in such a case can certainly negotiate to transfer the risk to the other party. But he may be deterred by the effect of even raising the issue on whether the negotiation will be successfully completed and on how profits will be divided. Thus, one can speak of a "burden of negotiation" that is very similar to a burden of proof.

A. Buyer's Damages: Allocation of Casualty Risk

. . . Seller's default raises several problems for courts. The failure of the contract may cause the failure of the buyer's enterprise, which was expected to cover the costs of the reliance and of the contract and to yield additional returns besides. Measurement of this enterprise expectation and of the associated reliance is difficult. There are questions of causality, as in the classical case of the horseshoe nail and the kingdom. Perhaps most seriously, the expectation doctrine, if not modified, may imply that large potential damages arise from a small contract. This seems inequitable to courts; the development of doctrines (such as that of certainty of damages) to limit these damages has been a recurrent judicial theme.

Of these doctrines, the most relevant one is that of Hadley v. Baxendale.[9] Defendant railroad had lost a mill shaft that it was shipping to the plaintiff's mill. Because of the loss, the mill was closed down for some days. Plaintiff sought to recover lost profits under the contract of carriage. The dilemmas are clear—to impose liability for these damages may require other railroad customers to bear costs that the mill could have prevented by holding an extra shaft in inventory; not to impose liability may require the mill to bear costs that the railroad could have prevented by using additional care.

The court's resolution is an ingenious one. The mill will receive these damages only if, at the time of contracting, it explained to the railroad the magnitude of risk that was at stake. This result effectively avoids the question of allocating a realized risk and replaces it by one of allocating efforts to avoid the realization of the risk. More explicitly, the resolution assumes that certain risks are borne by each party as a "normal form" of the transaction. If any other risks are to be transferred, they must be considered explicitly during the negotiation. It can be assumed—if the negotiation operates as the rule anticipates—that the party undertaking to bear such atypical risks will charge an appropriate insurance premium and exercise appropriate extraordinary care in the execution of the transaction.

What is most interesting about this resolution is that in effect it rejects both the incentive-maintenance and the expectation-protection policies. It says, "If you are *really* concerned that the other party may dishonor the contract, you may have to pay him extra!" And it reaches that position in part on the basis of an assumption that default is no longer willful and in part on the basis of an underlying concern with what is ultimately an economic allocation issue. Its result is exactly the duty to inform required to give the seller guidance when the negotiation is indeterminate. . . .

9. 9 Exch. 341 (1854).

B. Seller's Damages: Allocation of Market Risk

The typical example of seller's damages arises when, most likely because of a market shift, the entrepreneur finds the enterprise unprofitable and seeks to rescind the contract. . . .

If activity is conducted by a single firm, that firm's anticipated profit, as defined at any time during the course of performance, can be stated:

$$p_c = s_c - (c_i + c_c) - (r_i + r_c),$$

where *s*, *c*, and *r* refer to market prices, cost, and reliance expenditures respectively, and where subscript *i* refers to costs already incurred and subscript *c* to market price at completion time as projected at any point and to costs or expenditures that must still be incurred in order to complete. Hence all of these amounts are considered to be variable functions of time.[10] If the firm stops work at any time, its profit (loss) is given by

$$-c_i - r_i.$$

Economic optimality requires that the firm go on to complete if and only if its profit will be increased (or loss decreased) by completing. Assuming that all costs already incurred are irretrievably sunk, so that no mitigation is possible,[11] the condition for completing can be stated in terms of the difference between the two expressions:

$$s_c - c_c - r_c \geqslant 0. \qquad \text{Inequality 1}$$

If this inequality is satisfied, production should continue; if not, it should stop.

If the operation is now divided among two firms linked by contract, the same considerations still define whether it is optimal to complete performance or to terminate the contract. The question then becomes whether damage measures, d_m paid by manufacturer if he defaults and d_e paid by entrepreneur if he defaults, can be defined in such a way that they create an incentive to go ahead when the inequality is satisfied and to stop when it is not.

Each party will follow an analogous incentive pattern: he will go ahead if there is an increase in profits (or decrease in loss) compared with stopping, making allowance for damages. The inequalities, which hold when performance is to continue, are, for the manufacturer and entrepreneur respectively:

10. They can also be considered to be already discounted at an appropriate interest rate.

11. Presumably, the case in which mitigation is possible can be handled by considering the mitigation as an alternative performance to be compared with the planned performance on either a profit or a return-to-capital basis.

$$p - (c_i + c_c) \geqslant - (c_i + d_m) \text{ or } p - c_c \geqslant - d_m;$$

Inequality 2

$$s_c - p - (r_i + r_c) \geqslant - (r_i + d_e) \text{ or } s_c - p - r_c \geqslant -d_e.$$

Inequality 3

Treating the inequalities as equations and solving simultaneously, one is led to the following plausible measures, which do indeed solve the requirements just posed:

$$d_m = s_c - r_c - p$$

and

$$d_e = p - c_c.$$

The seller's damages are the traditional "sales price less cost to complete." The buyer's damages are lost profits from which expenditures already made in reliance are not deducted—in classical contract terms, both lost profits and lost reliance. This result is perhaps to be expected—an incentive-maintenance policy, being itself forward-looking, can consider only future expenditures and hence cannot consider sunk expenditures.[12]

Applying the second equation to the price change cases analyzed in the earlier part of this section, one can see the differences between the optimum-allocation and the incentive-maintenance approaches. The cost to complete is $c_a(n)$ (per unit). Hence, the damages under the incentive approach are $p - c_a(n)$. This bears no similarity to the formula for damages computed under the allocative approach.[13] In fact, without assuming a form for the cost function, one cannot even say which measure is larger. Nevertheless, plausible situations can be described in which damages determined under the allocative rule are inadequate to provide an incentive to complete performance, and these situations are probably the most typical ones. The existence of this situation may be one reason why business so strongly dislikes expectation damages (which may often be even bigger than incentive-maintenance damages).

. . . *It is impossible to define a single damage measure such that (a) optimal initial decisions are made while the ignorance of one party to the*

12. Note that in the commodity sales case, $r_c = 0$, $c_c = s =$ market price of the commodity, and our equations yield the traditional measures of damage: $d_m = p - s$, $d_e = s - p$.

13. [That formula, developed in a discussion omitted by the editors, is

$$d = \frac{pb}{b + \frac{\delta c_t(n)}{\delta n}},$$

which Barton states "will usually be a little greater than *b*, the classic measure of seller's reliance." 1 J. Legal Studies at 297. He goes on to note that if default occurs near completion of performance, the formula for damages under the allocative approach will include lost profits.]

contract is accepted and (b) incentives to contract performance are appropriate. It is sometimes possible, however, to distinguish situations in which one of the damage approaches is better than another. For example, where initial planning is not feasible and where business custom does not support contract performance, the incentive approach might be better. Where planning is feasible and where contractual ethics are high, the allocative approach would be better. For contracts among businessmen, the latter situation probably is more common, so that the optimum-allocation approach should normally be adopted. Reliance is placed on business ethics rather than on damage-law incentives.

Hence, . . . if a court concludes that the buyer should bear a particular risk, *the seller's damages should include his reliance costs plus a portion of expected profits varying from none to all depending on how far along seller is in performing the contract at the time of breach.*

Conclusion

The policy of contract damages changes substantially as contract law makes the transition from market transactions to non-market transactions. In particular, the contract-enforcement policy becomes almost irrelevant as does the expectation policy. Instead, one is led to view damages as a substitute for negotiated liquidated-damages clauses that can be used when only one party is likely to be aware of the risks and to be able to make allocative decisions in view of the risks.

If damages in the non-market transaction are calculated in accordance with this policy, one is led to specific measures which are remarkably similar to those developed intuitively by courts but which also avoid the conceptual difficulties associated with the concept of expectation. . . .

*Breach and Remedy for the Tender of Nonconforming Goods Under the Uniform Commercial Code: An Economic Approach**

George L. Priest

This article considers the manner in which courts have interpreted and applied the provisions of the Uniform Commercial Code

*Reprinted, by permission, from 91 Harv. L. Rev. 960, 963-967, 981, 983-984, 987, 989-990, 995-997 (1978), copyright 1978 by The Harvard Law Review Association.

giving a buyer the right to rescind a contract of sale when the goods tendered by the seller deviate from their description in the contract. It shows that, in general, courts regularly have applied a wide variety of statutory provisions in a way which is likely to enhance the efficiency of sales. Economic efficiency never has been recognized explicitly as a standard of Code interpretation and is seldom mentioned as a criterion of decision in judicial opinions. But the *results* of decisions interpreting the Code are consistent with minimization of long-run costs of formation of the contract, of delivery and handling of the goods, and of resolution of disputes arising under the contract. . . .

I. Minimizing the Cost Imposed by Nonconforming Tenders

A judgment awarding damages differs from a judgment returning the goods to the seller in two ways. First, to award damages, the buyer's loss from the defect must be calculated. Second, if the buyer recovers damages, he keeps the defective goods and must either adapt them for his use or dispose of them, while if the buyer returns the goods to the seller, the seller must dispose of them. Thus, the principal allocative costs of the damage remedy are the buyer's costs of adaptation, or his costs of disposal and cover, and the administrative cost of determining the buyer's loss. If the buyer adapts the goods, the costs are the expenditures the buyer must make to bring the goods into conformity with the contract or the adjustments he must make to use the nonconforming goods. If he resells the defective goods and covers by buying other goods—which will be the more efficient course of action if his costs of adaptation are greater than those of other firms in the market—the costs of breach are the difference between the resale and cover prices, plus the administrative costs to the buyer of effectuating the resale and procuring replacement goods. A damage remedy entails the calculation of these costs—a process which requires the expenditure of resources whether performed by a court or by the parties themselves in settlement negotiations. In addition, the calculation introduces a risk of error to the buyer and seller, respectively, of underestimating or overestimating the buyer's loss, which increases the cost of the damage remedy.

When the buyer is allowed to refuse the defective tender, different costs are incurred. They include the cost of returning the goods to the seller, the cost to the seller of reselling the defective goods, and the buyer's costs of purchasing substitute goods, i.e., the difference between the cover and contract prices plus the administrative costs of effectuating the purchase. If the buyer and seller negotiate toward the efficient remedy, they would likely agree to rescission where the sum of the costs of returning the goods is less than the total cost of the cheaper of the damage remedies.

Although the comparison of the costs of rescission and damages appears complicated, it can be simplified. Parties wishing to maximize the *joint* value of the transaction will prefer return of the goods to damages whenever the goods have a greater value in the seller's hands than in the buyer's. The value of the goods in the seller's hands is their market value less the seller's costs of retrieval and resale. The value of the goods in the buyer's hands is the greater of (1) their market value less the buyer's costs of resale, or (2) their value to the buyer after adaptation less the costs of adapting them. If the parties seek to conserve costs, they might first compare the value of the defective goods to the buyer with the market value of the goods. Where the loss from the defect is less to the buyer than to the market, returning the goods is generally not the cheaper remedy. If, however, the value to the buyer of the defective goods is less than the market value, the parties would agree to return the goods to the seller if the seller's costs of resale were lower than the buyer's by an amount greater than the retrieval costs. If the buyer's business involves the sale of defective as well as conforming goods, the buyer's and the seller's costs of resale may be equivalent, so that retrieval costs tip the balance in favor of a damage remedy. However, if the buyer is a consumer or is engaged solely in manufacturing, the value of managerial time necessary to resell the defective goods may be substantial. Then the advantages of the original seller—superior information about potential customers for defective goods and a superior distribution system—may offset the costs of retrieval and make rescission the preferable remedy.

In many cases, the cost of calculating damages may be decisive in determining which is the more efficient remedy, especially where there is no market in goods possessing the particular defect. Since in such cases the buyer's subjective valuation is difficult to ascertain, there is great danger both of the buyer's self-serving testimony and of a failure adequately to appreciate the particular tastes of the buyer. Where the latter factor is dominant, the remedy of returning the goods to the seller is the analogue of the equitable remedy of specific performance, which is awarded in sales of land or other "unique" forms of property because the legal remedy of damages is viewed as "inadequate."

The analysis thus far has ignored the distribution of the joint costs of breach between the buyer and seller. Because the choice of remedy can affect that distribution, each party may, for selfish reasons, prefer the remedy which, under the analysis so far, is less efficient. Moreover, each party may incur further allocative costs in negotiating or litigating toward the remedy which provides him the greatest personal benefit. Thus, the effects of the distribution of costs may affect not only the choice of remedy, but also the joint cost of the remedy chosen.

The remedy of rescission is designed to place the parties in their precontractual position: the goods are returned to the seller and the contract price is returned to the buyer. Damages, on the other hand, are designed to put the buyer in the position in which he would have been had the contract been performed. The measure of damages is the difference between the value of the goods as described in the contract and the value of the defective goods as tendered—with both values determined as of the time of tender. Consequently, where the value of the good has declined between agreement and tender, the buyer . . . has an incentive to conjure up defects or to exaggerate the materiality of real defects, and to demand rescission rather than damages, regardless of which remedy minimizes allocative costs. A similar incentive exists when the buyer realizes that he has chosen an unsuitable product. As long as the legal rules governing breach and remedy are sufficiently manipulable to offer the buyer a significant opportunity for distributional benefits, he will expend resources in negotiation or litigation in an attempt to gain them. . . .

II. Cost Minimization and the Courts: Code Jurisprudence, 1954-1976

In this Part, we examine various judicial decisions in cases arising under the Uniform Commercial Code to test the hypothesis that courts apply Code law so as to minimize the costs of sales. . . .

A. Rejection: Interpreting the Contract

. . . Where the buyer in a rejection case claims that the goods are defective with respect to a characteristic not explicitly described in the contract, a court is required to determine whether or not there has been a breach. The cost minimization hypothesis implies that the court will do so by comparing the cost to the seller of avoiding the alleged defect with the loss suffered by the buyer because of it.

Decisions in this area are consistent with efficiency. One, for example, inferred conformity of the tender from behavior of the buyer—reordering identical goods after discovery of the alleged defect. Here the costs of breach might have been avoided if the buyer had acted upon the information in his possession before the disputed order. . . .

B. The Reasonable Time for Rejection and Revocation of Acceptance

Part III [omitted in this reprinting] predicted that courts will define "reasonable time" [for rejection, under the Uniform Commercial Code] by balancing the cost to the buyer of discovering the defect with the cost to the seller of delay in discovery, typically depreciation of the goods prior to rejection or revocation, and that courts will deny relief where either the time or manner of the buyer's rejection or revocation indicates that the tender, though alleged to be defective, actually complied with the contract. In general, case law under the Code confirms these predictions. In Michael M. Berlin & Co. v. T. Whiting Manufacturing, Inc.,[1] for example, there was a contract for the sale of sheet steel, .090 inches thick. The first delivery was made on April 25, and other shipments were made in May. The buyer, however, did not inspect the steel until early June, when difficulties in its use led to the discovery that the steel was only .080 inches thick and therefore unsuitable for the buyer's purposes. The buyer attempted to reject by letter on July 29, but the seller, who was only a broker, refused to take back the steel, claiming that the original supplier refused responsibility because of the lapse of time. Upon the seller's suit to recover the purchase price, the court framed the legal question as the reasonableness of the buyer's conduct in delaying inspection of the goods until six weeks after delivery and in waiting another seven weeks before rejecting them. The court concluded that the buyer had not rejected within a reasonable time. . . .

[The] apparent judicial concern for the minimization of costs in the process of rejection has led one court to hold that the reasonable time for rejection expires immediately upon, or perhaps prior to, the seller's completion of the tender. In L. J. Robinson, Inc. v. Arber Construction Co.,[2] the seller tendered fill dirt for use at a construction site. Though a supervisory employee of the buyer was present during each delivery, it was not discovered until after 141 loads of dirt had been delivered that the dirt failed to meet contract specifications. The court denied rejection, finding that the buyer's employee could have inspected and discovered the nonconformities before the dirt had been spread and rolled in place.

It is important to note that the source of this holding is not the

1. 5 U.C.C. Rep. 357 (N.Y. Sup. Ct. 1968).
2. 292 A.2d 809 (D.C. 1972) (affirming trial court judgment).

text of the Code. Although section 2-606 establishes liability for the buyer's delay, it gives the buyer time to consider whether or not he will reject by providing that "acceptance does not occur until the buyer has had a reasonable opportunity to inspect [the goods]." If "delivery" is defined as the dumping of the dirt at the site, the reasonable time for inspection was practically zero because the dirt was rolled and spread immediately after dumping. On the other hand, delivery might have been defined as the entire process of dumping, rolling and spreading the fill dirt, since parts of the opinion indicate that the seller was responsible for the entire process. Under such an interpretation of "delivery," the court's decision implies that the reasonable time for rejection expired *before* completion of the tender—an interpretation directly at odds with the language of sections 2-606 and 2-602(1).

Either construction represents the subordination of the letter of the Code to the court's desire to minimize costs. In more typical sales cases, the costs of tender are sunk by the time the buyer becomes able to inspect the goods. Thus the Code provision giving the buyer a "reasonable time" to inspect and reject after tender is a useful tool for cost minimization. In cases like *Robinson*, however, the amount that the seller expends on tender depends on actions taken by the buyer. If the Code were interpreted literally in these cases to immunize the buyers from responsibility for their actions, resources might be expended on tender beyond the benefit to the contract. . . .

C. Rejection: Acts Inconsistent with the Seller's Ownership

The provision for construing acceptance from an act of the buyer inconsistent with the seller's ownership has been invoked in ways that minimize costs where the buyer's actions with respect to the goods—for example, his continued use or payment for the goods after rejection—indicate that the goods conform to his purposes. A second cost-minimizing function for the provision is to preclude rejection where some action of the buyer indicates that the remedy of damages is less costly than that of rejection. In Bowen v. Young,[3] for example, the buyer had ordered a mobile home in Texas to be delivered in South Carolina. Upon receipt, the buyer noticed various defects and immediately complained to both the seller and the manufacturer, neither of whom made any attempt to repair the defects. Later the buyer wired the seller to cancel the sale. But, failing to receive any response, the buyer moved into the mobile home, in-

3. 507 S.W.2d 600 (Tex. Ct. App. 1974).

vested $600 in repair and adaptation, and lived in it for over a year. He then had the home moved back to Texas, where he later brought suit seeking rejection. The court of appeals denied rejection but remanded the case for proof of damages, holding that the buyer's dominion over the home subsequent to his admittedly rightful rejection was an "act inconsistent." The central issue in the case was not whether the contract had been breached but whether rejection or damages was the appropriate remedy. The buyer's actions—living in the home and investing significant amounts accommodating it to his purposes—indicated a probability that he placed a value on the home higher than the resale value to the seller. To award the buyer rejection and to force a resale would reduce the joint value of the contract.

Although a buyer's continued possession of goods strongly suggests that he finds them useful, in some situations a buyer's continued use diminishes total costs. It supports the hypothesis of this article that in such situations courts have permitted rejection. For example, in Garfinkel v. Lehman Floor Covering Co.,[4] the buyer complained upon installation of the unsightly appearance of a carpet. Although the seller attempted to correct the condition, the buyer remained unsatisfied. Confronted with a finding that the carpet was defective, the seller argued that rejection should be denied because of the buyer's continued use of the carpet. The court, however, granted rejection, emphasizing that it would have been costly for the buyer to have removed, transported, and stored the defective carpet. . . .

D. The Substantive Grounds for Rejection and Revocation of Acceptance

This subsection examines the hypothesis of consistency of case law with cost minimization in a new way: it ignores the particular legal issue in the case and compares the judicial resolution of the disputes to the efficient resolution as determined from facts reported in the opinion.

Grants of rejection should be much less frequent than the broad language of section 2-601 might imply since the conditions under which rejection will minimize costs are quite limited. Of the sixty-two appellate rejection decisions announced between 1954 and 1976, rejection has been affirmed in only seventeen cases, equal to twenty-seven percent. This aggregate figure, of course, confirms the prediction in only a general way, for it conceals the presence or absence of the particular cost-minimizing conditions in individual

4. 60 Misc. 2d 72, 302 N.Y.S.2d 617 (Nassau County Dist. Ct. 1969).

cases. One refinement is to distinguish suits brought under section 2-601 by consumers from those brought by merchants. As discussed earlier, the cost minimization hypothesis implies that rejection should be awarded more frequently where the buyer is a consumer. Again, the findings are confirming. Rejection was awarded in eight of eighteen suits brought by consumer buyers (forty-four percent), but in only nine of forty-four suits brought by merchant buyers (twenty percent).

A second way of testing the hypothesis is to examine attempts to reject goods specially designed for the buyer. Since custom-made goods, even if defective in some respect, are likely to be more valuable to the buyer than to anyone else, damages are probably the cheaper remedy in cases involving such goods. Five rejection cases have been decided in which the goods were specially designed for the buyer, and rejection was denied in all but one. In Beco, Inc. v. Minnechaug Golf Course, Inc.,[5] a typical example, the seller had begun setting the first portion of specially designed restaurant equipment in position when the buyer refused to allow any further work. The seller voluntarily agreed to make alterations, but before they were completed the buyer rejected all of the equipment as nonconforming. The issue in the case was not whether the contract had been breached, but whether rejection was the appropriate remedy. Although there are no statutory grounds for such a holding, the court denied rejection but awarded the buyer damages for certain nonconformities. . . .

A final method of testing the cost minimization hypothesis for rejection cases is to look individually at the seventeen cases in which rejection was awarded. The hypothesis implies that in each, either the costs of reselling the defective goods will be higher to the buyer than to the seller or that the costs of calculating the buyer's damages will be high. We have already mentioned that the eight cases in which rejection was awarded to consumer buyers are generally consistent with the prediction. A closer look at these cases provides additional support. Five of the cases involved the purchase of a new automobile from a dealer. In general, it is plausible that a dealer will be able to resell a defective automobile more cheaply than the initial purchaser. These particular decisions, however, are notable for the court's emphasis in each on the relevance of the nature of the defect to the award of rejection. Each of the five cases involved defects of a very complex nature: the fusing of a differential to an axle, transmission failure, emission of smoke and fumes, or multiple defects costing several thousand dollars to repair. Two opinions draw attention to the difficulty to the consumer buyer of discovering the full extent

5. 5 Conn. Cir. Ct. 444, 256 A.2d 522 (1968).

of the defects, because of the likelihood that other parts of the auto had been affected. This difficulty, of course, increases both the cost of calculating the buyer's damages and the cost to the buyer of reselling the goods, especially relative to the cost of resale to an expert in automobile repair. In cases of this nature, rejection is likely to be the cost-minimizing remedy.

Eight of the nine cases in which rejection was awarded to merchant buyers are equally consistent with the hypothesis. The best example is Carl Beasley Ford v. Burroughs Corp.,[6] in which an automobile dealer purchased an electronic accounting system. The system was never accurate, and the seller was never able to correct the defects; so rejection appears to have been a cheaper remedy than damages. Resale by one of the parties was inevitable, and the manufacturer was more likely than the buyer to know about potential customers and alternative uses. Other cases are similar in that the court awarded rejection after evidence was presented showing that the defective goods were substantially valueless. Where goods are valueless, there is no resale advantage between the two parties. Therefore, rejection is the cheaper remedy since the court can avoid calculating the buyer's loss. . . .[7]

*Injury, Ignorance and Spite–The Dynamics of Coercive Collection**

Arthur Allen Leff

I. Settlement

Under the American law of contracts, after the other party has fully performed his obligations it is absolutely irrational for you fully to perform yours. If you, *D*, refuse voluntarily to repay v in full, C would always be better off accepting from you some lesser performance, $v - x$, so long as $(v - x) > (v - t_c)$.[1] Thus if v were 1000, and *D* could force C in recovering v to expend a t_c of 100 while suffering no

6. 361 F. Supp. 325 (E.D. Pa. 1973), aff'd, 493 F.2d 1400 (3d Cir. 1974).

7. [For a somewhat different treatment of the problem of nonconforming tenders, but one also based on economics, see Alan Schwartz, Cure and Revocation for Quality Defects: The Utility of Bargains, 16 B.C. Ind. & Com. L. Rev. 543 (1975).]

*80 Yale L.J. 1, 5-7, 11-12, 14-16, 26-29 (1970). Reprinted by permission of The Yale Law Journal Company and Fred B. Rothman & Company from The Yale Law Journal, Vol. 80, pp. 1 ff.

1. [Professor Leff uses these symbols as follows. *D* = debtor, the party owing payment; C = creditor, the party to whom payment is owed; v = the amount of the payment owed; t_c = the creditor's transaction costs in collecting payment; and t_d = the debtor's transaction costs in resisting payment.]

t_d himself, it would be rational for both *C* and *D* not to allow the coercive collection process to go to completion, but instead to settle on a repayment of anything between 901 and 999. . . .

. . . If one views coercive collection as a two-person game, and one takes account of the costs of playing it, it is not a two-person zero-sum game, but a two-person minus-sum game, and the parties can both gain by avoiding the play altogether, agreeing instead on [a] settlement.

When *D* has no t_d, he is comparatively indifferent as to whether the game is played or not; playing cannot make him worse off than not playing can. But what if *D* were forced to suffer, as part of the same coercive transaction which generated the t_c of 100, a t_d, perhaps one in excess of 100? . . . Again, playing the coercion game to completion would be minus-sum, and again both *C* and *D* would be well advised to . . . settle. But in this case *D* would no longer be indifferent as to whether the game were played or not, for a completed game, while hurting *C*, would hurt *D* more. Thus the ultimate settlement point [would tend to be] more to the taste of C. And if t_d could be made great enough relative to t_c, *D* might well decide to pay all of *v* in order to avoid the threatened playing of the game. Thus the actual posture of the parties will depend largely on the relative quantities of t_c and t_d which, in any particular context, coercive collection will predictably generate.

. . . [T]he "law," at least as embodied in legal process, is a very expensive mechanism for generating and channeling information and force.

One must to some extent be Hobbesian about it. If paid for and played from beginning to end, this expensive game does result in the acquisition of an immense bundle of power; behind every final judgment procured in any court in this country stands, ultimately, the United States Army, but even the intermediate mercenaries one buys—sheriffs, marshalls, judges—are usually sufficient unto the day. If someone has something that "belongs to" you and "the law" finally says so, so far as power can get it to you, that power will suffice. But the price one is supposed to pay for harnessing the Leviathan to one's cause is, essentially, the cost of moving it according to its own rather arcane principles, that is, the cost of due process.

The cost of due process is high for at least four reasons. First, due process demands that at the outset the court and its officers be wholly ignorant of what happened and it is expensive to educate them, at least using the pleading-and-playlet format of the common law. Second, the process of education cannot proceed on a generalized (mass-produced) basis; each case is theoretically hand-crafted.

Third, save in a court of small claims it is usually specialists (e.g., lawyers) who do the crafting. Fourth, because the courts do not allocate docket space by competitive bidding between plaintiffs, the creditor with the largest claim at stake must take his place in a "queue" behind plaintiffs with smaller claims. . . .

II. Repossession and Garnishment

. . . When *D* has defaulted in the performance he owes to *C*, there are two courses open to *C* under modern sales law. He may attempt via self-help to get back what he gave *D*, or he may at law attempt to get what *D* promised to give him. In some situations he may reclaim goods delivered under a contract (so far as that is physically feasible) and then, to the extent that that does not get him to where he would have been had the transaction gone through as planned, he may attempt to get additional things of value from *D* to make up the deficiency.

The attractiveness of the self-help process is obvious: it sometimes permits *C* to recover some large portion of v without incurring the usual expenses of going to law. It is, in effect, an opportunity to use state-of-nature power to get out of the *C* position without having either to buy off, or buy in, the Leviathan. It is not, of course, cost free; night work with tow trucks (or even with duplicate keys) entails expense, but seldom as much as a litigated lawsuit and subsequent execution. Moreover, it is possible in this way for *C* to recover all. This depends on the value to *C* of the goods seized and the amount of the debt outstanding at the time of the repossession, but given a high enough down payment and a low enough rate of depreciation for the goods, *C* may be made whole solely by retaking the goods.

But there are significant additional injuries inherent in self-help or judicially-ordered repossession which do not directly inure to *C*'s benefit but which may so increase t_d as to inhibit *D*'s breach. First is the loss which comes solely from being deprived of a good's use. Obvious examples are the repossessed fabricating machine, the padlocked plant and (in the context of non-business "productive" assets) the automobile which is the only access to work. This harm can be visited on *D* even if *C* does not get use and/or resale rights in the item, as the garageman's and lawyer's liens amply illustrate. Once deprivation is coupled with a power of resale, however, *D*'s loss increases and becomes more permanent. There are numerous things in the world that are worth much more to one person than they are to any other person. Consider the situation of a man owning a drill press which he uses in his business. He bought the press ten years ago and has used it since, not without problems, but by and large successfully. It has a slight tendency to yaw to the left and thus the operator must keep up a constant countervailing pressure. When used at top speed it tends to burn out its bearings. After some bitter experience all that is now known and integrated into its use pattern. What is also known and integrated is that it has no other material peculiarities; make but these few adjustments in use and it will drill press away to one's perfect satisfaction. The price of discovery has been spent. But put such a press up for sale, even in an honest, open auction market, and the sound buyer will discount his bid by the possibility of disaster. After all, it is a "ten-year-old press" of this manufacture and that appearance. It is a mystery. It may functionally be worth as much as it is, but it may be worth almost nothing. . . .

The potentiality of repossession and resale to increase strikingly the ratio of t_d to t_c by destroying value in *D*'s hands is manifest, often to a greater degree, in the operation of the other common execution technique, garnishment. But the attractiveness of garnishment from a creditor's point of view does not lie solely in its excitingly abusive possibilities. In theory, and often in practice, garnishment would be a lovely remedy to have even if it threatened no excess injury to the debtor. The way it is supposed to work is that the faucet whence liquid cash flows periodically to your debtor is directed to divert at least a little rivulet to you, at the faucet's cost and risk, until your cup runneth over. No need to grab possession of things, store them, manipulate them, push and shove them about until they turn into usable dereified value. No need to follow-up, time after time, the vicissitudes of sheriffs and auctioneers. Just wait, and to you all things will be given, slowly perhaps, but with interest. Indeed, from a creditor's point of view, garnishment is one of the most effective techniques for the noncooperative collection of debts ever devised.

But at least in certain circumstances, garnishment is additionally capable of inflicting grievous injuries upon a recalcitrant debtor that are frequently far in excess of the "injury" which paying the debt might entail. For though garnishment, like any lien, will interfere with the use of any liened property (a lien on a businessman's bank account will seriously interfere with his use of those liquid assets), the damaging impact of garnishment will likely be greatest if the debtor is a wage earner and the assets liened are his wages. One of the explanations for this is that a wage earner is likely to have a greater practical need for every penny of his wages than a businessman is likely to have for any particular liened asset; on the average, even with respect to equal-size garnishments there is a factor of differential marginal utility of money at work.

If, however, that were the only source of additional injury in wage garnishment it would be sufficient to do what has heretofore been done, severely limit the garnishable portion of a paycheck. The primary injury factor in wage garnishment lies elsewhere, however, in the effect of that legal process upon employer-employee relations. The trouble is that garnishment imposes transaction costs upon the employer. No one doubts that the mere processing of the writ costs the employer some money; the only dispute is about the amount. In addition there is always the risk of error in processing the writ and responding to it. Thus the garnished employer may find himself obligated to pay the same wages twice. In fact, it is precisely the cheapness and efficiency of the process from the creditor's (and even the debtor's) point of view which makes it so annoying to the employer. The reason it is so cheap is that it is the employer who organizes it, administers it, and risks its occasional errors. . . .

. . . [I]t is not surprising that employers frequently seek to dissociate themselves from the whole mess. Given the legal situation which makes reaction against the creditor difficult, if indeed at all possible, the employer is likely to take some kind of action against the employee-debtor. That does not mean that the garnished employer will always fire his employee. Frequently, one might guess, he acts by threatening the employee and pressuring him to extricate both of them by paying up. This is the course the creditor would prefer, at least as an economic matter. Or one can also imagine an employer taking the employee's part, either in fighting the claim with the employee or in supplying the wherewithal to settle it. But also with some frequency, the employer will fire the employee just to extricate himself from the whole garnishment *schreck*. And the same factors which militate in favor of such a decision simultaneously tend to maximize the brutal economic effect of any such discharge. . . .

III. Reputation

. . . If parties had perfect information about each other, the nature of collection law, perhaps even its existence, would be irrelevant. Picture a world without collection law, a peculiar exercise, but one not beyond the purview of useful analytic fantasy. After all, all one must do is imagine a society in which . . . the law did not enforce partly performed contracts at all, recognizing no claims on things of value except possession, or removal from possession by force or stealth. Would such an apparently massive change in American law make any difference? At first glance it would seem so, for in such a world the end-point of any collection game would seem to be identical with the walk-away point. In such a legal universe, it would appear at first glance to be irrational for sellers to enter into any credit transaction. Commerce would have to operate wholly through carefully planned instantaneous exchanges.

But that's silly. The decision about entrusting would still be made not on the basis of the *law's* effect on the rate of repayment, but on the basis of total experience with the *actual* rate of repayment, the shaping of which is a function of coercive law to only a limited extent. Partially executed contracts would for a variety of reasons continue to be completed some of the time despite the apparent legal and economic absurdity of such activity. Most people carry out their agreements because they carry out their agreements, not because awful things will happen to them if they don't. But equally important, even within an imaginary society which had credit transactions but no legal enforcement, there would still be a powerful source of non-ethical, rational impetus toward repayment. Assuming that trades involving temporal performance differentials are functional in the society, the power to take part in such transactions has value. It follows that exclusion from that system, or a disproportionally high entrance cost, both of which would follow from a reputation for default, is a species of rational economic coercion. That is, even if one's present purse is trash, one's good name may represent a large portion of any hope for a future purse.

"Reputation," then, for these purposes, may be defined as a measure of a particular person's positive or negative predicted deviation from the other party's average predicted [cost] of collecting from him. If information about a person's reputation were perfect, there would be no such thing as a collection problem. The sole "collection" practice would be precise pricing of the initial transaction. The endpoint of every individual credit transaction being identical with the price, no longer would any cheerfully quick repayer subsidize the slow, slovenly or evasive borrower.

Such prediction-perfecting information is impossible as a practical matter; generating it without cost is impossible even in theory. Even if such a state could eventually be approached by methods so efficient in gathering, correlating, evaluating and communicating information that the cost justified the expenditure, it might still be objectionable to do so on non-economic grounds: the loss of privacy and autonomy might itself be too high a "price" (on another but equally "real" scale) to pay. But that it is hopeless and maybe horrible to contemplate a world in which every individual's reputation was perfectly known hardly means that less than total information is valueless, or that it is not an important factor in collection strategy and efficiency. Since reputation has an effect upon the price at which one can deal on credit in the future, it is an asset subject to value fluctuation. Since reputation is a species of information, it can be modified by other information. Thus anyone who can deliver information which will modify a reputation, and communicate that reputation as modified to others, has the power to change the value of an item of another's property. Not only, then, can C threaten absolutely to decrease the value of *D*'s goods by repossessing them, or of his labor by garnishing his wages, but he can also threaten to depreciate the value of his reputation by communicating his displeasure. . . .

*Specific Performance**

Anthony T. Kronman

In an important article,[1] Calabresi and Melamed distinguish two different techniques for protecting legal entitlements. One they call a "property" rule and the other a "liability" rule. According to Calabresi and Melamed, a right or entitlement is protected by a property rule when it can be appropriated by a non-owner only if he first purchases permission to do so from the owner of the right. When a right is protected by a rule of this sort, one who appropriates it without the owner's permission will always be subject to a special sanction—typically, a fine or imprisonment. If a right is protected by a liability rule, in contrast, a non-owner who unilaterally appropriates it need only compensate the owner, after the taking, for any loss the owner suffers. The compensatory amount which a non-owner must pay for taking a right protected by a liability rule is set by a representative of the state rather than by the owner of the right in a voluntary transaction between owner and taker.

Calabresi and Melamed attempt to explain why some legal entitlements are protected by a property rule and others by a liability rule. They suggest that in certain cases the cost of negotiating the voluntary transfer of a right may be sufficiently high to frustrate the transfer. Where this is so, a property rule, which is intended to encourage transfers of this sort, is likely to promote an inefficient allocation of resources. This point is illustrated by automobile accidents and pollution torts. In both cases, a voluntary transfer of entitlements is almost certain to be prohibitively expensive: in the case of an automobile accident because of the cost of identifying the victim beforehand, and in the case of pollution torts because of

*Reprinted from 45 U. Chi. L. Rev. 351-375 (1978), by permission of the University of Chicago Law Review.

1. Guido Calabresi & Douglas Melamed, Property Rules, Liability Rules and Inalienability: One View of the Cathedral, 85 Harv. L. Rev. 1089 (1972).

free-rider and hold-out complications which are likely to make any negotiated settlement enormously difficult and time-consuming.

Where the costs of voluntarily transferring a particular entitlement are low, Calabresi and Melamed argue, economic considerations strongly support the use of a property rule to protect that entitlement. This argument is illustrated by the use of property rules in the criminal law: "[T]he thief or rapist . . . could have negotiated [a voluntary transfer of what he takes] without undue expense (at least if the good was one which we allowed to be sold at all) because we assume he knew what he was going to do and to whom he would do it."[2] In such cases, liability rules are inappropriate because they "represent only an approximation of the value of the object to its original owner and willingness to pay such an approximate value is no indication that it is worth more to the thief than the owner."[3]

In their discussion of property and liability rules, Calabresi and Melamed do not consider one very important species of legal right: the kind of right that is created by contractual agreement, the right to the performance of a promise. If one approaches the question from the theoretical perspective developed by Calabresi and Melamed, there are two considerations suggesting that all (or most) contract rights should be protected with a property rule. First, a contract typically involves only two parties. Where only two parties are involved, the special hold-out and free-rider difficulties that plague multiparty negotiations do not arise. Second, and more important, the parties to a contract already know one another and so need not worry about the special problems of identification arising, for example, in the case of automobile accidents. These considerations suggest that the costs of negotiating a voluntary transfer of contract rights are likely to be low. Following Calabresi and Melamed, this should be regarded as a reason for protecting rights of this sort with a property rule.

This view, however, appears to have had little influence in shaping our law of contract remedies. The normal remedy for breach of contract is, of course, money damages. Specific performance is exceptional. The Anglo-American law of contracts protects most contract rights with a liability rule, only a few with a property rule.

It is natural to wonder whether the peculiar mix of property and liability rules in the law of contracts can be explained on economic grounds. Although a great deal has been written about the efficiency of our law of contract damages, this more basic question has been largely ignored.

2. Id. at 1127.
3. Id. at 1125.

I. The "Uniqueness" Test

Specific performance is an equitable remedy which a court, in its sound discretion, may grant a promisee whose money damages remedy is inadequate. The situations in which courts are prepared to order specific performance are heterogeneous. Typical situations include contracts for the sale of land; contracts for the sale of heirlooms, antiques, and certain licenses and patent rights that can only be obtained from the promisor; contracts for the sale of a majority of shares in a particular corporation; and long-term output and requirements contracts. Occasionally, an employment or construction contract will also be specifically enforced.

The most important common feature of these diverse cases is the central role played by the idea of "uniqueness." If the "subject matter of [a] contract is unique in character and cannot be duplicated" or if obtaining "a substantial equivalent involves difficulty, delay, and inconvenience,"[4] a court will be more apt to compel specific performance. "The fact that such a duplicate or equivalent cannot be so obtained does not necessarily show that money damages are not an adequate remedy, but is a fact that tends strongly in that direction."[5] Conversely, if the subject matter of a contract is such that "its substantial equivalent for all practical purposes is readily obtainable from others than the defendant in exchange for a money payment, this fact will usually in the absence of other factors be sufficient to show that money damages are an adequate remedy for breach."[6]

In common discourse "unique" means without a substitute or equivalent. In the framework of conventional economic analysis, however, the concept of uniqueness is troublesome. Although it might seem reasonable to define the economic uniqueness of a good in terms of its attributes or properties, this is not the definition economists employ. Economists recognize this sort of uniqueness—they call it "technological" uniqueness—but they do not define the substitutability of goods in these terms. For the purposes of economic theory, the substitutability of a particular good is determined by observing consumer behavior, not by cataloguing the various properties of the good. If an alteration in the relative price of one good affects the demand for another, then these two goods are said to be economic substitutes. The degree of their substitutability is measured by what economists call the "cross-elasticity of demand."[7]

4. 5A Arthur Corbin, Contracts §1142 (1964).
5. Ibid.
6. Ibid.
7. George J. Stigler, The Theory of Price 31-33 (3d ed. 1966).

On this view, every good has substitutes, even if only very poor ones. Because all goods compete for consumer attention, a substantial change in the relative price of any good always affects the consumption of other goods. Economists are interested in determining how great a change in the price of one good is required to effect a change of given magnitude in the consumption of certain other goods. But these are really questions of degree, resting on the underlying assumption—fundamental to economic theory—that all goods are ultimately commensurable. If this assumption is accepted, the idea of a unique good loses meaning.

This point may be illustrated by a case that under present law would almost certainly be held to involve a unique good. Suppose that *A* contracts with Sotheby's to purchase the handwritten manuscript of Hobbes's Leviathan. If Sotheby's refuses to perform—perhaps because it has a more attractive offer from someone else—*A* will undoubtedly be disappointed. Yet no matter how strong his affection for Hobbes, it is likely there are other things that would make *A* just as happy as getting the manuscript for the contract price. For example, *A* may be indifferent between purchasing the manuscript at the specified price and having twenty-five hours of violin lessons for the same amount. If so, then *A* will be fully compensated for the loss he suffers by Sotheby's breach upon receiving the difference between the cost of twenty-five hours worth of violin lessons and the contract price. However, despite the fact that the manuscript has an economic substitute, a court would be likely to order specific performance of the contract (assuming Sotheby's still had the manuscript in its possession) on the ground that the subject matter of the contract is unique.

Pursuing the matter further, it is not difficult to see why *A*'s money damages remedy is likely to be inadequate and on the basis of this insight to develop an economic justification for the uniqueness test. Under a money damages rule, a court must calculate the amount Sotheby's is required to pay *A* to give *A* the benefit of his bargain. The amount necessary to fully compensate *A* is equal to the amount he requires to obtain an appropriate substitute. So in fixing the amount Sotheby's must pay *A*, the court must first determine what things *A* would regard as substitutes and then how much of any particular substitute would be required to compensate him for his loss.

In the hypothetical case, however, it would be very difficult and expensive for a court to acquire the information necessary to make these determinations. Perhaps some information of this sort would be produced by the parties. For example, *A* could introduce evidence to establish a past pattern of consumption from which the court might draw an inference as to what would be a satisfactory substitute for the manuscript. Sotheby's could then attempt to rebut the evidence and establish some alternative theory of preferences and substitutes. But of course it would be time-consuming to produce information this way, and any inference a court might draw on the basis of such information would be most uncertain.

Moreover, this uncertainty cannot be avoided by simply looking to the selling price of other manuscripts or even the expected resale price of the Hobbes manuscript itself (unless, of course, *A* is a professional dealer). It would be risky to infer the value *A* places on the Hobbes manuscript from the value placed on it by others, and riskier still to infer it from the value others place on the manuscripts of, for example, Harrington's Oceana or Locke's Second Treatise. If a court attempts to calculate *A*'s money damages on the basis of such information, there is a substantial probability that the award will miss the mark and be either under- or over-compensatory.

Of course, if a court could accurately identify a substitute for the manuscript, it could disregard the fact that *A* may value the manuscript in excess of the price that he, or anyone else, has agreed to pay for it. But where it is difficult to identify a satisfactory substitute (as I assume it is here), the goal of compensation requires that an effort be made to determine the value the promisee places on the promisor's performance, as distinct from what the promisee, or anyone else, has offered to pay for it.

Although it is true in a certain sense that all goods compete in the market—that every good has substitutes—this is an empty truth. What matters, in measuring money damages, is the volume, refinement, and reliability of the available information about substitutes for the subject matter of the breached contract. When the relevant information is thin and unreliable, there is a substantial risk that an award of money damages will either exceed or fall short of the promisee's actual loss. Of course this risk can always be reduced—but only at great cost when reliable information is difficult to obtain. Conversely, when there is a great deal of consumer behavior generating abundant and highly dependable information about substitutes, the risk of error in measuring the promisee's loss may be reduced at much smaller cost. In asserting that the subject matter of a particular contract is unique and has no established market value, a court is really saying that it cannot obtain, at reasonable cost, enough information about substitutes to permit it to calculate an award of money damages without imposing an unacceptably high risk of undercompensation on the injured promisee. Conceived in this way, the uniqueness test seems economically sound.

The following case will illustrate this point. *A* contracts with *B* for the purchase of 100 ball bearings. *B* breaches his promise to deliver, and *A* sues. If there are two or more sellers of ball bearings, and if there is substantial empirical evidence indicating that the cross-elasticity of demand is very high for ball bearings offered by different sellers, a court is warranted in assuming that most purchasers of ball bearings regard those sold by one seller as a satisfactory substitute for those sold by any other. For this reason, a court may also justifiably assume that a compensatory damages payment to *A* which enables him to purchase ball bearings from someone other than *B* (without incurring costs in excess of those he had originally anticipated), is likely to put *A* in precisely the position he would have been in had *B* performed his promise. The better the evidence that most buyers regard one brand of ball bearings as a substitute for another, the more confident a court can be that it has correctly calculated the magnitude of the promisee's loss.

It is of course true that even with very complete information about substitutes, a court may err in calculating money damages. It might be that *A* prefers *B*'s ball bearings to those of any other seller because he believes they will last longer. Normally this preference would be reflected in the market price for *B*'s ball bearings; if one brand of ball bearings lasts longer than others, it should command a premium of some sort. But this may not be the case. It may be that *A*'s knowledge and experience with *B*'s ball bearings are not shared by other purchasers. If *A* attaches some special value to *B*'s ball bearings not reflected in their price, he will be undercompensated if his damages are calculated on the assumption that the cost of a substitute is the cost of obtaining ball bearings from another seller. To prevent undercompensation, *A* must prove that he will suffer a special loss as a result of *B*'s breach, but this may be difficult and costly to establish.

The conclusion to be drawn from this analysis is a simple one. Whenever a court calculates money damages, there is some risk that it will undercompensate the injured party. But the magnitude of this risk is inversely related to the completeness and reliability of the information on which the court bases its award. At one extreme, where there is a well-developed market generating evidence of substitutability, this risk is minimal. At the other extreme, where there is no market or at most a few isolated transactions, this risk is substantial. There is a point, between these two extremes, at which the risk becomes unacceptably large (or, what amounts to the same thing, at which the risk can only be reduced by incurring unacceptable costs). This is the point separating those contracts that are specifically enforceable from those that are not—the point to which the uniqueness test obliquely refers.

There is an additional, perhaps less obvious, reason why money damages are most likely to be undercompensatory when the subject matter of a contract is unique. In searching for a particular good, a consumer will almost always incur certain costs—the costs of locating the good, obtaining information about it, and so on. When these costs are incurred before formation of a contract, they are generally not compensable under a money damages rule. Under a money damages rule, a disappointed promisee is usually unable to recover precontractual search costs, and is limited, instead, to compensation for the increased cost of obtaining a substitute after the promisor breaches.

Where a good is not unique, information acquired in searching for the good is likely to have some independent usefulness, which will survive a breach by the promisor. For example, if *A* wishes to purchase ball bearings, he will first obtain information about the ball bearing market. If he then makes a contract with *B*, which *B* breaches, *A* will of course have to obtain some additional information before he can arrange for a substitute purchase. But much of the information acquired prior to his contract with *B* will still have value for *A*—it will still be economically useful. On the other hand, where *A* contracts for the purchase of a unique good, say, a one-of-a-kind stamp, this is less likely to be the case. *A* may have expended a substantial sum in locating the stamp, and although it is possible that some of the information acquired in the course of his search will be generally useful, it is more likely that much of the information is valuable to *A* only because it aided the discovery of the particular stamp.

Under a money damages rule, *A* will not be compensated for these search costs if his seller breaches. But of course he will be compensated (that is, he will obtain the desired return) if he can compel specific performance of the contract. That precontractual search costs are not compensable under a money damages rule is less worrisome when the information generated by the search represents a capital stock that can be exploited in subsequent transactions. But when it does not, the likelihood is increased that money damages will be undercompensatory.

The economic justification for the uniqueness test consists in showing that the test draws the line between specific performance and money damages in the way that most contracting parties would draw it were they free to make their own rules concerning remedies for breach and had they deliberated about the matter at the time of contracting. If this is true, the uniqueness test promotes efficiency by reducing the costs of negotiating contracts.

II. Specific Performance and the Ex Ante Interests of Promisor and Promisee

When would the parties to a contract freely agree to a judicially enforceable provision giving the promisee an option to specifically enforce the other party's promise? Other things equal, a promisee will always prefer to have such a provision included in his contract for it gives him an additional right which he would not otherwise possess. Other things equal, a promisor will always prefer a contract without such a provision—a contract, in other words, which he may unilaterally breach on the condition that he make a subsequent compensatory payment to the promisee. Consequently, a promisee intent upon writing a specific performance provision—a property rule—into the contract will have to pay to secure the promisor's consent. Similarly, a promisor must make a payment of some sort in order to exclude a provision for specific enforcement from the contract. If and only if the benefit which the promisee realizes from a specific performance provision exceeds the cost of the provision to the promisor will the provision be included in the final contract.

When the subject matter of a contract is unique, the risk is greater that the promisee's money damage remedy will be under-compensatory. Since a right to compel specific performance reduces this risk, promisees—as a class—should be willing to pay more for a provision giving them a right of this sort when there is no developed market generating information about the value of the subject matter of their contract.

However, if a specific performance provision is likely to be more beneficial to a promisee when the subject matter of his contract is unique, it is also likely to be more costly to his promisor under the same circumstances. In the first place, a right in the promisee to compel specific performance increases the probability of costly negotiations for transfer of the promisee's contract rights. This of course always reinforces the promisor's preference for a money damages rule. However, a promisor is likely to regard this reason as especially compelling where the subject matter of his contract is unique, since the lack of information about substitutes will almost certainly make the parties' negotiations longer and more complicated and thus more costly.

Second, if the promisee is entitled to specifically enforce the promisor's obligation, the promisor who wishes to breach will have to make a release payment to the promisee and buy his way out of the contract. The amount of the release payment demanded by the promisee will be greater than what the promisor would have to pay the promisee under a money damages rule. This is so whether or not the subject matter of the contract is unique. But the difference between what the promisee would accept in exchange for a release and what he may be expected to receive under a court-administered money damages rule is likely to be larger where the subject matter of his contract is unique because the risk that court-awarded damages will be undercompensatory is greater. For these two reasons, a specific performance provision will be more expensive to the promisor when the subject matter of his contract is unique.

Thus far, it would appear that the benefits to the promisee and the costs to the promisor of a specific performance provision are proportional; both are greater when the subject matter of the contract is unique. There is, however, an additional consideration influencing their ex ante deliberations that provides some basis for thinking that the parties to a contract will be more likely to provide for specific performance when the subject matter of their agreement is unique.

The cost of a specific performance provision to the promisor will be determined, in part, by his own estimate of the likelihood that he will want to breach the contract. If he fully intends to perform, and thinks breach unlikely, a promisor will be less hostile to a contract with a specific performance provision than he would otherwise be. One important factor influencing the promisor's thinking in this regard is the probability that he will receive a better offer for his goods or services in the interim between formation of the contract and performance. The higher the probability, the greater the likelihood he will want to breach. The probability of receiving an attractive alternative offer may be especially low where the subject matter of the contract is unique. In this case there is by definition no developed market, transactions are spotty at best, and therefore a promisor will often justifiably think it highly unlikely that he will receive any alternative offer (let alone a better one) for the promised goods or services. Indeed, where the subject matter of his contract is genuinely unique, a promisor may estimate the likelihood of a preferable alternative offer as close to zero, and thus be nearly indifferent as to what remedies the promisee will enjoy in the highly unlikely event of breach.

Although the promisor thinks breach highly improbable, the promisee may not. Despite the promisor's insistence that he intends to perform, the promisee may be skeptical. As long as he is anxious about the promisor's performance, the promisee will be concerned about the adequacy of his own remedies, and where the subject matter of his contract is unique he will likely have a decided preference for a contract that gives him the right to specifically enforce the other party's promise. Consequently, in the case of a contract for a unique good or service, the benefits the promisee derives from a specific performance provision are apt to outweigh its costs to the promisor, who, free of doubts about his own reliability, may regard the inclusion of such a provision as a relatively costless way of enticing the promisee to enter the contract on advantageous terms.

In the case of a contract for non-unique goods or services, by contrast, the existence of a developed market increases the likelihood that the promisor will receive alternative offers before he has performed the contract. The promisor will therefore be anxious to retain the freedom and flexibility enjoyed under a money damages rule.

Moreover, where the subject matter of his contract is not unique, the promisor will be especially anxious to avoid the additional transaction costs that would be incurred if he had to negotiate a voluntary transfer of the promisee's contract rights. Although these costs will tend to be smaller where the subject matter of the contract is not unique, they can never be less than some fixed minimum (the cost of contacting the promisee, notifying him of an intention to breach, obtaining a release statement of some sort, and so on). If there is an established market in the goods or services involved, prices will ordinarily be grouped rather closely around a single point. The probability is therefore greater that any alternative offer the promisor does receive will not be sufficiently high to cover the cost of negotiating a release plus the amount he must pay the promisee for the release. Thus the likelihood increases that a promisor who has agreed to a specific performance provision will find himself in the undesirable position of having to decline an alternative offer that he would accept under a money damages rule. In some cases the alternative offer will cover the release payment but will be refused solely because the transaction costs of negotiating a transfer of the promisee's contract rights are prohibitively high. The promisor should therefore be willing to make a small payment to the promisee, perhaps in the form of a slightly reduced contract price, in order to exclude a specific performance provision and thus avoid these potential transaction costs. Because the transaction costs avoided by the promisor would not have benefited the promisee, the latter will be better off with the reduced contract price if he regards the risk of undercompensation under a money damages rule as minimal. The promisee will generally regard this risk as slight where there is a developed market generating information about suitable substitutes.

III. Specific Performance and Freedom of Contract

I have argued that ex ante considerations provide some basis for thinking the uniqueness test is economically rational. The argument attempted to show that if contracting parties were entirely free to select their own remedies, their choice would generally correspond to the mix of property and liability rules adopted by the law of contracts. But ex ante arguments for the efficiency of a particular legal rule assume that individuals remain free to contract around that rule, and a legal system that denies private parties the right to vary rules in this way will tend to be less efficient than a system that adopts the same rules but permits contractual variation.

This raises an important question. If, under the uniqueness standard, a promisee does not have the right to specifically enforce a particular promise, can he create a right of this sort by private agreement? It is easy to imagine situations in which a promisee might wish to do this. For example, *A* may wish to enter a specifically enforceable contract for the purchase of ball bearings because he believes that special considerations, which will be difficult to establish in a lawsuit, are likely to make his normal money damages remedy undercompensatory. Similarly, some sellers of ball bearings may be willing to agree to a specific performance provision in order to secure a better contract price or a new customer. For example, a new entrant in an industry, lacking an established reputation, may conclude that agreeing to a specific performance is the least costly way to communicate to prospective clients his confidence in his ability to perform.

In the well-known case of Stokes v. Moore,[8] the plaintiffs, partners operating a small loan business, hired and later dismissed defendant Stokes. They then sued to enforce a covenant not to compete, which had been incorporated in the contract of employment. The contract contained a clause stating that if Stokes breached his promise not to compete, "a restraining order or injunction [might] be issued and entered against [him] in any court of equity jurisdiction."[9] Although it affirmed the trial judge's decision to issue a temporary injunction, the Supreme Court of Alabama viewed unfavorably the parties' attempt to create a right to injunctive relief by private agreement:

> We do not wish to express the view that an agreement for the issuance of an injunction, if and when a stipulated state of facts arises in the future, is binding on the court to that extent. Such an agreement would serve to oust the inherent jurisdiction of the court to determine whether an injunction is appropriate when applied for and to require its issuance even though to do so would be contrary to the opinion of the court.[10]

8. 262 Ala. 59, 77 So. 2d 331 (1955).
9. Id. at 61, 77 So. 2d at 334.
10. Id. at 64, 77 So. 2d at 335.

The court added, however, that "the provision for an injunction is important in its influence upon an exercise of the discretionary power of the court to grant a temporary injunction."[11]

Perhaps judicial unwillingness to honor provisions such as the one in *Stokes* reflects a desire to avoid private abuse of a powerful and intrusive remedy. This is a legitimate concern. But if the purpose in scrutinizing a private agreement of the *Stokes* variety is to prevent abuse by an overreaching promisee, this end could be served as adequately and more directly by other legal tools—for example, by traditional common-law doctrines of fraud, duress, and good faith. If the concern is abuse of the contracting process, courts should focus on the voluntariness of the parties' agreement.

It may be, however, that courts prohibit the private creation of injunctive remedies not because specific performance provisions evidence some procedural unfairness in the parties' dealings, but rather because they are perceived to be substantively unacceptable limitations on personal freedom. A provision of the kind involved in *Stokes* might be viewed as a modified contract of self-enslavement,[12] an attempt to transfer an entitlement whose transfer is prohibited by law (an "inalienable" right or entitlement in the scheme proposed by Calabresi and Melamed). This idea is echoed in some of the older specific performance cases involving construction and employment contracts.

Such an argument carries little weight in a case like *Stokes*, where the promise to be enforced is a negative one—a promise to refrain from doing something. More importantly, the argument is overdrawn. It is true that certain forms of domination (for example, slavery and peonage) are regarded as inherently bad. Our legal system prohibits these forms of domination, whether they are created by consensual act or by force. On the other hand, there are many relations of domination recognized and protected by law so long as they are voluntarily established and maintained. The relation created by a contract of employment is an important example of legally protected domination.

The nature, completeness, and duration of self-imposed limitations on personal freedom determine their legal and moral acceptability. Slavery is objectionable because it approaches total control. By contrast, the domination an employer exercises is partial and limited—the employer only controls certain aspects of his employee's life. Nevertheless, employees are not generally required by judicial order to submit to employer control. The judicial order, it may be argued, makes a crucial difference: if the employment relation is

11. Ibid.
12. [See p. 256 infra.]

created or maintained by the threat of judicial sanctions, it is almost certain to be plagued by acrimony and ill will. But although the unpleasantness of a forced employment relation should certainly be taken into account by an employer contemplating a suit for specific performance, it should not be a basis for refusing to impose such a relation upon parties who have agreed to an injunctive provision in their contract. Moreover, if the party in breach anticipates that the relation will be unbearable, he can buy his release from the contract.

There is another common explanation for the reluctance of courts to enforce private injunctive agreements: the specific enforcement of contracts (especially employment and construction contracts) entails special administrative costs which normally can be avoided under a money damages rule, and private individuals should not be allowed to shift the special costs associated with this form of relief to the taxpayers who subsidize the legal system. The assumption on which this argument rests, however, may be mistaken. It is ancient dogma that specific performance necessarily means increased judicial involvement in the enforcement and supervision of contractual duties. This might be true, but so might the opposite conclusion: if all promises were specifically enforceable, or if private parties were permitted to contract into a specific performance rule at their discretion, a resulting increase in the voluntary transfer of contract rights might lower the number of breaches—and perhaps even of lawsuits—and in this way reduce the actual involvement of courts in contractual relationships.

In comparing the administrative costs, broadly defined, of a property rule mandating specific performance with a liability rule directing an award of money damages, the following factors must be taken into account: (1) the frequency of litigation under both rules; (2) the administrative cost of resolving litigated disputes under both rules; (3) the portion of the administrative costs involved in dispute resolution borne by the parties and the portion borne by society under both rules; (4) the likelihood and administrative cost, under each rule, of pretrial settlement; and (5) special institutional costs, such as the potential loss in court prestige that results from noncompliance with a direct order to perform, and the cost of invoking the court's contempt powers.

To say the least, it is unclear how these administrative costs add up under the two rules. Until these questions have been explored, it is unwise to assume that the legal invalidity of private agreements purporting to create a right of specific enforcement is justified on the ground that specific relief is a more costly remedy than money damages and that a greater portion of the costs of specific performance is borne by third parties.

A promisee could attempt to achieve indirectly the special protection associated with a property rule by insisting, as a condition of entering the contract, that the other party promise to pay a penalty upon breach—a penalty in excess of any damages payment necessary to compensate the promisee. A provision of this sort, if enforceable, would have the same effect as the sanctions that back up both injunctive orders and criminal prohibitions: it would encourage the prospective taker of an entitlement to purchase the entitlement from its owner in a voluntary market transaction. However, a contractual provision that is deliberately designed to be penal will not be enforced. The legal prohibition of penal clauses is an important obstacle facing parties who wish to contract into a property rule.[13]

*Liquidated Damages, Penalties and the Just Compensation Principle: Some Notes on an Enforcement Model and a Theory of Efficient Breach**

Charles J. Goetz & Robert E. Scott

For more than five centuries, strict judicial scrutiny has been applied to contractual provisions which specify an agreed amount of damages upon breach of a base obligation. Although the standards determining the enforceability of liquidated damage clauses have developed novel and labyrinthine permutations, their motivating principle has remained essentially immutable. For an executory agreement fixing damages in case of breach to be enforceable, it must constitute a reasonable forecast of the provable injury resulting from breach; otherwise, the clause will be unenforceable as a penalty and the non-breaching party will be limited to conventional damage measures. . . .

The continuing vitality of the penalty doctrine can best be explained by examining the assumptions underlying the application of the "just compensation" principle to liquidated damage provisions. The central assumption is that enforcing an in terrorem clause overcompensates the non-breaching party. The current penalty rule is therefore envisioned as a protection against (1) unfair recovery in excess of justifiable reliance, and (2) the performance of a contract through fear of the penalty, where it would be more efficient economically to breach. The assumption of overcompensation, however,

13. [See pp. 260-261 infra.]

*Reprinted, by permission, from 77 Colum. L. Rev. 554, 556, 559-562, 572-573, 578-588, 594 (1977).

is gratuitous. We argue below that its uncritical application frequently induces a costly reexamination of the initial allocation of risks and may also deny the non-breaching party either adequate compensation for the harm caused by the breach or the opportunity to insure optimally against such harm. . . .

I. The Role of Damage Agreements Under the Just Compensation Standard

. . . [C]ontracting parties have incentives to negotiate liquidated damages clauses whenever the costs of negotiating are less than the expected costs resulting from reliance on the standard damage rule for breach. There are two primary factors which might induce the decision to negotiate:

> (1) The expected damages are readily calculable, but the parties determine that advance stipulation will save litigation or settlement costs;
>
> (2) The expected damages are uncertain or difficult to establish and the parties wish to allocate anticipated risks.

Of course, these factors may be present singly or in combination.

Pre-breach agreements will not be legally enforceable, however, unless two requirements coincide. First, the agreement must be a reasonable forecast of just compensation for the anticipated harm that would be caused by the breach. Second, the possible damages which might result from the breach must be uncertain and difficult to estimate. However, liquidated damages provisions have seldom been voided solely because the damages were easy to estimate. Instead, courts have considered the degree of uncertainty an influential factor in determining the reasonableness of the estimate. If the conditions inducing damage agreements are viewed on a continuum, the application of the penalty rule becomes clearer: as the uncertainty facing the contracting parties increases, so does their latitude in stipulating post-breach damages.

. . . The traditional justification for post-breach inquiry is prevention of "unjust" punishment to the breacher, i.e. compensation exceeding the harm actually caused. This justification has been expressed in two distinct forms. One basis for invalidation is the presumption of unfairness: liquidation damage provisions are unreasonable—a penalty—whenever the stipulated sum is so disproportionate to provable damages as to require the inference that the agreement must have been effected by fraud, oppression, or mistake. The other major basis for invalidating agreed remedies is that, since the courts set damages based upon the principle of just compensation, parties should not be allowed to recover more than just compensation from the courts through a privately concocted alternative arrangement, even one fairly negotiated.

The common theme of these decisions is that a disproportion between the stipulated and the anticipated damage justifies an inference of overcompensation. In turn, overcompensation implies either bargaining unfairness or an objectionable in terrorem agreement to secure performance. This line of reasoning suggests two benefits which may be expected from the current rule invalidating penalties. First, the cost of identifying unfairness may be reduced by a standard rule-of-thumb based on disproportion. Second, an enforceable in terrorem clause might discourage promisors from breaching and reallocating resources where changed circumstances would ordinarily create efficiency gains from this behavior. Inducing performance under these conditions is a misallocation which prevents the net social gain that would result from non-performance.

. . . However, this analysis incorrectly assumes that, rather than negotiating out of the penalty, the promisor who is subject to an in terrorem clause will inevitably undertake an inefficient performance. In addition, there is no basis for the apparent assumption that the premium placed by the promisee on performance is valueless. Indeed, the market paradigm on which the compensation standard is based requires a contrary presumption; a promisee has a recognizable utility in certain in terrorem provisions and this utility is frequently reflected in willingness to pay a price for such clauses. . . .

[The authors next develop a model of efficient contract damages, demonstrating as Barton had, p. 154 supra, that a rule of damages that compensates the victim of the breach for the losses caused by the breach is the efficient rule. They show, however, that it does not follow that an agreed-upon penalty clause is inefficient even though the penalty is expected to exceed the amount required for compensation. While it might seem that such a clause might induce the performing party not to breach even when, because the gains from breach exceeded the losses (i.e. the amount that would be due under a compensation rule), breach was more efficient than performance, the authors demonstrate that this reasoning is unsound. If the performing party agrees to split his gains from breach with the paying party, the latter will be better off with such a deal than he would be by insisting on performance; the deal will be made; and hence the contract will not be performed, no matter how great the penalty for nonperformance was. Besides showing that an agreed-upon penalty clause is not inefficient even though it deviates from the compensation principle of contract damages, the authors demonstrate that the compensation principle itself, as implemented in the law of contracts, is inadequate from an economic standpoint because it fails to take account of real, but not readily monetizable, elements of loss from breach of contract.]

. . . Why have ex post legal sanctions been adopted in which subjective damage elements may not be recognized? Optimal systematic rules establishing post-breach compensation may require some limiting assumptions concerning the extent of harm caused by contract breach. These assumptions reduce the direct or administrative costs of implementing the compensation principle through the legal mechanism, but purchase these advantages at the price of breaking the equivalency between the damage rule and the actual subjective harm which is difficult to assess. In assessing damages, two limiting assumptions—valuation and foreseeability—may operate to prevent the recovery of idiosyncratic value. The rule requiring the loss to be foreseeable, designed to control for causation and remoteness, can be overcome in some circumstances by pre-contract disclosure of the causal relation between the loss and the breach and of the parameters of reasonable foresight. The requirement of valuation, given the existence of a market, is a more rigid barrier to the recovery of subjective losses. First, the "value" of a promised performance is generally limited to "the amount of money that can be obtained in exchange for it in some market." Second, where the exchange value is conceded to be inadequate, and "value to the owner" is substituted, any "fanciful or sentimental" value will be excluded on the grounds that such losses are too speculative and uncertain. Together, these valuation and certainty limitations may well preclude the non-breacher's recovery of idiosyncratic value[1]. . . .

II. An Enforcement Hypothesis: A Model of the Most Efficient Insurer

Applying an efficiency analysis to contract damage rules suggests the following enforcement hypothesis:

In the absence of evidence of unfairness or other bargaining abnor-

1. . . . A classic example of the denial of idiosyncratic value as compensation for breach is provided in Carpel v. Saget Studios, Inc., 326 F. Supp. 1331 (E.D. Pa. 1971). In *Carpel,* the court granted defendant's motion for summary judgment in a diversity action for breach of a contract to take wedding photographs on the ground that plaintiff's allegations of sentimental value were, as a matter of law, insufficient to achieve the monetary jurisdictional limits of the federal court. The court held that "the alleged lost sentimental value of the pictures is so highly speculative that it is not a proper element of damages for consideration by the jury. There are no guidelines available to aid the jury in determining a dollar value for this loss. . . . Since in this case the photographs never came into existence, there is the additional question of whether they would have had any sentimental value at all."

malities, efficiency would be maximized by the enforcement of the agreed allocation of risks embodied in a liquidated damages clause.

This hypothesis is based on the assumption that liquidated damage provisions will (1) reduce transaction costs where the parties determine that the costs of negotiation are less than the expected costs of litigation upon breach; and (2) reduce the error costs produced upon breach when the promisee is denied recovery for his non-provable idiosyncratic value. It follows, unless enforcement produces other inefficiencies, that enforcing agreements negotiated ex ante will enhance efficiency by permitting the parties to minimize the costs of transacting. The current penalty rule seems to produce significant inefficient effects by limiting the possibilities of mutually beneficial exchange. In addition, negotiated damage agreements are now subject to post-breach attack as penal sanctions. This increases the direct costs of litigation in all cases—even where the agreement is upheld.

The situational model which will be used to test the hypothesis can be illustrated by the hypothetical Case of the Anxious Alumnus. Assume the following facts: Dean Smith, a 1957 graduate of the University of Virginia, is a loyal, some would say fanatical, fan of the University of Virginia Cavalier college basketball team. For the 1976 season, after years of second division performances in the highly competitive Atlantic Coast Conference, the Cavaliers finally produce a team that advances to the finals of the conference championship tournament at the end of the season. Through hard work and financial sacrifice, Smith acquires twenty-five tickets to the conference championship game in Landover, Maryland. Smith enters into contract negotiations with the Reliable Charter Service, Inc. to arrange for a bus to transport himself and twenty-four other Virginia fans to Landover on the day of the game. The standard price for this service is $500.

Smith considers his attendance at the game to be of supreme importance and does not relish the thought of anxious and sleepless hours worrying whether the bus will arrive and successfully accomplish the desired purpose. He is eager to quiet his fears by securing adequate protection in case Reliable fails to perform. However, under the current legal rule Smith cannot protect his unprovable reliance either by securing fully compensating post-breach damages or a bargained-for stipulation of the value of performance. Consequently, he is forced to consider other protective alternatives.

One option is to attempt to insure against the subjective consequences of breach with a third party (Lloyd's of London, for example). Assuming that a policy could be secured and enforced up to the assessed valuation of performance, adding the proceeds of the policy to the award of provable expectation damage which Smith could recover under existing law would provide him with full recovery for his idiosyncratic value upon breach by Reliable.

Alternatively, Smith could negotiate for direct insurance from Reliable or any of its competitors offering the same service. Dean might propose to pay Reliable $1,000 for the charter service if, in return for the additional premium, Reliable would agree to a penal sanction of $10,000 upon failure of performance. The stipulated sum of $10,000 would represent that amount at which Dean would be indifferent between performance and breach. Unfortunately, insurance purchased directly from the promisor, Reliable, is not a real alternative; the mere labelling of the idiosyncratic damages as pursuant to an "insurance" contract is unlikely to prevent a perceptive court from recognizing that such payments are de facto equivalent to a penalty. Hence, legally enforceable insurance for damages not recoverable as breach damages is in practice obtainable only from third parties.

This insurance model and the enforcement hypothesis pose the following issues for resolution:

(1) As between the third-party insurance company and the promisor, which is the more efficient provider of insurance?

(2) To what extent do the rationales supporting the "indemnity principle" suggest significant additional social costs due to enforcement of agreements at stipulated values?

(3) Assuming changed conditions after an insurance agreement has been negotiated, such that the value of performance to the promisor is reduced, does enforcement of a penal sanction produce a high probability of inefficient effects?

(4) What presumptions of unfairness can be developed to cope with those special classes of cases where bargaining abnormalities would produce inefficient effects if stipulated damage provisions were enforced?

A. The Efficient Insurer Model

Identifying the efficient insurer requires an analysis of the costs of providing insurance. At what price would a profit-making commercial enterprise be willing to offer Smith $10,000 worth of protection against the contingency of bus failure en route to the fabled final game of the championship?

Perhaps the overwhelming element in the cost of this insurance would be the expected value of the underwriting loss to the insurer. This expected value is defined as the product pR where p is the probability of non-performance and R is the recovery payable to the insured. In addition, an insurer will also have other transactions costs, such as the costs of ascertaining the true probability p and the costs of negotiation and communication with the insured. These transaction costs will be subsumed in the portmanteau variable T, so that the total cost C of a policy paying R on the occurrence of an event with probability p can be summarized as

$$C = pR + T.$$

We assume that since the services in question are marketed competitively in the presence of alternative sellers, the cost of breach insurance to Smith will be $(1 + \alpha)\ C$ where α is the competitive rate of return or profit for the insurer. The question, then, is whether C would differ between the bus company and the third-party insurer.

An obvious focal point of interest is the transaction cost element T. Here, it is tempting to argue that the advantage lies with the bus company. In the first place, the bus company is in a superior position to know the breakdown probability p. Secondly, many of the other transactions costs normally incident to customer communication may be negligible when communication is already being undertaken relative to the carriage service itself. Hence, T may be lower for the bus company and thus so would C and the offering price of the insurance to Smith.

Actually, however, the transactions cost element is not the strongest argument in favor of the bus company as the most efficient insurer. The bus company's main advantage derives from its power to exercise some control over the breakdown probability p. This can be illustrated by examining how the rational enterprise will make the maintenance and repair decisions which affect the breakdown probability.

Figure [10] reflects the fact that there is an inverse relationship between the probability of breakdown and the level of maintenance.[2] Each additional "dose" of maintenance reduces p, presumably by smaller and smaller amounts as the maintenance level increases.

In Figure [11], the technological facts of Figure [10] are converted into their investment implications. If D is the damage liability upon non-performance (here $10,000), the *expected* damages decline as increasing maintenance decreases the probability of breakdown. Since these expected damages are pD, the saving in expected damage costs attributable to a marginal unit of maintenance is rD where r is the marginal reduction in p brought about by the maintenance increase. Hence, the "marginal damage reduction" curve in Figure [11] is simply a schedule of the value rD for alternative maintenance

2. "Maintenance" is used as a summary word for all bus company activities which potentially affect the breakdown probability.

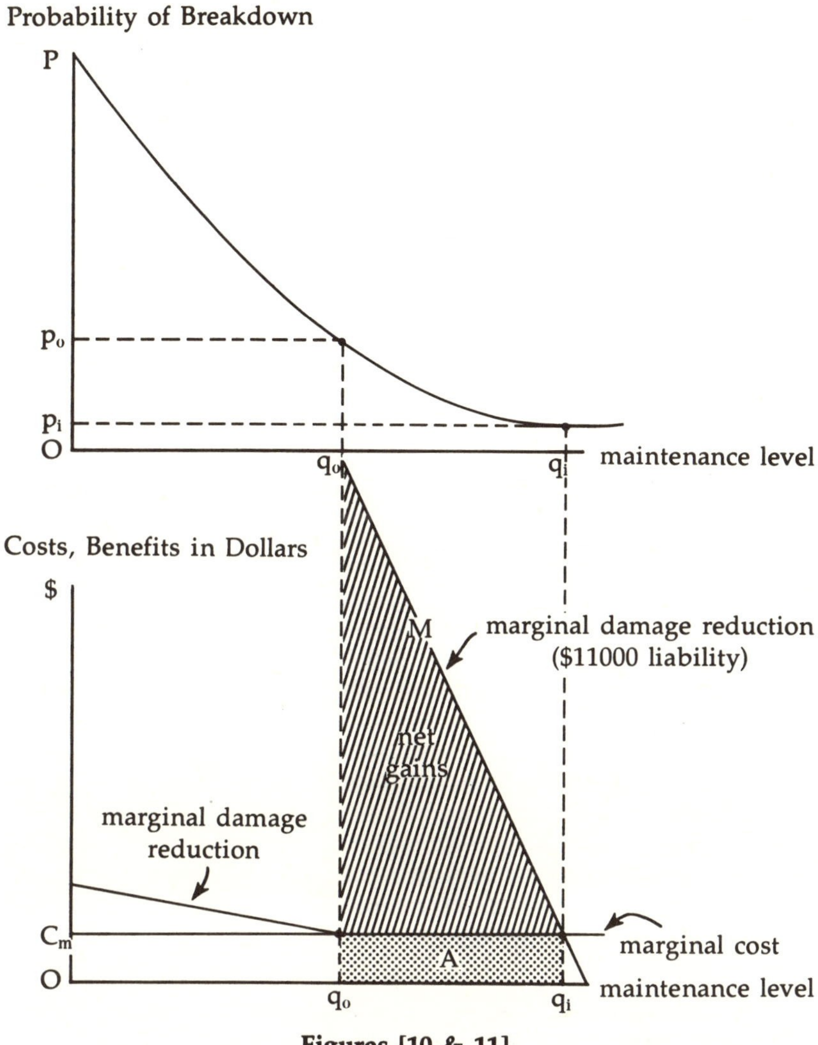

Figures [10 & 11]

levels.[3] The "marginal cost" curve is, in turn, a reflection of the incremental costs incurred as the maintenance level is varied.[4] The firm will maintain the buses up to the point where the last or marginal unit of maintenance is "just worth it," i.e. where the

3. This is an inverse relationship as it is closely related to the curve in Figure [10]. As the maintenance increases (from q_0 to q_1), the marginal damage reduction decreases, eventually tending to zero, a point where increased maintenance does not reduce the probability of breakdown at all.

4. In Figure [11], this marginal cost is a constant. Each additional unit of maintenance has the same cost.

marginal damage reduction curve intersects the marginal cost curve at quantity q_0.[5]

Absent the \$10,000 liquidated damage agreement, the bus company anticipates that D will embody only the standard objective damage recoverey which, let us assume, amounts to \$1,000 for the Smith bus trip. This anticipation underlies the marginal damage reduction curve in Figure [11] and is the ultimate basis for the p_0 breakdown probability. In computing the expected underwriting loss, the third party insurance company will therefore arrive at a value ($p_0 \cdot \$10{,}000$).

Suppose, however, that the bus company can offer the same insurance. The expected value of damages is now based, not on a D of \$1,000, but on a D of \$1,000 actual provable damages plus \$10,000 insurance recovery. Therefore, the new marginal damage reduction curve (M) for maintenance will be exactly eleven times higher than the original one. The company will expend additional maintenance costs A, equivalent to the shaded area in Figure [11] or $C_m \cdot (q_1 - q_0)$, and the breakdown probability will consequently decline to p_1.

What are the implications of these adjustments on cost? For the bus company, the insurance cost must now be modified to reflect the net benefits of possible risk-avoidance efforts. Hence, the appropriate cost function for the provision by the bus company of \$10,000 coverage is

$$C = (p_0 \cdot \$10{,}000) - [\$11{,}000\,(p_0 - p_1) - A] + T$$

where the terms in the square bracket are net gains from adjusting maintenance levels: $(p_0 - p_1)$ is the change in breakdown probability, its product with \$11,000 is the expected damage reduction, and A is the added cost of maintenance.[6] We know that these net gains are

5. If the company would continue to maintain the buses, spending another unit of maintenance beyond q_0, it would cost C_m but reduce the expected damage liability by an amount less than C_m. This would clearly be uneconomical for the bus company.

Note that this decision of q_0 maintenance also determines the probability p_0 in Figure [11], the probability of breakdown when the bus company stops its maintenance and the bus actually sets out.

6. Note that the relevant cost function for the bus company is the expected loss *due to the provision of the insurance.* The present expected loss to the bus company is

$$C_1 = (\$11{,}000 \cdot p_1) + A + T.$$

In computing the insurance premium, the pre-insurance expected loss of

$$C_0 = \$1{,}000 \cdot p_0$$

(provable damages upon breach multiplied by probability of breach) must be deducted. The cost function is thus

$$C_1 - C_0 = (\$11{,}000 \cdot p_1) - (\$1{,}000 \cdot p_0) + A + T.$$

positive from the nature of their computation and that they would not be achieved when the third-party insurance is purchased. Hence, even where the transaction cost component T is identical for the alternative insurers, the bus company has an efficiency advantage equal to the square-bracketed term in the equation above. (Graphically, this quantity is represented in Figure [11] by the crosshatched triangular area of net gains above the shaded area of incremental costs A and below the new marginal benefits curve M.)

The preceding argument has been that non-enforcement of liquidated damages provisions has the result of inducing individuals to protect against otherwise non-recoverable losses through special third-party insurance. This is likely to be an extremely inefficient alternative since there are strong economic arguments that suggest that the vendor is the lowest-cost insurer against non-performance. Although our argument has been framed in terms of the bus company example, a similar conclusion may be generalized to all cases in which the vendor has some control over the probability of externally caused non-performance.

In sum, many people may not want to make deals unless they can shift to others the risk that they will suffer idiosyncratic harm or otherwise uncompensated damages. To the extent that the law altogether prevents such shifts from being made or reduces their number by unnecessarily high costs, it creates efficiency losses; that is, it prevents some welfare-increasing deals from being achieved.

B. The Indemnity Principle: The Problems of Wagering and Moral Hazard

The preceding model assumed that legal principles governing the formation and enforcement of aleatory contracts would permit the promisee to secure third-party insurance to cover unprovable idiosyncratic value. We concluded that the third-party option is likely to be relatively inefficient. The availability of even the inefficient option must be examined more carefully, however, in light of the principle of indemnity. Since a contract insuring property rights is a contract of indemnity only, payment upon loss is generally based not upon the face value of the policy, but upon the provable economic loss. Does this general limitation on recovery suggest reasons

---

The equation in the text is equivalent to this one. It is presented in a more complicated form to demonstrate the relationship between the bus company's insurance and the third party's. The first term is equal to the cost function of the insurance company ($p_0 \cdot \$10,000$). The bracketed term, which is positive, is then subtracted which indicates that the bus company's insurance is less expensive by this amount than the third-party insurance.

against enforcing insurance of idiosyncratic value? The policies enjoining wagering and moral risk are traditionally identified as the reasons supporting the indemnity rule. Examining these policies, however, reveals adequate substitutes for controlling the increased social costs of the enforcement hypothesis.

Traditional analysis distinguishes a gambling contract which creates risk, from a valid insurance contract which merely allocates existing risk to a third party for a price. The indemnity principle prevents parties who shift existing risk by contract from creating additional risk through over-valuation of the insured object. Collection of insurance coverage for an over-valued "loss" yields a net gain to the insured. Such a contract is therefore viewed as a gamble by the insured on the occurrence of such a "loss."

Clearly, the policy against wagering is potentially inconsistent with the enforcement hypothesis. Assuming that the bargaining process is fair, the hypothesis requires enforcing all stipulated agreements without inquiry into the nature of the underlying risks. An additional post-breach inquiry would increase transaction costs by requiring proof of valid risk allocation by the promisor. This issue, however, appears collateral to the central question of enforcement. If it is determined that wagering contracts are violative of public policy, a stipulated damages provision used to disguise a gambling transaction would be unenforceable. Without empirical data indicating that wagering contracts are prevalent in liquidated damages provisions, a presumption of legitimate risk allocation would appear to reflect more accurately the use of stipulated damage provisions in commercial contracts. The danger of wagering seems sufficiently remote to leave invalidation to explicit proof of a gambling transaction, rather than using it as a rationale for invalidating all agreements which allocate risks based on unprovable reliance.

The second rationale supporting the indemnity principle is the perceived moral hazard that accompanies the allocation of idiosyncratic risk to a third-party insurer. The very nature of unprovable value heightens the risk that the assessed valuation will overcompensate the insured, providing incentives for fraudulent claims of loss. Limiting the recovery to provable loss, irrespective of the stipulated value, will reduce the moral hazard by some amount. Again, the choice that must be resolved is whether the savings produced by reducing the frequency of fraudulent claims of loss exceeds the increase in enforcement costs due to undercompensation and reduced contracting flexibility. Absent empirical evidence, there is no persuasive reason to invalidate an entire range of legitimate bargains in order to produce an indeterminate reduction in moral risk. . . .

. . . The valued policy doctrine permits parties to an insurance contract to avoid the limitations of the indemnity principle by stipulating a valuation which will be payable upon proof of loss. Stipulated value policies originated in marine insurance because valuation based on indemnity was too imprecise to insure full recovery. They are commonly used to insure items of tangible personalty where market value is not a reliable indicator of subjective worth.

This valued policy alternative indicates that the indemnity principle can be efficiently applied. Where the expected costs of undervaluation exceed the benefits in reducing the probability of fraud or wagering, the legal system will enforce insurance contracts covering nonprovable idiosyncratic value. We conclude, therefore, that existing legal restraints on fraud and gambling are adequate substitutes for controlling the increased social cost resulting from the enforcement hypothesis.

C. Changed Conditions: Inefficient Performance and Induced Breach

The enforcement hypothesis proves a persuasive basis for a new legal doctrine as long as the assumption of fairly-bargained exchange justifies confidence in end-result efficiency. A challenge to that assumption is posed, however, by the problem of changed economic conditions. The nature of the problem can be illustrated by examining the case of Rockingham County v. Luten Bridge Co.[7] In *Rockingham* the county contracted with the bridge company to construct a bridge to provide a connecting link with a hard surface road to be constructed simultaneously. Subsequently, the construction of the road was terminated during a political dispute, and the county moved to repudiate the bridge contract. At the time of repudiation, the company had incurred $2,000 in reliance costs. The company continued work on the bridge until six months after repudiation and then instituted action against the county for $18,500 representing work performed under the contract.

Denying recovery for the work performed after repudiation, the court applied classic mitigation principles in holding that, "it is inflicting damage on the defendant without benefit to the plaintiff to allow the latter to insist in proceeding with the contract."[8] The court in *Rockingham* correctly identified and applied the just compensation principle to the changed conditions problem. Any further recovery would have produced a disincentive to efficient breach, and prevented a preferred reallocation of resources by the promisee.

7. 35 F.2d 301 (4th Cir. 1929).
8. Id. at 307.

Assume, however, that in the initial contract the county attached a substantial, nonprovable value to full performance, and secured a promise by the company that upon nonperformance it would pay a stipulated damage of $20,000. The cancellation of the road building project reduced the value of the performance to the county to $1000. Assume further that a change in raw material prices will produce an estimated $15,000 loss to the bridge company if full performance is required. Under the current legal rule, the in terrorem $20,000 damage clause would be unenforceable and the parties would be left to conventional damage measures. This would induce a breach by the bridge company, and the payment of $1000 expectation damages—an efficiency-maximizing result. However, under the enforcement hypothesis the county is provided with an incentive to demand full performance by the company and simultaneously attempt to induce breach in order to collect the $20,000.

Inefficient performance is the first problem posed by the changed conditions dilemma. The efficiency criterion indicates that the bridge should not be built where the return performance is no longer valued by the promisee. Given ordinary market assumptions, however, the bridge never will be built. Since performance has become less valuable to the promisee he is induced to negotiate with the promisor to permit him to buy out from performance. The county would be willing to accept any payment over $1,000, and the bridge company would be willing to pay any amount less than $15,000. These sums represent the respective gain and loss which will accrue to each party if the bridge is completed. At some point, they will negotiate an agreement to divide the gains from breach that would be captured entirely by the breaching bridge company under the current legal rule.

Clearly, renegotiation produces transaction costs that would not arise under the penalty rule. It is tempting to measure these costs against the expected savings in litigation costs and propose whichever rule promotes the least costly alternative. However, since this measurement can only be made ex post by the legal mechanism, taking this approach would produce additional litigation costs in all cases. The enforcement hypothesis is the more efficient rule, because it permits an ex ante measurement of the expected costs. The parties must be assumed to have taken all the expected costs into consideration at the time they elected to negotiate an agreed damages provision. In sum, the very existence of a freely negotiated agreed damages provision is compelling presumptive evidence that it constitutes the cost-minimizing alternative. This analysis is consistent with contract rules which assign responsibility for allocated risks, and excuse performance only where circumstances indicate risk was unassigned.

The second problem posed by the changed conditions dilemma is the increased incentive that the promisee has to induce breach in order to capture the $19,000 premium contained in the in terrorem clause. The prospective payoff would encourage the county to urge full performance and then attempt to induce a breach rather than negotiate an efficient release from the contract. The enforcement hypothesis would produce an increase of some amount in the social costs of policing against fraud or non-cooperation by the promisee. However, absent empirical data indicating the extent of these costly effects, the least restrictive assumption—invalidation for induced breach when those facts are identified—is suggested again. In any event, the moral risk produced by the changed conditions dilemma is reduced where the promisor provides the insurance. Third-party insurance in this situation would produce the heightened risk of collusive breach between the contracting parties. . . .

III. Conclusion

Challenging the penalty rule demonstrates that it has numerous costly effects. First, the rule denies true compensation to the promisee with non-provable idiosyncratic wants, inducing him either to protect those wants with inefficient third party insurance or to suffer exposure to inefficient breaches. Secondly, assuming that cases of non-compensable idiosyncratic value are rare, the rule produces a more significant cost by inducing review of the entire continuum of cases where liquidated damages provisions are intended to reimburse true losses which are to any extent uncertain.

The modern development of unconscionability as a unifying fairness principle presents a less costly alternative to the sweeping invalidation powers exercised under the penalty rule. With our present enhanced access to information and consequential greater accuracy in individual risk evaluation, an enforcement model which facilitates the recovery of difficult-to-prove values would appear to maximize the allocative efficiency of the contracting process.

In sum, contemporary cost-benefit analysis suggests that the traditional penalty rule is anachronistic for several reasons: (1) the efficiency costs of the rule are now apparent in the light of modern analysis; (2) the market imperfections once addressed by the rule have become empirically less important; and (3) more selective legal doctrines, such as unconscionability, have developed as remedies for those market imperfections which retain practical importance.

*Seller's Recovery of Overhead Under UCC Section 2-708(2): Economic Cost Theory and Contract Remedial Policy**

Richard E. Speidel & Kenneth O. Clay

. . . [C]onsider [Figure 12] and assume that the market is purely competitive, that is, price is not influenced by this seller's actions. At the time of contracting the seller's average fixed costs (overhead) will decrease proportionately for every additional unit of production secured. Put another way, as volume increases the seller can spread his fixed costs over more units to produce cost savings. On the other hand, the seller's average variable cost (*AVC*) and average total cost (*ATC*) will be decreasing or increasing depending upon the volume of production. Initially, average variable cost will decrease, but at some point in overall operation it will begin to rise.[1] When the increase in average variable cost equals and exceeds the per unit decrease in average fixed cost (*AFC*), average total cost will begin to rise. Still assuming a purely competitive market, if at the time of contracting both average fixed and variable costs are decreasing, the seller is in what we call stage I. If average variable cost is increasing but average total cost is still decreasing, then the seller is in what we call stage II. If average variable cost is rising and average total cost is either constant or rising, so that increases in average variable cost equal or exceed the per unit decrease in average fixed cost, then the seller is in what we call stage III.

Our thesis is that if the seller is in stage III, the allowance of overhead as damages will put him in a better overall position than if the buyer had fully performed. In stage III relieving the seller of the necessity of incurring increasing variable costs will at least equal the savings that the seller could have achieved if permitted to spread overhead costs to particular units of production covered by the con-

*Reprinted, by permission, from 57 Cornell L. Rev. 681, 695-697, 703-707, 711-712 (1972).

1. Average variable cost will decrease at first because of increased efficiency or because additional resources can be procured at lower prices. Assume, for example, that a certain factory is designed to employ approximately 100 workers. Further assume that labor is the only variable resource. If only one worker is employed, the output will be extremely small. If one additional person is employed, the output will more than double because of the resultant division and specialization of labor. If the doubling of variable cost results in a greater than proportionate increase in output, average variable cost decreases. Throughout stage I, the added variable cost results in a more than proportionate increase in output and average variable cost decreases. At some point, however, the addition of more workers will result in less output per worker, largely because of the law of diminishing returns. . . . At this point, average variable cost begins to increase. . . .

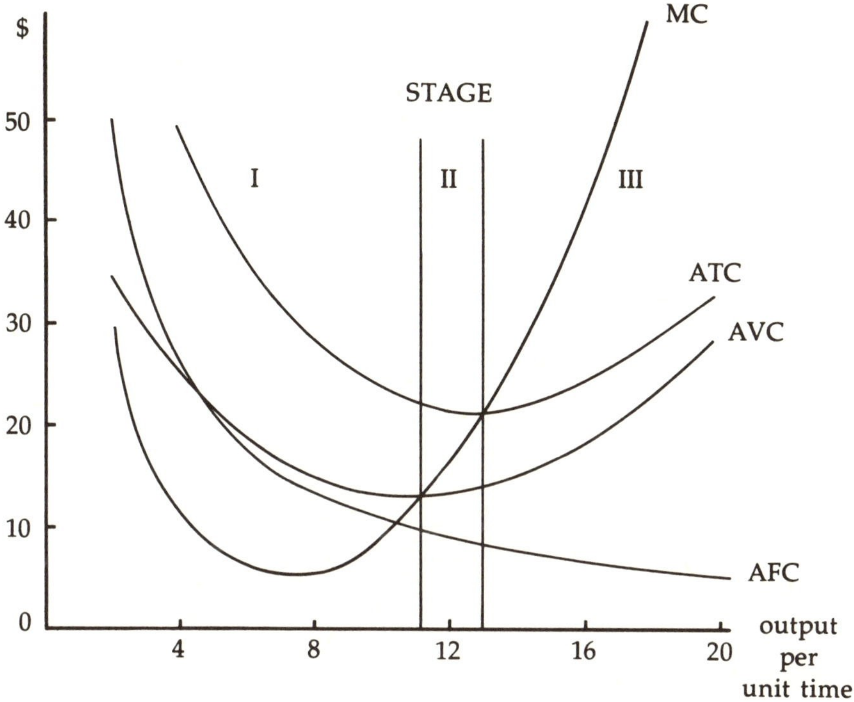

Figure [12] Short run average and marginal cost functions.

tract. Put another way, since average variable costs increase more than average fixed costs decrease in stage III, the reallocation of overhead to other work upon breach, although increasing the aliquot share of overhead costs to some extent, will be exceeded by the savings in not having to incur the projected variable costs. Thus for the seller in stage III, which is the most likely place for the rational firm seeking to recover total costs and earn a profit, the recovery of overhead results in overcompensation because it places the seller in a better overall profit position than could have been achieved by full performance. . . .

Under economic cost theory the propriety of allowing overhead as damages for breach of contract depends upon two conditions at the time of contracting: the competitive character of the market and the stage of production in which the seller finds himself. The stage of production can readily be determined from the particular seller's cost curves. A detailed determination of the competitive character of the seller's market would require an examination of the demand sector of the economy. For purposes of this analysis, however, competitive character can be determined by comparing the relative level of market prices to the average variable cost for the stage I seller and the average total cost for the stage II seller. The comparison is not necessary for the stage III seller, since the competitive character of the market does not affect the propriety of his overhead recovery. When the market price is higher than the average variable cost for the stage I seller or the average total cost for the stage II seller at the relevant level of output, the market is not purely competitive. If the market price for the relevant level of output is lower than the average variable cost for the stage I seller or the average total cost for the stage II seller, the market can be treated as though it were purely competitive. Let us now combine stages of production with competitive character to test, in general, the propriety of overhead recovery.

In stage I, both the average fixed and average variable cost curves are decreasing at the time of contracting. Under purely competitive conditions, it is unlikely that the rational seller would choose to produce in stage I because the contract price will not cover even the variable expenses incurred in production, not to mention overhead. If, however, a contract was entered into under these conditions and breached by the buyer, the stage I seller still should not recover overhead. Although the savings lost through the inability to spread overhead to additional units of production would not be equalled or exceeded by the savings retained by elimination of additional variable costs, the projected loss on full performance precludes reimbursement for fixed costs. In a noncompetitive market, however, the rational seller would operate in stage I if the market price exceeded average variable cost, which is the purely competitive price ceiling. Upon breach, then, the seller should recover unsalvaged variable costs plus all of the overhead allocated to the contract and, depending upon the relationship of the contract price to average variable and average total cost curves, these costs plus any lost profit.

In stage II, the average variable cost curve is increasing but the average total cost curve is still decreasing. Under purely competitive conditions, the rational seller might choose to produce in stage II since the contract price, even though less than average total cost, would cover all variable costs incurred and some portion of the aliquot share of overhead. No profit, however, could be earned because the market price would not exceed average total cost. However, upon breach by the buyer, the seller should recover as damages all overhead allocated to the contract plus variable costs actually incurred up to the breach, subject to an adjustment for any loss that would have been suffered on full performance. In a noncompetitive market, the price may be higher than average total cost. Thus upon full performance the seller would have recovered all of the costs plus a profit. Upon breach, the seller should recover only that part of the overhead allocated to the contract which is not neutralized by the savings he retains in being relieved of incurring variable costs, and because full performance would not produce a loss.

In stage III both the average total and average variable cost curves are rising. Under both purely competitive and noncompetitive conditions, the market price will exceed average total cost and the seller, by full performance, may recover all fixed and variable costs plus some profit. Upon breach, however, the loss to the seller in being unable to spread overhead to another unit of production is neutralized or exceeded by the savings realized in being relieved of the need to incur variable costs for full performance. This is because the average fixed cost curve is decreasing and the average variable cost curve is increasing. Thus if the seller is not harmed by the inability to spread overhead further, overhead recovery upon breach by the buyer results in overcompensation and is inconsistent with the primary purpose of compensatory damages.

In Vitex Manufacturing Corp. v. Caribtex Corp.,[2] the Vitex Corporation was engaged in the business of chemically treating cloth for duty free importation into the United States. For this purpose, Vitex maintained a plant in the Virgin Islands and was entitled to process a specified quantity of material under the Virgin Islands quota system. Caribtex was in the business of importing cloth into the Islands, securing its processing, and exporting it to the United States.

In the fall of 1963 Vitex, with an unused portion of its quota but no customers, closed its plant. Caribtex acquired some Italian wool and the parties entered a contract in which Vitex agreed to process 125,000 yards of the Caribtex woolen material. Subsequently, Vitex reopened its Virgin Islands plant, ordered the necessary materials, recalled its work force, and made the necessary preparations to begin performance. Caribtex repudiated before performance had started, and Vitex brought suit to recover lost profits. The Third Circuit, after stressing the difference between fixed and variable costs, upheld the recovery of overhead as necessary to put the seller in the same position as if full performance had occurred, noting that "the successful businessman must set his prices at sufficient levels to recoup all his expenses, including overhead, and to gain profits."[3]

The economic cost theory developed in this article provides a framework for critical evaluation of the propriety of this overhead recovery. As previously suggested, recovery of part or all of the overhead upon breach by the buyer is proper only if the seller is in a market that is not purely competitive in stages I or II, or in a market

2. 377 F.2d 795 (3d Cir. 1967).
3. Id. at 798.

that is purely competitive in stage II subject, however, to adjustment for losses that the seller would have incurred on full performance. In those situations the rational seller would not contract unless the price was sufficiently high to recover all of his variable costs and have some return to his fixed resources, as either an aliquot share of overhead or as profits. Even so, the seller would be at a competitive disadvantage in stages I or II and would continue there only if faced with a limited demand for his product. Presumably, the rational buyer would contract on this basis only if he had no choice in selecting the seller or if he were unable to contract at a price that would exist in a purely competitive market.

Although the *Vitex* opinion recites no facts conclusive as to the seller's stage of production or the competitive character of the market, the probabilities are that Vitex was in stage III of a noncompetitive market. First, Vitex may have already processed sufficient quantities of wool to place it in stage III for the relevant time period before closing the plant. This suggestion is reinforced by the incentive to operate in stage III rather than stages I or II. Second, the character of the market is indicated by the fact that to meet the needs of Caribtex, Vitex opened a plant previously closed for lack of orders. Limited demand is strong evidence of a noncompetitive market. Based upon these data, economic cost theory would not support the recovery of overhead.

Without sufficient data, however, conclusions based upon probabilities as to what rational sellers and buyers would do are rather thin. In fact, because of limited demand and excess capacity, Vitex may very well have been in either stage I or stage II in a noncompetitive market even though the rational seller would have preferred to be elsewhere. The point is that the court's conclusion based upon legal analysis would be consistent with economic cost theory only under a limited set of circumstances; the probabilities are against the existence of those circumstances in *Vitex*. . . .

The overhead dilemma is most sharply posed when the buyer repudiates a contract for the sale of manufactured goods and the seller, after properly stopping performance, seeks damages under UCC section 2-708(2). Under economic cost theory, overhead recovery is proper only when the seller at the time of contracting is either in a noncompetitive market in stages I or II, or in a purely competitive market in stage II, subject to adjustment for losses that would have been incurred upon full performance. It is not proper for the stage III seller since the savings realized from not having to incur variable costs equal or exceed the loss from being unable to spread fixed costs over one more unit of production. The overall profitability of the firm will not be reduced by reallocating these fixed costs to other units of production. Thus, unless the "reasonable overhead" language of UCC section 2-708(2) is interpreted to deny overhead recovery to the stage III seller, the damage award will put the seller in a better overall profit position than he would have gained from full performance.

Under this interpretation, new problems of proof are presented for the seller. In addition to proving variable costs saved with reasonable certainty, the seller will be required to produce empirically estimated cost curves to refute the probability that he is operating in stage III. These curves are also relevant in determining both the competitive character of the market and the extent to which the estimate of net profit prevented was realistic. Since only the seller has ready access to the data necessary to develop these curves, the burden of production should arguably fall on him. A failure to produce these curves, then, should limit the seller's recovery to variable costs actually incurred at the time of breach, as adjusted for reasonable salvage and reallocation to other jobs. . . .

*Microeconomics and the Lost-Volume Seller**

Student Note

To a considerable extent, the question of how to treat the lost-volume seller presents a problem in economics. The arguments asserted for providing him a remedy in excess of the traditional contract-price-minus-market-price damages are anchored to the peculiar economic characteristics of his market, characteristics which cause him theoretically to "lose" a sale whenever one of his buyers breaches. Briefly stated, these critical characteristics are (1) a limited number of potential buyers, each of whom will eventually buy from the seller if he can supply them, and (2) a present capacity to supply all of these potential buyers at the going price. . . .

Over the long run each producer has considerable latitude in choosing the combination of production inputs (such as plant capacity, equipment, and laborers) that he will utilize in manufacturing products. But in the short run, which is the period over which the producer will "lose" a sale if he is to lose one, his latitude is considerably decreased. To expand the rate of production in the short run, the producer's only option may be to increase the size of his work force or the amount of overtime worked.

*Reprinted, by permission, from 24 Case Western Reserve L. Rev. 712-719, 728-729 (1973). Copyright 1974 by Case Western Reserve University.

As the producer continues to expand his rate of output, by increasing the size of his work force, for example, without corresponding increases in his plant or equipment, he will eventually reach a point where overall efficiency is sacrificed, where the increase in total product brought about by each new worker gets smaller and smaller. . . . Translated into terms of dollar expenditures, it means that as output is increased beyond the point of diminishing marginal product, if *W* represents the dollar amount of wages paid to each worker, for each additional *W* expended the resulting addition to total output constantly decreases. Phrased differently, the *marginal cost* of producing each additional unit of output increases. What results is a marginal cost (*MC*) curve similar to the one depicted in figure [13]. The horizontal axis measures flow of output, in terms of units produced over a given time period. The vertical axis measures costs per unit. At the level represented by point Q_1, diminishing marginal returns set in. The curve designated *AFC* represents the average fixed costs (such as interest payments, depreciation on plant and equipment, and a reasonable amount of total profit) per unit of output and can be used as an approximation for "reasonable overhead" as used in section 2-708(2) [of the Uniform Commercial Code]. At low levels of output, this curve slopes sharply downward as fixed costs are divided among an increasing number of units; as output increases this slope tapers off significantly. The *AVC*

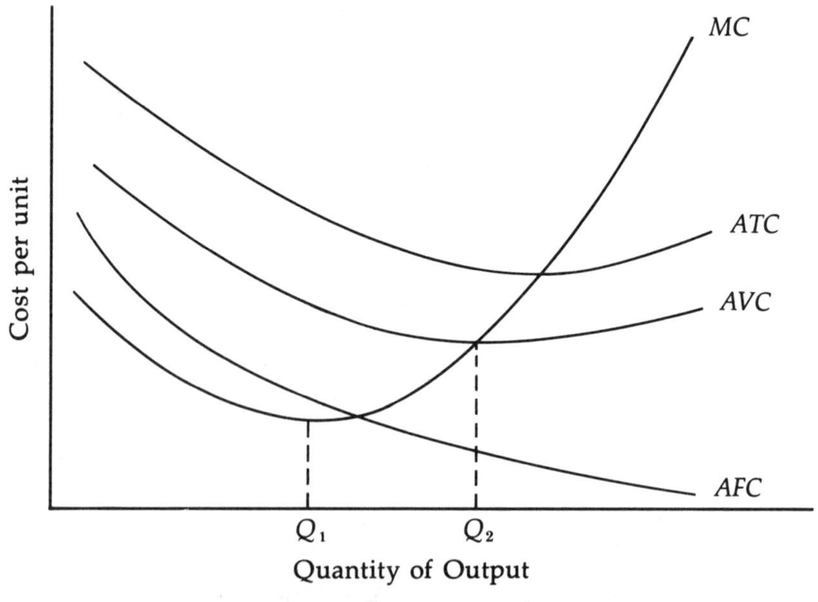

Figure [13] Shortrun Cost Curves

curve signifies the average variable cost incurred in producing a given level of output. Average variable cost initially decreases, reflecting the low marginal cost of making additions to total output. The curve continues to decline even after the point of diminishing marginal returns is reached and up until the point Q_2 where average cost is no longer in excess of marginal cost. The average total cost (*ATC*) curve represents the sum of average fixed costs and average variable costs. Like the *AVC* curve, the *ATC* curve has its minimum point at its intersection with the *MC* curve.

An industry is said to embody *pure competition* when it is comprised of numerous firms producing a standardized product. The critical element is that each producer's share of the total output of the industry is so insignificant that, in his view, his decisions as to the amount of output to produce and ultimately to sell have no impact upon the price he is to receive for his goods. A good example is the small grain farmer. The price to be paid for his grain is determined by the aggregate supply and demand for the entire industry's product. At this market price, the individual grain farmer believes he can sell as much (or as little) output as he chooses to produce. In other words, the demand curve for the product of each individual farmer is horizontal, as represented in figure [14], with price equal to the prevailing market price P^*.

The analysis of how much output an individual firm will decide to produce over a given period rests on the assumption that the firm will make its output decisions with the objective of maximizing the total amount of profits it expects to receive. Because total profits are equal to total revenues minus total costs (fixed and variable), increasing output results in increased profits only so long as the increment in total revenue derived from selling each additional unit exceeds the increment in total costs incurred in manufacturing it.

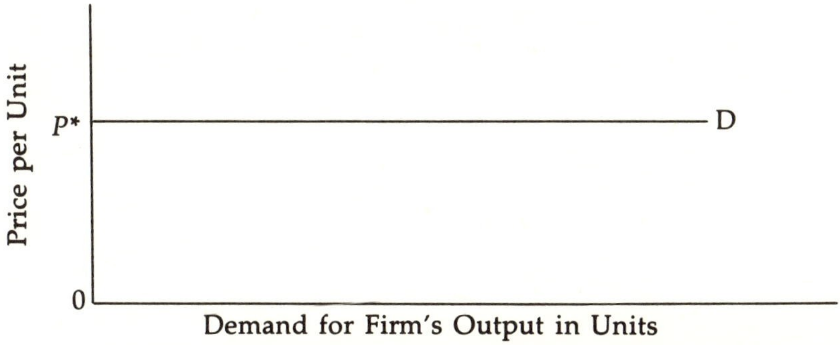

Figure [14] Demand Curve for Individual Firm

Consequently, the firm should expand its production to the point where the marginal revenue from manufacturing a new unit is no longer greater than the marginal cost, or, phrased differently, to the point where marginal profit is reduced to zero.

For the firm operating under pure competition, like the small grain farmer, the marginal revenue derived from selling each unit is constant. Since the firm can sell as many units as it pleases at the going market price, the marginal revenue of the *n*th unit as well as the marginal revenue of the first unit is equal to that market price. To maximize its profits the firm should therefore produce that level of output where the marginal cost of the last unit produced equals the going market price. This is illustrated in figure [15]. Marginal reve-

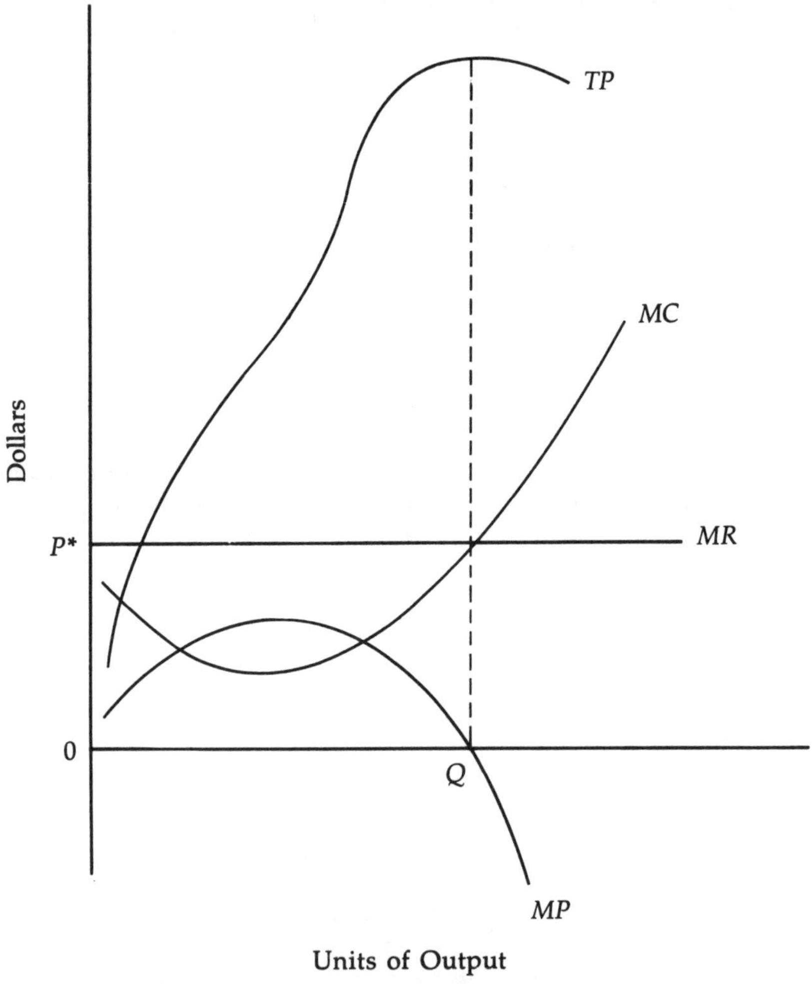

Figure [15]

nue (MR) is equal to P^*, the going market price, at all levels of output. The MC curve is taken from figure [13]. The MP curve, signifying marginal profits, represents the difference between MR and MC at each level of output. The TP curve is total profit, which can be viewed as cumulated marginal profit. From the graph it can be seen that the firm will maximize its total profits by producing Q units, which is the output level at which $MP = 0$ and the MC curve intersects the MR curve.

This pure-competition model, while providing a useful heuristic for analyzing the firm's production decisions, does not accurately depict the situation which has been postulated as facing the lost-volume seller. In pure competition, there can never be a "lost" sale, since by definition the firm can dispose of whatever output it produces at the going market price. If the lost-volume seller is to have any existence whatsoever it must be in an industry where the market and the market price is somewhat sensitive to the quantity of product which the seller is marketing. But after these problems with applying the model have been recognized, the pure-competition framework still sheds light on some of the issues critical to the lost-volume problem.

One of these issues is the notion . . . that many sellers have an unlimited capacity to supply their product at the market price. If the profit-maximization hypothesis has validity, it follows that a firm with price and cost curves similar to those depicted in figure [15] will decide to produce and sell Q units and Q units only, notwithstanding the fact that it can sell more and notwithstanding the fact that it possesses the physical capacity to produce more. While the hypothetical firm could expand its rate of production to sell $Q + 1$ units in a given period, to do so would prove unprofitable. The clear result of this reasoning is that in the event one of the firm's buyers breaches a sales contract, and the firm goes ahead and produces and sells Q units over the time period in question, as it should in order to maximize its total profits, the firm should not be entitled to recover a profit from the breaching buyer. Even if the firm could somehow prove that the buyer's breach caused it to "lose" the sale of what would have been the $(Q + 1)$th unit, the firm should not recover the profits from the $(Q + 1)$th sale, because, for profitability reasons, the $(Q + 1)$th sale would never have been actually made.

The inequity of allowing the pure-competition firm to use section 2-708(2) to collect an extra profit for the $(Q + 1)$th sale is demonstrated in figure [16]. In that diagram, C equals the average total cost of producing Q units. Since it is assumed that the industry in which the firm is operating is in longrun equilibrium, C is equal to the price P^*, and the only profit which the firm earns is its normal profit. Operating at its profit-maximization point Q, where MC equals MR,

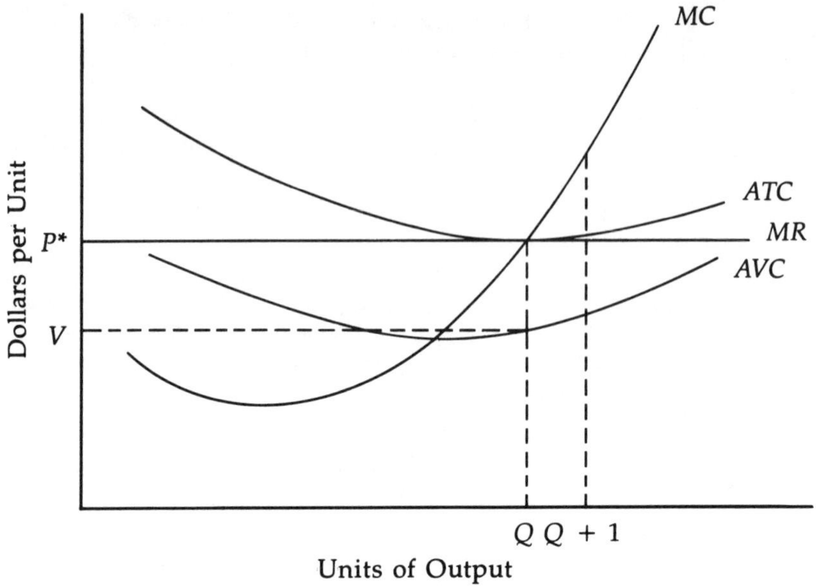

Figure [16]

the firm has average variable costs equal to V, and generates total revenues ($P^* \times Q$) which exceed total variable costs by an amount sufficient to pay the firm's fixed costs and return to the firm a normal profit. Had the firm actually sold and been forced to produce $Q + 1$ units, this total excess would have been decreased by the amount by which the marginal cost of producing the ($Q + 1$)th unit exceeds P^*. Moreover, because ATC is greater than P^* at $Q + 1$, the ($Q + 1$)th sale would have reduced the firm's total profits below a normal rate of return.

The clear implication of the preceding analysis is that the firm should not be allowed to recover a profit because it did not make the ($Q + 1$)th sale. But unfortunately for the breaching buyer, a court of law, if presented with this case and persuaded that the firm "lost" a sale because of the buyer's breach, is unlikely to employ this economically correct marginal-profit analysis. Instead, it would probably estimate the profit that was foregone on the lost sale by the average profit and contribution to overhead earned by the firm on the sales it did make. If this is the case, the firm will be awarded damages in the amount of $P - V$, an undeserved recovery, since had the sale in fact occurred, the firm would have lost money.

Admittedly, it does not follow from the preceding discussion that every sale which a profit-maximizing firm loses would actually have caused a reduction in total profits if it had been carried out. Had the hypothetical firm been able to produce and sell only $Q - 2$ units because of breaching buyers, then, since the firm could profitably have made the Qth and $(Q - 1)$th sales if it had had the opportunity, it could correctly be said that the firm was deprived of a profit. The important point, though, is that even if the firm did lose a sale and profit, the recovery it could receive under section 2-708(2) is likely to prove excessive. Applying that Code section to the firm described in figure [16], a court would probably look at the amount by which price exceeds *average* variable costs and incorrectly conclude that each additional unit of output would make a healthy contribution to profit and overhead. Recognizing that court and counsel lack the tools and the data to conduct the sort of marginal cost and revenue analysis employed in the preceding discussion on a case-by-case basis, the more reasonable working presumption is that the firm is attempting to maximize its profits and is therefore operating at a level of output where the high marginal cost of producing the lost-sale units would have offset most of the marginal revenue that would have been received had the buyers not breached, and in fact may have exceeded it. . . .

[The author's detailed analysis of the lost-sale question in a monopolized market is omitted.]

Summary of Conclusions

If the seller is operating in a market characterized by pure competition, where there are numerous small sellers producing a standardized product, he cannot properly be viewed as "losing" a profit as a result of one of his buyers breaching a sales contract. First, in pure competition, the seller can by definition dispose of as much output at the going market price as he chooses to produce. Second, even if the pure-competition seller was somewhow forced to lose a sale because of the breach, it is doubtful that the lost sale would create an appreciable reduction in the seller's total profits. The reason is that for any profit-maximizing firm (whether it is operating in pure competition or not) the marginal sales, which are the ones that will be "lost," will probably either produce only insignificant amounts of profit or be unprofitable. Thus, in cases of pure competition, the need to fashion for the seller a lost-profits remedy does not exist.

If the seller is operating under imperfect competition, on the other hand, that is, if the structure of his market is either monopolistic, oligopolistic, or monopolistically competitive, he cannot sell any amount of output he chooses at the going price. But nonetheless he should not "lose" a sale because of the buyer's breach, since he has the power to lower his price to a level that will induce a new buyer to purchase the unit. While his revenues will not be as great as they would have been had the original buyer performed, the seller does not forego a sale. This conclusion that the seller can dispose of his entire output by reducing his price is subject to two exceptions, however. One is the rare situation where there is some finite limit on the number of potential buyers. The second and probably more frequent exception is where the reduction in total revenues that will result from decreasing the price exceeds the corresponding increase in revenues derived from selling the additional unit. In these two instances the lost-volume phenomenon does in fact exist in the real world and there follows the necessity to provide the seller with an appropriate remedy under section 2-708(2).

There may be one other economic situation, which may be viewed as something of a hybrid of pure and imperfect competition, where lost-volume theory will be applicable. This occurs when the seller is not operating under pure competition, and therefore faces a finite demand for his output at the going price, but for some reason is prevented from reducing his price in order to increase his sales volume. The "standard-priced" goods mentioned in the comments to section 2-708(2) might fit into this category. But to qualify for lost-volume treatment under this theory, it would seem that the seller not only must be prohibited from varying the market price of his product but must also be precluded from offering any other forms of inducement to potential buyers that might enable the seller to dispose of his stock. And such a case of complete seller inflexibility would appear unlikely.

*Money Sanctions for Breach of Contract in a Communist Economy**

Bernhard Grossfeld

. . . In a communist economic system the payment of damages can by no means compensate completely the damage incurred. The damage to the society as a whole, for example, cannot be compensated, for every breach of contract disturbs a certain established pattern and demands an increased effort to overcome its conse-

*Reprinted from 72 Yale L.J. 1326, 1330-1332, 1334, 1336 (1963). Reprinted by permission of The Yale Law Journal Company and Fred B. Rothman & Company from The Yale Law Journal, Vol. 72, pp. 1326 ff.

quences and to re-create order. The liquidation of the damages absorbs additional energy and time which could have been better used—if the damage had not occurred—for constructive activity. Moreover, the goods which could not be produced as a result of the breach of contract are missing in the final balance of the plan, or can be produced only at the expense of other goods. The fact that these arguments might equally be given in a western legal system throws some doubt on the contention that the most important goal of the money sanctions for breach of contract is compensation; the relevance of these arguments is at least not restricted to the law of a planned communistic economy. But there is another—I am inclined to say "unique"—feature in a communist economy that makes compensation itself virtually impossible—the existence of a comprehensive plan by which the economy is ruled. In a free, competitive economy, with free access and exchange of goods, nearly every good can be evaluated and replaced by a certain amount of money. Consequently, in such an economic system a purchaser whose supplier breaches a contract can generally purchase the same goods from another supplier, provided the damages he sustained are compensated. Thus in our western legal systems a purchaser very often does not have a vital interest in the specific performance of the contract; whether he receives from the seller the goods he wanted or their money value may make little difference to him. This is not the case in a completely planned economy where there does not exist a free flow of goods available on the open market. If one particular producer or supplier fails to perform his contractual duties there are no others to whom the buyer can turn. Money, therefore, is no equivalent for the product itself. Thus the tasks imposed upon the enterprise by the plan cannot be accomplished when the enterprise receives money instead of the goods it needs for production, and from this it follows that in such an economy actual performance of every contract is of greatest importance. This "principle of specific performance" is the basic principle of the communist system of contracts. It represents the categorical demand of the law that the goods which are to be delivered must not be replaced by money damages. Thus even an express agreement between the parties to a contract concluded under the plan that specific performance will be waived in favor of an equivalent in money is void. The money compensation is conceived exclusively as an "emergency measure," a "last resort" when specific performance is virtually impossible.

These unique features of the economic system demonstrate that the main purpose of the money sanctions for breach of contract cannot be compensation for losses. Rather, the emphasis shifts to prevention of losses or "education." The main task of money sanctions becomes the enforcement of contractual discipline, for the understanding is that the more difficult it is to compensate damage the more must be done to prevent it. The money sanctions serve their purpose best, therefore, when they prevent occurrence of a breach of contract. When a party does fail to perform the contract and has to pay damages, they function as a "form of social criticism," as a means of "education through the Mark." Simultaneously, of course, there is a compensatory effect, but, in direct contrast with the Western systems, compensation is warranted *only* if it can serve an educational purpose. Moreover, the effects of the money sanction go far beyond the particular contract in question, because the contract and the plan stand in very close nexus. Through the contracts the necessary combination between the central direction of the economy by the state and the economic independence of the enterprises is realized. When concluding contracts within the framework of the plan, each enterprise determines the precise content of its share in the implementation of the plan. The contract is thus a means of economic planning, an instrument by which the purposes of the state can be realized. Compensation for damages, then, is not paid for the benefit of the injured party, but constitutes an attempt by the state to use the individual interest as a tool to achieve social control, to secure the fulfillment of the plan. The party to the contract who sues for damages fulfills a "public" task; his own interest is satisfied only where it serves the greater goals of the society.

Liability is based on the fault principle. . . . The general tendency is to make the responsibility as severe as possible within the framework of the fault principle. This tendency is reflected clearly by the measure of care which is required from every enterprise in the performance of its contracts. The standards for testing whether a breach of contract was avoidable are extremely rigorous. Rather than relating to the abilities of the particular individual or enterprise in question, they are objective standards—the objective demands of commerce. It is not the "reasonably prudent man" who serves as the "objective" standard in a case involving an individual but the worker in a socialist enterprise displaying the greatest success in production. As to the responsibility of the enterprise, the standard requires a duty to make the utmost efforts and to display the highest possible concern for the fulfillment of the contract. A maximum exertion by the enterprise, even an extraordinary effort, is necessary, and this effort is evaluated from the standpoint of the society and its objective needs. Thus, for instance, an enterprise cannot contend as a defense that its technical equipment does not meet the present high standards of technology and science. The defendant is relieved from liability only when the breach is traceable to "unavoidable forces" or when the injured party himself was the cause. . . .

. . . [T]he fault principle in the system is based on the assumption that every mistake—except those stemming from "unavoidable forces"—can be avoided and that every mistake that *can* theoretically be avoided *must* be avoided in practice. It goes without saying that this axiom and the demand drawn from it do not correspond to reality, and that very often the liability for breach of contract becomes strict liability in practice. The line between liability based on fault and strict liability in this system is by necessity very thin, and the dilemma it creates seems insoluble. On the one hand standards must be very high, bordering on strict liability, because there should be an inducement to exercise the utmost care. On the other hand this borderline must not be crossed, lest the educational purpose be frustrated. Yet the law creating such a dilemma seems itself unavoidable by the very nature of the basic economic system. The plan establishes a highly complicated system which is very sensitive to every disturbance. Even slight disarrangements can have serious consequences on the economy as a whole. Unlike a free, competitive economy where the risk is divided among many independently-operating, self-adjusting economic units, a completely planned economy does not have great elasticity, no "built-in buffers" which alleviate and limit losses. That is why the utmost care to avoid even minor failures is necessary. Only an élite is capable of meeting these demands; the average man with his mistakes, his deficiencies and his lack of social discipline has no place in this system. But this is only one side of the coin. The law cannot disregard completely the fact that most people are near average. There is a broad gap between the ideal, conceived as the standard, and reality. This gap must be closed by education or even stronger pressures, and the larger the gap the stronger must be the pressure to close it. Such pressures raise the danger, however, that people withdraw into resignation. Thus, ironically, the high standard of care which is indispensable to produce the necessary educational effect may be at the same time the greatest obstacle to its attainment. . . .

NOTES AND QUESTIONS

1. What do Leff's paper on collection, Goetz and Scott's on liquidated damages and penalty clauses, and Kronman's on specific performance have in common? Is there any sense in which all three papers are concerned with the same problem?

2. The courts will enforce an arbitrator's order compelling specific performance in cases (e.g., of promises to render personal services) where the courts, applying the doctrines discussed in Kron-

man's article, would not. See Staklinski v. Pyramid Electric Co., 6 N.Y.2d 159, 160 N.E.2d 78, 188 N.Y.S.2d 541 (1959); Grayson-Robinson Stores, Inc. v. Iris Construction Corp., 8 N.Y.2d 133, 166 N.E.2d 377, 202 N.Y.S.2d 377 (1960). Is this evidence that the refusal of the courts to enforce an agreement of the parties to a contract for specific performance in the event of breach is inefficient?

3. Goetz and Scott appear to overlook the *informational* role of penalty clauses. Suppose *A* wants a building built for him, and is eager for completion by a specified date. Contractor *B* wants this contract very much but is new to the field and has no reputation for prompt performance; nonetheless he is confident he can perform by the specified date. How is *B* to communicate this information convincingly to *A*? One way, perhaps the only effective way, is for *B* to agree to pay a substantial penalty if he fails to complete construction on time. The penalty may bear no relation to the actual costs to *A* of delayed completion, for the purpose of the penalty is not to estimate damages, whether market or idiosyncratic, but to induce *A* to take a chance on contracting with a firm of uncertain reputation. (As an inducement, how does this differ from *B*'s simply offering a lower price to *A* than established contractors would?)

Could Goetz and Scott reply that the information argument is in fact an aspect of their idiosyncratic-value argument for penalty clauses—that our hypothetical in fact assumes that *A* attaches an idiosyncratic value to completion by the specified date?

4. For a suggestion that the traditional hostility of the common-law judges toward liquidated-damages clauses may be related to the old practice of paying judges out of litigant fees, see William M. Landes & Richard A. Posner, Adjudication as a Private Good, forthcoming in 8 J. Legal Studies (1979).

5. Logically, should Goetz and Scott favor enforcement of a clause providing that in the event of default the breaching party would become the indentured servant of the promisee for a period of seven years? See pp. 256-260 infra.

6. A recent paper tries to show that the policy of not enforcing penalty clauses is actually consistent with efficiency. See Kenneth W. Clarkson, Roger LeRoy Miller & Timothy J. Muris, Liquidated Damages vs. Penalties: Sense or Nonsense?, forthcoming in the Wis. L. Rev. The authors point out that where, because of the inclusion of a penalty clause, a promisee has more to gain if the promisor breaches than if he performs, the promisee will have an incentive to expend resources in procuring a breach; and these resources, plus those the promisor expends to counter the promisee's efforts, are socially wasted. The authors argue that where the danger of the promisee's attempting to precipitate a breach is significantly enhanced by a penalty clause, the courts will not enforce the clause.

The refusal to enforce a penalty clause on this ground seems difficult to reconcile with efficiency. If the inclusion of the clause would create a real danger of the promisee's trying to provoke the promisor to breach, this danger will be reflected in the parties' negotiations over the contract price or other terms of the contract. If the penalty clause survives the negotiating process, that is presumably because the benefits to the promisee exceed the costs to the promisor. However costly a contract containing a penalty clause may be, all of the relevant costs are fully borne by the contracting parties and therefore all will be taken into account in the negotiation. Only if it is believed that the parties will fail to assess these costs correctly is there a basis for intervention; the basis, however, is paternalism rather than efficiency.

However, Clarkson et al. argue that if the courts refuse to enforce penalty clauses where the danger of induced breach is substantial, they save contracting parties the costs of having to specify that their penalty clauses are not to be enforced where such a danger is present or to add provisions designed to reduce the danger. Do you find this argument convincing?

7. Are Speidel and Clay correct in arguing that overhead should normally not be part of the damage award in a breach of contract action? The question may be stated slightly differently: where the buyer breaches before the seller has begun to perform, is the proper measure of damages the contract price minus the incremental cost of performing the contract—that is, the cost the seller saves by not having to fulfill it—or should there also be deducted from the damage award whatever allowance for overhead the seller allocated to the contract? Only the former measure is proper because only it will place the seller in the position he would have been in had the contract been performed according to its terms. This measure may include something denominated by the seller as an allowance for "overhead" but it is a matter of indifference whether the seller calls the difference between the contract price and the additional cost to him of performing the contract overhead, profit, or something else.[1]

To illustrate, imagine that a manufacturer has only two costs: debt of $10,000, and materials. Existing output is 10,000 widgets. He contracts to supply 10,000 additional widgets at a price of $2 per widget, and it will cost him $10,000 in extra materials to produce them, i.e., $1 per widget. In figuring the price, the manufacturer will allocate $1 to cost of materials, $.50 to overhead (i.e., the fixed debt

1. A bit of terminology may be helpful here. An "incremental" cost is the cost incurred by some increment of output, e.g., another 10,000 widgets. "Marginal" cost, a related term, describes the cost incurred by a very small increment of output. A "fixed" cost is a cost that is not affected by how much or how little the firm produces; an example would be a fixed debt of $1000.

that, by our severely simplifying assumption, is the only overhead cost of the firm, divided by the total units produced), and $.50 to profit. If the contract is terminated before production commences, the manufacturer should, under an expectation theory of damages, be entitled to a damage award of $10,000—the revenues lost ($20,000) minus the costs saved from not performing the contract ($10,000 worth of materials). No overhead costs are saved by nonperformance because, by definition, these costs are invariant with regard to the number of widgets the manufacturer produces. Does the author of the Case Western note consider this a feasible damage method? How must this method of damage computation be modified if the manufacturer has begun to produce under the contract?

The principal value of the Speidel and Clay article is as a warning that automatically awarding the seller the difference between the contract price and the *average* total costs of production over all of his contracts would often overcompensate him. If the seller faces a rising marginal-cost curve, meaning that the cost of his output rises with the amount he produces (see p. 151 supra), the cost of performing a given contract may be higher than the average cost of performing all of his contracts. Concretely, if he is already operating at optimal capacity and makes another sale, he may have to hire less skilled workers or buy more costly machinery to perform the new contract, and the cost to him of performing the contract will be higher than the cost of performing his previous contracts.

Speidel and Clay assume an economy in which all sellers are operating beyond optimal full capacity so that additional production always adds more to total costs than to average total costs. Consider Figure 17, a simplified version of their Figure [12]. In a competitive market in which all firms have identical costs, firms sell at a price equal to the lowest point on their (identical) average total cost curves for that point, which is also equal to the firms' and hence (under the assumption that all firms have the identical costs) the industry's marginal costs, is the price at which the total costs of supplying the market are minimized. At that point, *pq* in our variant of Speidel and Clay's Figure [12], marginal cost must be rising, to offset the decline in average total costs that is due to spreading the firm's fixed costs (which by definition are invariant to the level of output) over a greater output. Speidel and Clay assume that normally firms operate to the right of *pq* (i.e., that price is higher than *p*), but there is no basis for this assumption.[2] Moreover, whether the firm is operating

2. If the firms are indeed identical, the assumption is clearly incorrect. If the firms are not identical—if some firms have lower costs than others—the lower-cost firms will be operating in a region of rising marginal costs (can you see why?). Any unexpected shift in the conditions of demand and supply could cause all or some of the firms in a market temporarily to operate either to the right or left of *pq*.

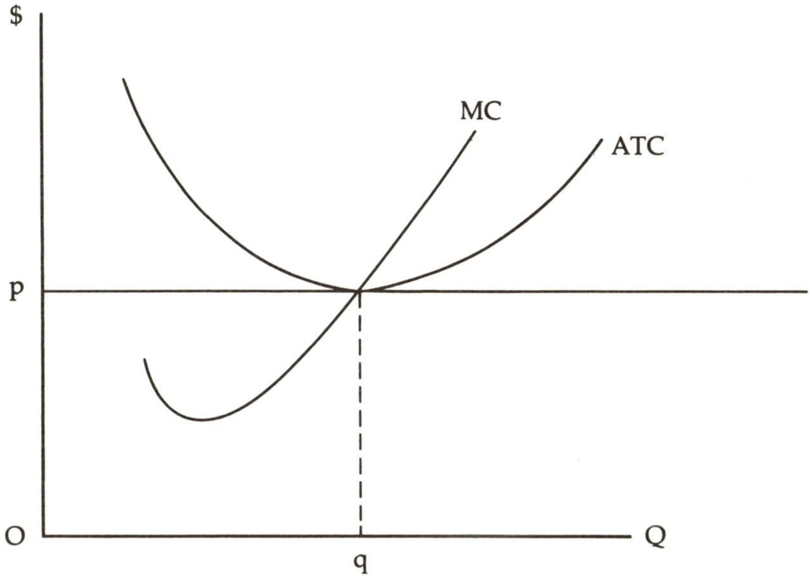

Figure [17]

to the right or left of this point, under an expectation theory of damages the firm is entitled to the difference between the contract price and the costs saved (i.e., marginal costs) from not performing the contract when the buyer terminates. The only difference between being to the right or left of *pq* is that to the right marginal costs are a higher fraction of the contract price than they are to the left.

8. How does the Case Western note differ in its analysis of the overhead-cost recovery question from the Speidel and Clay article? Specifically, what is the difference between Figure [12] in the latter article and Figure [16] in the former? Notice the strong conclusion in the Case Western note: if a seller loses a sale through breach, that breach will enable him to make a new sale to another buyer; it will not reduce his volume or profits because his volume is fixed at point *Q* in Figure [16]. What assumption drives the Case Western note to this conclusion?

Would the following rule regarding recovery of overhead in a contract-damage action represent a good compromise between the desire for an economically correct measure of damages and the administrative costs of attempting to achieve economic sophistication in a contract action? The rule is: if the seller sells a fungible product at a uniform price, let him recover the difference between that price and his average total costs; but if the seller negotiates each sale separately, estimating the incremental or marginal costs attributable to that sale, let him recover only the difference between the contract price and those incremental costs.

Does this discussion suggest why the defense that a contract is in violation of the antitrust laws is sometimes said to be disfavored, notwithstanding the general principle that illegal contracts are unenforceable?

9. Suppose in an apartment building which has no vacancies one of the tenants breaks his lease and the owner promptly leases to a new tenant on the same terms as to the old. What are the owner's damages? Suppose *A*, a producer of widgets, a fungible industrial input, contracts to sell 10,000 widgets to *B*. *B* defaults and *A* enters into a new contract to sell 10,000 widgets to *C*. What is the measure of damages in this case? How would you model these two cases in terms of Figure [16] of the Case Western note?

10. Suppose that Seller agrees to sell Buyer one ton of wheat for $100. The agreement is made on January 1; the wheat itself is to be delivered on May 1. Buyer pays Seller $50 on January 1, and agrees to pay the remaining $50 when the wheat is delivered. On May 1, Seller announces that he has no intention of performing. At the time of Seller's breach, the market price of wheat is $75 a ton. Buyer sues Seller to recover the $50 he has prepaid. Seller responds by saying that Buyer is only entitled to recover $25 since this is all Buyer needs to be put in the position he would have been in if Seller had performed. What is the basis of Seller's argument? Is it economically sound? See Bush v. Canfield, 2 Conn. 485 (1818).

11. Answer the following questions: (a) Do reliance losses in law correspond to marginal costs in economics? (b) Is a loss of expectation a real economic loss? (c) In a competitive market in equilibrium, are the reliance and expectation interests the same?

12. In Hadley v. Baxendale: A Study in the Industrialization of the Law, 4 J. Legal Studies 249, 282-283 (1975), Richard Danzig questions the economic efficiency of the rule of Hadley v. Baxendale:

> Resting the seller's liability on whether the type of damages incurred was "normal" (or, in the UCC's words, whether it was a type of damage of which the seller has "reason to know"), seems undesirable because it lets an all-or-nothing decision ride on an indicator about which many sellers cannot, at the time of breach, speculate with confidence. Further, if the recoverability of a type of damages is established, a seller may often have no reasonable basis for determining the magnitude of the damages involved. On this dimension—obviously critical to any calculus of the care warranted to avoid breach—the rule has nothing to say. Lastly, if the rule were truly finely geared to optimizing the allocation of resources, it would place its emphasis on the damage known to the seller at the time of breach, rather than at the time of contract, at least where the breach was voluntary. When the rule was framed stress had to be placed on communication at the time

> of the making of a contract because that was the only occasion on which information exchange could be coerced without fear of imposing enormous transaction costs. Now the telephone and vastly improved telegraphic facilities make it possible to mandate discussion at the time of breach. Would it be desirable to move the focus of the rule to this point? On this question, some empirical evidence would be desirable. Do the average transaction costs associated with information exchange at the time of the contract multiplied by the number of instances in which such information is exchanged exceed the average transaction costs of information exchange at the time of voluntary breach multiplied by the number of occasions when breach is seriously considered? If so, there is much to be said for a revision in the rule.

Do Danzig's observations about the ease of communication at the time of breach lend support to the view that there is an economic case to be made for requiring the specific enforcement of *all* contracts? See pp. 181-187 supra.

13. Grossfeld's paper on communist contract law brings out the neglected point that Anglo-American contract law, at least, is a regime of strict liability. Not only is the victim of a breach not required to prove that the breach was the product of negligence on the part of the breaching party, but, except within the limits of impossibility and cognate excuse doctrines, the breaching party cannot defend by showing that his breach was, in tort terminology, an "unavoidable accident." The comparative economic properties of strict liability and negligence in tort law are the subject of a growing literature. See, e.g., John Prather Brown, Toward an Economic Theory of Liability, 2 J. Legal Studies 323 (1973); Richard A. Posner, Economic Analysis of Law 137-142 (2d ed. 1977). Can you think of any economic reasons why strict liability plays a larger role in contract than tort law? See id. at 142.

14. Grossfeld notes that in a communist economy, the parties to a contract cannot waive their right to specific performance "in favor of an equivalent in money." In our legal system, the parties to a contract cannot voluntarily create a right to specific performance even if they wish. What explains this difference? Which rule is more consistent with the principle of freedom of contract?

Chapter 7

Freedom of Contract: Philosophical Perspectives on Economic Analysis

*Freedom and Coercion**

Max Weber

The development of legally regulated relationships toward contractual association and of the law itself toward freedom of contract, especially toward a system of free disposition within the framework of regulated legal type transactions, is usually regarded as signifying a decrease of constraint and an increase of individual freedom. It is clear from what we have been saying, in how relative a sense this opinion is formally correct. The possibility of entering with others into contractual relations the content of which is entirely determined by individual agreement, and likewise the possibility of making use in accordance with one's desires of an increasingly large number of type forms rendered available by the law for purposes of consociation in the widest sense of the word, has, as compared with the past, been immensely extended in modern law, at least in the spheres of

*Reprinted by permission of the publishers, from Max Weber on Law in Economy and Society 188-191, Max Rheinstein trans. & ed., Edward Shils trans., Cambridge, Mass.: Harvard University Press, copyright © 1954 by the President and Fellows of Harvard College.

exchange of goods and of personal work and services. However, the extent to which this trend has brought about an actual increase of the individual's freedom to shape the conditions of his own life or the extent to which, on the contrary, life has become more stereotyped in spite, or, perhaps, just because of this trend, cannot be determined simply by studying the development of formal legal institutions. The great variety of permitted contractual schemata and the formal empowerment to set the content of contracts in accordance with one's desires and independently of all official form patterns, in and of itself by no means makes sure that these formal possibilities will in fact be available to all and everyone. Such availability is prevented above all by the differences in the distribution of property as guaranteed by law. The formal right of a worker to enter into any contract whatsoever with any employer whatsoever does not in practice represent for the employment seeker even the slightest freedom in the determination of his own conditions of work, and it does not guarantee him any influence on this process. It rather means, at least primarily, that the more powerful party in the market, i.e., normally the employer, has the possibility to set the terms, to offer the job "take it or leave it," and, given the normally more pressing economic need of the worker, to impose his terms upon him. The result of contractual freedom, then, is in the first place the opening of the opportunity to use, by the clever utilization of property ownership in the market, these resources without legal restraints as a means for the achievement of power over others. The parties interested in power in the market thus are also interested in such a legal order. Their interest is served particularly by the establishment of "legal empowerment rules." This kind of rules does no more than create the framework for valid agreements which, under conditions of formal freedom, are officially available to all. Actually, however, they are accessible only to the owners of property and thus in effect support their very autonomy and power positions.

It is necessary to emphasize strongly this aspect of the state of affairs in order not to fall into the widely current error that that type of decentralization of the lawmaking process which is embodied in this modern form of the schematically delimited autonomy of the parties' legal transactions is identical with a decrease of the degree of *coercion* exercised within a legal community as compared with other communities, for instance, one organized along "socialist" lines. The increasing significance of freedom of contract and, particularly, of enabling laws which leave everything to "free" agreement, implies a relative reduction of that kind of coercion which results from the threat of mandatory and prohibitory norms. Formally it represents, of course, a decrease of coercion. But it is also obvious how advantageous this state of affairs is to those who are economically in the position to make use of the empowerments. The exact extent to which the total amount of "freedom" within a given legal community is actually increased depends entirely upon the concrete economic order and especially upon the property distribution. In no case can it be simply deduced from the content of the law. Enabling laws of the sort discussed here would certainly play a slight role in a "socialist" community; likewise, the positions from which coercion is exercised, the type of coercion, and those against whom it is directed, will also be different from what they are in an order of private economy. In the latter, coercion is exercised to a considerable extent by the private owners of the means of production and acquisition, to whom the law guarantees their property and whose power can thus manifest itself in the competitive struggle of the market. In this type of coercion the statement "coactus voluit"[1] applies with peculiar force just because of the careful avoidance of the use of authoritarian forms. In the labor market, it is left to the "free" discretion of the parties to accept the conditions imposed by those who are economically stronger by virtue of the legal guaranty of their property. In a socialist community, direct mandatory and prohibitory decrees of a central economic control authority, in whichever way it may be conceived, would play a much greater role than such ordinations are playing today. In the event of disobedience, observance will be produced by means of some sort of "coercion" but not through struggle in the market. Which system would possess more real coercion and which one more real personal freedom cannot be decided, however, by the mere analysis of the actually existing or conceivable formal legal system. So far sociology can only perceive the qualitative differences among the various types of coercion and their incidence among the participants in the legal community.

A (democratically) socialist order (in the sense current in present-day ideologies) rejects coercion not only in the form in which it is exercised in the market through the possession of private property but also direct coercion to be exercised on the basis of purely personal claims to authority. It would recognize only the validity of agreed abstract laws, regardless of whether they are called by this name. Formally, the market community does not recognize formal coercion on the basis of personal authority. It produces in its stead a special kind of coercive situation which, as a general principle,

1. "Coactus voluit" (it is his wish, although coerced)—Romanist phrase to describe the situation of an individual who has engaged in a legal transaction under the influence of coercion, in contrast to the situation in which a person is used as the mere physical tool of another, for instance, where the latter forcibly grabs the former's hand and moves it so as to go through the physical motions of writing a signature. . . .

applies without any discrimination to workers, enterprisers, producers and consumers, viz., in the impersonal form of the inevitability of adaptation to the purely economic "laws" of the market. The sanctions consist in the loss or decrease of economic power and, under certain conditions, in the very loss of one's economic existence. The private enterprise system transforms into objects of "labor market transactions" even those personal and authoritarian-hierarchical relations which actually exist in the capitalistic enterprise. While the authoritarian relationships are thus drained of all normal sentimental content, authoritarian constraint not only continues but, at least under certain circumstances, even increases. The larger a structure whose existence depends in some specific way on "discipline," for instance a capitalistic industrial plant, the more relentlessly can authoritarian constraint be exercised in it, at least under certain conditions. It finds its counterpart in the shrinkage of the circle of those in whose hands the power to use this type of constraint is concentrated and who also hold the power to have that former power guaranteed to them by the legal order. A legal order which contains ever so few mandatory and prohibitory norms and ever so many "freedoms" and "empowerments" can nonetheless in its practical effects facilitate a quantitative and qualitative increase not only of coercion in general but quite specifically of authoritarian coercion.

*The Ideology of the Economic Analysis of Law**

C. Edwin Baker

. . . On one level, Posner's analysis [in The Economic Analysis of Law] purports merely to describe the allocative effects of legal rules and institutions. But both in his choice of categories and in his continual recommendations of policies intended to simulate the results of a costless market, Posner has adopted a market model as the ideal for both allocative and distributive purposes. The market model assumes the sovereignty of the consumer, which means that the consumers' choices must be accepted. Interference with the individual's orientations, desires, and economic power is rejected. Consumer sovereignty and Posner's definition of value are rooted in the status quo in the same way (and for the same reasons): in

*Reprinted from 5 Phil. & Pub. Affairs 3, 32-41 (1975). Reprinted by permission of Princeton University Press.

accepting as the proper standard willingness and ability to pay, both accept existing orientations or desires and the existing distribution. Most defenses of the consumer-sovereignty market ideal fall into two categories. First, some defenses maintain that under ideal conditions a market maximizes something worth maximizing—e.g. welfare or satisfaction or utility; these are essentially "utilitarian" defenses. Second are defenses which challenge any non-neutral government interference with individual decisions as unjustified. These view the market as the paradigm or embodiment of individual freedom and equate distributive justice with the results of market transactions among property holders. Such defenses are based on ideas of freedom and justice.

. . . Some criticisms of the two defenses of the market model now will be sketched in order to discover whether any positive, alternative concept of value can be found. If so, the sufficiency of the alternative can be tested by investigating its success in transcending the failings of the market concept of value.

The utilitarian or maximizing defense takes either a vacuous analytic or semi-empirical form. The analytic version claims that "value" is optimized when no more trades would be made in a free, costless market. However, "value" is defined as subjective desire for which a person is willing and able to pay to satisfy, i.e. is defined in terms of what trades people would make in a costless market. Since value is defined by the same behavior which the economist praises for creating value, no policy significance can be attributed to the creation of value without an independent defense of the behavior. However, the independent defense either turns into a combined empirical-ethical argument which equates economic "value" with a desirable (possibly the only?) goal of human institutions—welfare or human satisfaction—or turns into an ethical defense of consumer sovereignty.

Even if human satisfaction were accepted as the only goal of human institutions, the attempt to make an empirical argument is doomed. Consumer sovereignty based on any existing, nonegalitarian distribution systematically fails to maximize human satisfaction.[1] . . . Likewise, there is no evidence to indicate that people's existing orientations are those most conducive to their greatest happiness or greatest satisfaction. The necessary demonstration would require the same type of (interpersonal) comparisons which the economists will not make. With the recognition that desires are not static but that the market itself influences the changes, comparisons

1. [Professor Baker attempts to demonstrate this point in an earlier part of the article from which this selection is excerpted.]

between the satisfactions resulting from tastes generated by market and by alternative nonmarket processes become necessary. Moreover, any nontautological defense of the market as a value maximizer must claim that, at least in principle, all goods or values can be handled by the market.

A "social value"—"any experience or state of affairs whose definition makes essential reference to reciprocal states of awareness among two or more persons"—is an example of a good which even the ideal market could not handle. Work, collective decision-making, and personal relations are among the processes of interaction which present situations in which people can and do value the mutual awareness of each other's participation and each other's concerns and needs. Not merely outcomes but also the process and form of interaction are crucial aspects of social values. Hence, the processes or structures of interaction in which social values exist have more than instrumental value.

In a market transaction, what is bought or sold must be an object, a commodity. The buyer or seller (the subject) relates only to an object: all orientations are subject-object, never subject-subject. In a market transaction, everything is treated as a "private value"—an object of interest involving the consciousness in only one person—and everything is reduced to an "object" or "commodity." A market "efficiently" allocates "goods" among "want centers" (individuals)—but how can it allocate processes whose value does not lie in satisfying an individual "want" but in making connections in consciousness between different people's "wants" and "aspirations" and "being"? No optimum production or distribution of these values can be expected as a direct result of market transactions since such values can not be encapsulated in a market transaction.

The market theorist counters that only as a single person can one "value" (receive satisfaction from) a "social value." If various social values develop within certain structures of interaction, ignoring probably insurmountable public goods and transaction costs problems, individuals could purchase nonmarket structures within which these values exist.

But how can the existing distribution of resources and the existing tastes be expected to provide for the choice of value-maximizing amounts of nonmarket forms of interaction? In fact, the existence of forms of interaction whose value is based in part on their independence from market treatment suggests that the market criteria of existing distribution and existing tastes are properly bypassed in decisions as to how much "production" of these forms of interaction is desirable. For example, an important social value exists in the political realm in which people interact on the basis of their recognized equality as persons while making decisions about mutual goals, the structure of common activities, and, implicitly, their concept of man. Should the choice of boundaries for this political realm be based on any existing distribution of wealth? Or, on the contrary, should the boundaries and rules of the market be determined by the decisions of a political collective based on equality? This question merely reformulates the earlier problem of finding criteria for comparing and evaluating the welfare effects of different distributions. No empirical grounds indicate whether satisfaction would be greater when value decisions use willingness-to-pay criteria or represent political choice based on equality in participation rights (formally equal distribution). The simple claim that the market maximizes value begs the question; it fails to justify the way or amount an individual's evaluation is weighted in determining value. Furthermore, existing tastes often reflect the structural requirements of a given system. When tastes are molded by the needs of the capitalist market system—e.g. only choices compatible with the secure control by the capitalists or managers are made available—evaluation from the perspective of consumer sovereignty merely sanctifies the status quo. From this market perspective, social values characteristically would be valued less than from certain alternative perspectives. Again, however, no Archimedean point appears from which to judge what tastes or what structures should be assumed as a starting point. For this reason, although the empirical defense of the market perspective appears ungrounded, no preferable alternative emerges.

Compared with the utilitarian defense which tries to evaluate "results," an ethical defense of the market as a "process" appears more promising. Since no objectively correct values exist, the state has no basis for promoting one set of values over another. The choice is left to the individual who realizes his own subjective values to the extent possible within a market—the market being the paradigm of voluntary, noncoerced interchange. Freedom is maximized because no constraints are placed on an individual except that no one is allowed to interfere coercively with others. Interference by the state constitutes a denial of individual freedom. (The implication is that without this interference, the individual is free.) Thus, interference requires a special justification—the most important justifiable interferences being (1) to protect the system and (2) to simulate the results of the market when it breaks down.

Objections to this ethical defense are too numerous to discuss. However, one line of attack will be developed in order to find how it suggests an alternative to the market notion of value.

The starkest failure of the ethical defense results from its necessary assumption of the neutrality of the market vis-à-vis individual values. The supposed freedom exists only if all choices are made by individuals while the structure imposes no values. However, no structure is value-neutral; all social structures affect both what people get and also how they interact; that is, affect both end-results and processes. Any structure, but more specifically the market and consumer sovereignty, shapes tastes and distributions, organizes the processes of realizing values, and embodies a concept of value and of man.

Clearly, people's tastes are to a great extent formed within their social setting. Advertising and the availability of goods (and past consumption habits) clearly affect people's desires. The economic analysis concerned with value and efficiency may take tastes as given, but business, as it tries to increase sales (selling people more of what they are willing to pay more for), attempts to mold people's tastes. The dynamic resulting from the business goal of increasing sales (and profits) is integral to the free market model of allocating to the most "valuable" use. The structurally created dynamic also influences tastes. For example, while trying to increase sales and profits, a business enterprise will want to create tastes that are (1) cheapest to develop or stimulate and (2) for which palliatives can be produced, but (3) which are never completely satisfied and do not cause other desires to be satiated. The business goal of increasing "value" through increasing sales requires the creation of these tastes; only by molding people to be willing to pay for more commodities can business increase sales, profits, and "value." As long as value is measured by willingness to pay, a system structured to increase value necessarily results in the stimulation of this taste for commodities.

Accepting this market definition of value and the goal of increasing or maximizing value requires the controversial judgment that a certain type of man—one who is oriented toward certain types of desires—should be created and is desirable. The model leaves no room for most people to consider and approve the judgment that these tastes—and the corresponding type of man—should be created. Clearly, the market structure and Posner's concept of "value" are anything but value-neutral.

Likewise, a market structure patterns the unequal distribution in certain ways—e.g. on the basis of who "happens" to have the skills and resources needed as palliatives for the desires created. This pattern is neither neutral nor justified. A radical critic would argue that the pattern of rewards (distributions) is unjustifiable and also, given a separation of labor from resource ownership, that the process systematically exploits certain groups and systematically underproduces certain values (e.g. social values—the relative absence of which is often described as a form of alienation). The critic also notes that if freedom means self-determination, such freedom exists only within the constraints and the opportunities generated and allowed by the market—but the most important social facts are determined by that structure. If freedom is identified with a person's power or ability to exercise his human capacities, the critic will argue that the patterns and, more importantly, the conditions of distribution within a capitalist market system are inconsistent with such developmental freedom. Nevertheless, even if correct, this specific criticism does not suffice. After demonstrating that the market system, consumer sovereignty, and the corresponding notion of value are not neutral structures or concepts, this critique fails to provide an alternative standard for evaluation.

As used here, a right exists when a person is justified in making a claim, either to a specific entitlement or to a feature of the collective framework of interaction, which should be satisfied irrespective of whether he could or would satisfy the claim by purchases on the market. Rights, like "social values," would be incomprehensible if not for man's joining together in communities. A right implies a justifiable claim. In making a claim a person asserts some relationship with those to whom the claim and the justification is addressed; and the content of the relationship forms an integral part of the commonality in which the appeal must be rooted. Modern western moral and political philosophy asserts, and our most basic and most praised political and legal practices embody, the assumption of the equality in moral worth of human beings. Even attempted justifications of Benthamite utilitarianism (or "value" maximization) and of the ethical defense of the market were predicated on the supremacy of the rights of liberty and equal treatment; this defense argued that the market criteria of value were the necessary result of recognizing the centrality of those rights. When the assumption of a natural inequality of moral worth is rejected as a satisfactory basis for human interaction, any attempt to justify legal or political obligation almost inevitably requires the recognition of individual rights. For example, before an individual can be expected to accept the legitimacy of community decisions regarding the advancement of the general welfare, that community must respect his autonomy and dignity as a free and equal moral agent. The historically evolving requirements implicit in respecting this autonomy and dignity of the individual define the present content of specific rights.

This notion of rights provides a vital key in the search for criteria with which to judge alternative conceptions of value. In addition to the integrity of the body, freedom of speech, equality under law, etc., any proposed list of individual rights would probably be headed by a right to participate in the collective choices which inevitably shape one's being. The most lofty claim made in behalf of the market is that the market protects individual choice and self-determination. However, that exalted claim rings hollow when one realizes that the market structure of interaction itself embodies a specific concept of value and influences the opportunities for, the inclinations of, and the concept of the self. A right to define and determine one's being must include equal and real opportunities to participate in collective constitutive decisions as well as certain liberties pertaining to individual development and expression. From the perspective of the collectivity—the group to which the economic analysis of law is addressed—value must not have an a priori technical economic meaning but must be defined within the political arena on the basis of equality.

The failure to find an analytic or empirical basis for judging the adequacy of Posner's concept of value could have been expected. Criteria of judgment grow out of practices which we accept. The grammar of judgment is rooted in agreement in forms of life. Recognition of man's equality—everyone counts as one—and freedom as a moral agent underlie our various competing political theories and our most praised political and legal practices. Accepting these premises, the authority of criteria used in our collective judgments is strengthened as the criteria are grounded in forms of interaction which increasingly manifest human equality and human freedom and decreasingly embody structures of domination. Recognition of rights, and more relevantly, the right to participate in collective constitutive choices is an important practice which exemplifies this form of interaction. (Once the market may have represented at least a formal advance in equality and freedom over previous forms of interaction. However, as we saw, in the market, choices were not based on equality and freedom did not extend to the realm of possibly man's most important, constitutive decisions.) Not the ideal market but the ideal polity manifests individual equality and freedom to choose a "valued" world. Any failure of the actual polity to have these characteristics does not mean that the market properly maximizes (or defines) value or provides for freedom but merely indicates that our judgments and notions of value are presently inescapably arbitrary—arbitrary to an extent precisely proportional to the extent of the failure of the polity to allow choice on the basis of equality and freedom. However, the constantly sought vantage point from which to judge between competing criteria of value must be found in the collective practices and choices of a political sphere based on equality. . . .

*Anarchy, State, and Utopia**

Robert Nozick

I. The Entitlement Theory

If the world were wholly just, the following inductive definition would exhaustively cover the subject of justice in holdings.

1. A person who acquires a holding in accordance with the principle of justice in acquisition is entitled to that holding.
2. A person who acquires a holding in accordance with the principle of justice in transfer, from someone else entitled to the holding, is entitled to the holding.
3. No one is entitled to a holding except by (repeated) applications of 1 and 2.

The complete principle of distributive justice would say simply that a distribution is just if everyone is entitled to the holdings they possess under the distribution.

A distribution is just if it arises from another just distribution by legitimate means. The legitimate means of moving from one distribution to another are specified by the principle of justice in transfer. The legitimate first "moves" are specified by the principle of justice in acquisition. Whatever arises from a just situation by just steps is itself just. The means of change specified by the principle of justice in transfer preserve justice. . . .

. . . The general outlines of the entitlement theory illuminate the nature and defects of other conceptions of distributive justice. The entitlement theory of justice in distribution is *historical*; whether a distribution is just depends upon how it came about. . . .

II. Patterning

. . . [To better understand the precise character of the entitlement principles of justice] we shall distinguish them from another subclass of the historical principles. Consider, as an example, the principle of distribution according to moral merit. This principle requires that total distributive shares vary directly with moral merit; no person should have a greater share than anyone whose moral merit is greater. (If moral merit could be not merely ordered but measured on an interval or ratio scale, stronger principles could be formulated.) Or consider the principle that results by substituting "usefulness to

*Reprinted, by permission, from Anarchy, State, and Utopia, pp. 151, 153, 155-164 (1974).

society" for "moral merit" in the previous principle. Or instead of "distribute according to moral merit," or "distribute according to usefulness to society," we might consider "distribute according to the weighted sum of moral merit, usefulness to society, and need," with the weights of the different dimensions equal. Let us call a principle of distribution *patterned* if it specifies that a distribution is to vary along with some natural dimension, weighted sum of natural dimensions, or lexicographic ordering of natural dimensions. And let us say a distribution is patterned if it accords with some patterned principle. . . .

Almost every suggested principle of distributive justice is patterned: to each according to his moral merit, or needs, or marginal product, or how hard he tries, or the weighted sum of the foregoing, and so on. The principle of entitlement we have sketched is *not* patterned. There is no one natural dimension or weighted sum or combination of a small number of natural dimensions that yields the distributions generated in accordance with the principle of entitlement. The set of holdings that results when some persons receive their marginal products, others win at gambling, others receive a share of their mate's income, others receive gifts from foundations, others receive interest on loans, others receive gifts from admirers, others receive returns on investment, others make for themselves much of what they have, others find things, and so on, will not be patterned. . . .Though the resulting set of holdings will be unpatterned, it will not be incomprehensible, for it can be seen as arising from the operation of a small number of principles. These principles specify how an initial distribution may arise (the principle of acquisition of holdings) and how distributions may be transformed into others (the principle of transfer of holdings). The process whereby the set of holdings is generated will be intelligible, though the set of holdings itself that results from this process will be unpatterned. . . .

To think that the task of a theory of distributive justice is to fill in the blank in "to each according to his ______" is to be predisposed to search for a pattern; and the separate treatment of "from each according to his ______" treats production and distribution as two separate and independent issues. On an entitlement view these are *not* two separate questions. Whoever makes something, having bought or contracted for all other held resources used in the process (transferring some of his holdings for these cooperating factors), is entitled to it. The situation is *not* one of something's getting made, and there being an open question of who is to get it. Things come into the world already attached to people having entitlements over them. From the point of view of the historical entitlement conception of justice in holdings, those who start afresh to complete "to each according to his ——" treat objects as if they appeared from nowhere, out of nothing. A complete theory of justice might cover this limit case as well; perhaps here is a use for the usual conceptions of distributive justice.

So entrenched are maxims of the usual form that perhaps we should present the entitlement conception as a competitor. Ignoring acquisition and rectification, we might say:

> From each according to what he chooses to do, to each according to what he makes for himself (perhaps with the contracted aid of others) and what others choose to do for him and choose to give him of what they've been given previously (under this maxim) and haven't yet expended or transferred.

This, the discerning reader will have noticed, has its defects as a slogan. So as a summary and great simplification (and not as a maxim with any independent meaning) we have:

From each as they choose, to each as they are chosen.

III. How Liberty Upsets Patterns

It is not clear how those holding alternative conceptions of distributive justice can reject the entitlement conception of justice in holdings. For suppose a distribution favored by one of these nonentitlement conceptions is realized. Let us suppose it is your favorite one and let us call this distribution D_1; perhaps everyone has an equal share, perhaps shares vary in accordance with some dimension you treasure. Now suppose that Wilt Chamberlain is greatly in demand by basketball teams, being a great gate attraction. (Also suppose contracts run only for a year, with players being free agents.) He signs the following sort of contract with a team: In each home game, twenty-five cents from the price of each ticket of admission goes to him. (We ignore the question of whether he is "gouging" the owners, letting them look out for themselves.) The season starts, and people cheerfully attend his team's games; they buy their tickets, each time dropping a separate twenty-five cents of their admission price into a special box with Chamberlain's name on it. They are excited about seeing him play; it is worth the total admission price to them. Let us suppose that in one season one million persons attend his home games, and Wilt Chamberlain winds up with $250,000, a much larger sum than the average income and larger even than anyone else has. Is he entitled to this income? Is this new distribution D_2, unjust? If so, why? There is *no* question about whether each of the people was entitled to the control over the resources they held in D_1; because that was the distribution (your favorite) that (for the purposes of argument) we assumed was acceptable. Each of these persons *chose* to give twenty-five cents of their money to Chamberlain. They could have spent it on going to the movies, or on candy bars, or on copies of Dissent magazine, or of Monthly Review. But they all, at least one million of them, converged on giving it to Wilt Chamberlain in exchange for watching him play basketball. If D_1 was a just distribution, and people voluntarily moved from it to D_2, transferring parts of their shares they were given under D_1 (what was it for if not to do something with?), isn't D_2 also just? If the people were entitled to dispose of the resources to which they were entitled (under D_1), didn't this include their being entitled to give it to, or exchange it with, Wilt Chamberlain? Can anyone else complain on grounds of justice? Each other person already has his legitimate share under D_1. Under D_1, there is nothing that anyone has that anyone else has a claim of justice against. After someone transfers something to Wilt Chamberlain, third parties *still* have their legitimate shares; *their* shares are not changed. By what process could such a transfer among two persons give rise to a legitimate claim of distributive justice on a portion of what was transferred, by a third party who had no claim of justice on any holding of the others *before* the transfer? To cut off objections irrelevant here, we might imagine the exchanges occurring in a socialist society, after hours. After playing whatever basketball he does in his daily work, or doing whatever other daily work he does, Wilt Chamberlain decides to put in *overtime* to earn additional money. (First his work quota is set; he works time over that.) Or imagine it is a skilled juggler people like to see, who puts on shows after hours.

Why might someone work overtime in a society in which it is assumed their needs are satisfied? Perhaps because they care about things other than needs. I like to write in books that I read, and to have easy access to books for browsing at odd hours. It would be very pleasant and convenient to have the resources of Widener Library in my back yard. No society, I assume, will provide such resources close to each person who would like them as part of his regular allotment (under D_1). Thus, persons either must do without some extra things that they want, or be allowed to do something extra to get some of these things. On what basis could the inequalities that would eventuate be forbidden? Notice also that small factories would spring up in a socialist society, unless forbidden. I melt down some of my personal possessions (under D_1) and build a machine out of the material. I offer you, and others, a philosophy lecture once a week in exchange for your cranking the handle on my machine, whose products I exchange for yet other things, and so on.

(The raw materials used by the machine are given to me by others who possess them under D_1, in exchange for hearing lectures.) Each person might participate to gain things over and above their allotment under D_1. Some persons even might want to leave their job in socialist industry and work full time in this private sector. I shall say something more about these issues in the next chapter. Here I wish merely to note how private property even in means of production would occur in a socialist society that did not forbid people to use as they wished some of the resources they are given under the socialist distribution D_1. The socialist society would have to forbid capitalist acts between consenting adults.

The general point illustrated by the Wilt Chamberlain example and the example of the entrepreneur in a socialist society is that no end-state principle or distributional patterned principle of justice can be continuously realized without continuous interference with people's lives. Any favored pattern would be transformed into one unfavored by the principle, by people choosing to act in various ways; for example, by people exchanging goods and services with other people, or giving things to other people, things the transferrers are entitled to under the favored distributional pattern. To maintain a pattern one must either continually interfere to stop people from transferring resources as they wish to, or continually (or periodically) interfere to take from some persons resources that others for some reason chose to transfer to them. (But if some time limit is to be set on how long people may keep resources others voluntarily transfer to them, why let them keep these resources for *any* period of time? Why not have immediate confiscation?) It might be objected that all persons voluntarily will choose to refrain from actions which would upset the pattern. This presupposes unrealistically (1) that all will most want to maintain the pattern (are those who don't, to be "reeducated" or forced to undergo "self-criticism"?), (2) that each can gather enough information about his own actions and the ongoing activities of others to discover which of his actions will upset the pattern, and (3) that diverse and far-flung persons can coordinate their actions to dovetail into the pattern. Compare the manner in which the market is neutral among persons' desires, as it reflects and transmits widely scattered information via prices, and coordinates persons' activities.

. . . Any distributional pattern with any egalitarian component is overturnable by the voluntary actions of individual persons over time; as is every patterned condition with sufficient content so as actually to have been proposed as presenting the central core of distributive justice. . . .

*The Buying and Selling of Labor-Power**

Karl Marx

The change of value that occurs in the case of money intended to be converted into capital, cannot take place in the money itself, since in its function of means of purchase and of payment, it does no more than realise the price of the commodity it buys or pays for; and, as hard cash, it is value petrified, never varying. Just as little can it originate in the second act of circulation, the re-sale of the commodity, which does no more than transform the article from its bodily form back again into its money-form. The change must, therefore, take place in the commodity bought by the first act, M—C, but not in its value, for equivalents are exchanged, and the commodity is paid for at its full value. We are, therefore, forced to the conclusion that the change originates in the use-value, as such, of the commodity, i.e., in its consumption. In order to be able to extract value from the consumption of a commodity, our friend, Moneybags, must be so lucky as to find, within the sphere of circulation, in the market, a commodity, whose use-value possesses the peculiar property of being a source of value, whose actual consumption, therefore, is itself an embodiment of labour, and, consequently, a creation of value. The possessor of money does find on the market such a special commodity in capacity for labour or labour-power.

By labour-power or capacity for labour is to be understood the aggregate of those mental and physical capabilities existing in a human being, which he exercises whenever he produces a use-value of any description.

But in order that our owner of money may be able to find labour-power offered for sale as a commodity, various conditions must first be fulfilled. The exchange of commodities of itself implies no other relations of dependence than those which result from its own nature. On this assumption, labour-power can appear upon the market as a commodity only if, and so far as, its possessor, the individual whose labour-power it is, offers it for sale, or sells it, as a commodity. In order that he may be able to do this, he must have it at his disposal, must be the untrammelled owner of his capacity for labour, i.e., of his person. He and the owner of money meet in the market, and deal with each other as on the basis of equal rights, with this difference alone, that one is buyer, the other seller; both, therefore, equal in the eyes of the law. The continuance of this relation

*Reprinted from Capital, Vol. I, pp. 185-196, 215-216 (Moore & Aveling transl., Modern Library ed. 1906).

demands that the owner of the labour-power should sell it only for a definite period, for if he were to sell it rump and stump, once for all, he would be selling himself, converting himself from a free man into a slave, from an owner of a commodity into a commodity. He must constantly look upon his labour-power as his own property, his own commodity, and this he can only do by placing it at the disposal of the buyer temporarily, for a definite period of time. By this means alone can he avoid renouncing his rights of ownership over it.

The second essential condition to the owner of money finding labour-power in the market as a commodity is this—that the labourer instead of being in the position to sell commodities in which his labour is incorporated, must be obliged to offer for sale as a commodity that very labour-power, which exists only in his living self. . . .

For the conversion of his money into capital, therefore, the owner of money must meet in the market with the free labourer, free in the double sense, that as a free man he can dispose of his labour-power as his own commodity, and that on the other hand he has no other commodity for sale, is short of everything necessary for the realisation of his labour-power.

The question why this free labourer confronts him in the market, has no interest for the owner of money, who regards the labour market as a branch of the general market for commodities. And for the present it interests us just as little. We cling to the fact theoretically, as he does practically. One thing, however, is clear—nature does not produce on the one side owners of money or commodities, and on the other men possessing nothing but their own labour-power. This relation has no natural basis, neither is its social basis one that is common to all historical periods. It is clearly the result of a past historical development, the product of many economical revolutions, of the extinction of a whole series of older forms of social production.

. . . The historical conditions of [the existence of capital] are by no means given with the mere circulation of money and commodities. It can spring into life, only when the owner of the means of production and subsistence meets in the market with the free labourer selling his labour-power. And this one historical condition comprises a world's history. Capital therefore, announces from its first appearance a new epoch in the process of social production.[1]

1. The capitalist epoch is therefore characterised by this, that labour-power takes in the eyes of the labourer himself the form of a commodity which is his property; his labour consequently becomes wage labour. On the other hand, it is only from this moment that the produce of labour universally becomes a commodity.

We must now examine more closely this peculiar commodity, labour-power. Like all others it has a value.[2] How is that value determined?

The value of labour-power is determined, as in the case of every other commodity, by the labour-time necessary for the production, and consequently also the reproduction, of this special article. So far as it has value, it represents no more than a definite quantity of the average labour of society incorporated in it. Labour-power exists only as a capacity, or power of the living individual. Its production consequently presupposes his existence. Given the individual, the production of labour-power consists in his reproduction of himself or his maintenance. For his maintenance he requires a given quantity of the means of subsistence. Therefore the labour-time requisite for the production of labour-power reduces itself to that necessary for the production of those means of subsistence; in other words, the value of labour-power is the value of the means of subsistence necessary for the maintenance of the labourer. . . . His natural wants, such as food, clothing, fuel, and housing, vary according to the climatic and other physical conditions of his country. On the other hand, the number and extent of his so-called necessary wants, as also the modes of satisfying them, are themselves the product of historical development, and depend therefore to a great extent on the degree of civilisation of a country, more particularly on the conditions under which, and consequently on the habits and degree of comfort in which, the class of free labourers has been formed. . . .

In order to modify the human organism, so that it may acquire skill and handiness in a given branch of industry, and become labour-power of a special kind, a special education or training is requisite, and this, on its part, costs an equivalent in commodities of a greater or less amount. This amount varies according to the more or less complicated character of the labour-power. The expenses of this education (excessively small in the case of ordinary labour-power), enter pro tanto into the total value spent in its production. . . .

One consequence of the peculiar nature of labour-power as a commodity is, that its use-value does not, on the conclusion of this contract between the buyer and seller, immediately pass into the hands of the former. Its value, like that of every other commodity, is already fixed before it goes into circulation, since a definite quantity of social labour has been spent upon it; but its use-value consists in the subsequent exercise of its force. The alienation of labour-power

2. "The value or worth of a man, is as of all other things his price—that is to say, so much as would be given for the use of his power." (Th. Hobbes: "Leviathan" in Works, Ed. Molesworth. Lond. 1839-44, v. iii., p. 76.)

and its actual appropriation by the buyer, its employment as a use-value, are separated by an interval of time. But in those cases in which the formal alienation by sale of the use-value of a commodity, is not simultaneous with its actual delivery to the buyer, the money of the latter usually functions as means of payment. In every country in which the capitalist mode of production reigns, it is the custom not to pay for labour-power before it has been exercised for the period fixed by the contract, as for example, the end of each week. In all cases, therefore, the use-value of the labour-power is advanced to the capitalist: the labourer allows the buyer to consume it before he receives payment of the price; he everywhere gives credit to the capitalist. That this credit is no mere fiction, is shown not only by the occasional loss of wages on the bankruptcy of the capitalist, but also by a series of more enduring consequences. Nevertheless, whether money serves as a means of purchase or as a means of payment, this makes no alteration in the nature of the exchange of commodities. The price of the labour-power is fixed by the contract, although it is not realised till later, like the rent of a house. The labour-power is sold, although it is only paid for at a later period. It will, therefore, be useful, for a clear comprehension of the relation of the parties, to assume provisionally, that the possessor of labour-power, on the occasion of each sale, immediately receives the price stipulated to be paid for it.

We now know how the value paid by the purchaser to the possessor of this peculiar commodity, labour-power, is determined. The use-value which the former gets in exchange, manifests itself only in the actual usufruct, in the consumption of the labour-power. The money owner buys everything necessary for this purpose, such as raw material, in the market, and pays for it at its full value. The consumption of labour-power is at one and the same time the production of commodities and of surplus value. The consumption of labour-power is completed, as in the case of every other commodity, outside the limits of the market or of the sphere of circulation. Accompanied by Mr. Moneybags and by the possessor of labour-power, we therefore take leave for a time of this noisy sphere, where everything takes place on the surface and in view of all men, and follow them both into the hidden abode of production, on whose threshold there stares us in the face "No admittance except on business." Here we shall see, not only how capital produces, but how capital is produced. We shall at last force the secret of profit making.

This sphere that we are deserting, within whose boundaries the sale and purchase of labour-power goes on, is in fact a very Eden of the innate rights of man. There alone rule Freedom, Equality, Property and Bentham. Freedom, because both buyer and seller of a commodity, say of labour-power, are constrained only by their own free will. They contract as free agents, and the agreement they come to, is but the form in which they give legal expression to their common will. Equality, because each enters into relation with the other, as with a simple owner of commodities, and they exchange equivalent for equivalent. Property, because each disposes only of what is his own. And Bentham, because each looks only to himself. The only force that brings them together and puts them in relation with each other, is the selfishness, the gain and the private interests of each. Each looks to himself only, and no one troubles himself about the rest, and just because they do so, do they all, in accordance with the preestablished harmony of things, or under the auspices of an all-shrewd providence, work together to their mutual advantage, for the common weal and in the interest of all.

On leaving this sphere of simple circulation or of exchange of commodities, which furnishes the "Free-trader Vulgaris" with his views and ideas, and with the standard by which he judges a society based on capital and wages, we think we can perceive a change in the physiognomy of our dramatis personae. He, who before was the money owner, now strides, in front as capitalist; the possessor of labour-power follows as his labourer. The one with an air of importance, smirking, intent on business; the other, timid and holding back, like one who is bringing his own hide to market and has nothing to expect but—a hiding.

. . . [T]he value of labour-power, and the value which that labour-power creates in the labour process, are two entirely different magnitudes; and this difference of the two values was what the capitalist had in view, when he was purchasing the labour-power. The useful qualities that labour-power possesses, and by virtue of which it makes yarn or boots, were to him nothing more than a conditio sine qua non; for in order to create value, labour must be expended in a useful manner. What really influenced him was the specific use-value which this commodity possesses of being *a source not only of value, but of more value than it has itself*. This is the special service that the capitalist expects from labour-power, and in this transaction he acts in accordance with the "eternal laws" of the exchange of commodities. The seller of labour-power, like the seller of any other commodity, realises its exchange-value, and parts with its use-value. He cannot take the one without giving the other. The use-value of labour-power, or in other words, labour, belongs just as little to its seller, as the use-value of oil after it has been sold belongs to the dealer who has sold it. The owner of the money has paid the value of a day's labour-power; his, therefore, is the use of it for a day; a day's labour belongs to him. The circumstance, that on the one hand the daily sustenance of labour-power costs only half a day's labour, while on the other hand the very same labour-power can work during a whole day, that consequently the value which its use during one day creates, is double what he pays for that use, this circumstance is, without doubt, a piece of good luck for the buyer, but by no means an injury to the seller. . . .

*The Transformation of American Law**

Morton J. Horwitz

. . . [C]hanges in contract law . . . were necessary to meet the needs of the newly emerging market economies in England and America. There is evidence, however, that the change from the eighteenth to the nineteenth century also involved a pervasive shift in the sympathies of the courts. In the eighteenth century the subjection of individual bargains to the extensive supervisory powers of courts and juries expressed the legal and ethical culture of the small town, of the farmer, and of the small trader. In the nineteenth century, the will theory of contract was part of a more general process whereby courts came to reflect commercial interests. The changing alliances are painfully obvious in nineteenth century courts' discriminatory application of the recently discovered chasm between express and implied contracts.

The most important class of cases to which this distinction applied was labor contracts in which the employee had agreed to work for a period of time—often a year—for wages that he would receive at the end of his term. If he left his employment before the end of the term, jurists reasoned, the employee could receive nothing for the labor he had already expended. The contract, they maintained, was an "entire" one, and therefore it could not be conceived of as a series of smaller agreements. Since the breach of any part was therefore a breach of the whole, there was no basis for allowing the employee to recover "on the contract." Finally, citing the new orthodoxy proclaimed by the treatise writers, judges were led to pronounce the inevitable result: where there was an express agreement between the parties, it would be an act of usurpation to "rewrite" the

*Reprinted by permission of the author and the publishers from The Transformation of American Law, 1790-1860, pp. 186-188, by Morton J. Horwitz, Cambridge, Mass.: Harvard University Press.

contract and allow the employee to recover in quantum meruit for the "reasonable" value of his labor.

Courts in fact seemed driven to resolve all ambiguity in contracts in favor of the employer's contention that they were "entire." It made no "difference . . . whether the wages are estimated at a gross sum, or are to be calculated according to a certain rate per week or month, or are payable at certain stipulated times, provided the servant agree for a definite and whole term." Under these circumstances, it should be emphasized, the assumption that the agreement was "for a definite and whole term" was simply a judicial construction not required by the terms of the agreement. Moreover, it did not "make any difference, that the plaintiff ceased laboring for his employer, under the belief that, according to the legal method of computing time, under similar contracts, he had continued laboring as long as could be required of him." Nor did it matter that the "employer, during the term, has from time to time made payments to the plaintiff for his labor." The result of the cases was that any employee not shrewd or independent enough to demand immediate payment for his work risked losing everything if he should leave before the end of the contract period. The employer, in turn, had every inducement to create conditions near the end of the term that would encourage the laborer to quit.

The disposition of courts ruthlessly to follow conceptualism in the labor cases was not, however, quite matched in cases involving building contracts. Building contracts are similar to labor agreements in that there is no way of restoring the status quo after partial performance. Nevertheless, nineteenth century courts allowed builders to recover "off the contract" when they had committed some breach of their express obligation. The leading case is Hayward v. Leonard[1] (1828), in which the Supreme Judicial Court of Massachusetts held that a builder could recover in quantum meruit "where the contract is performed, but, without intention, some of the particulars of the contract are deviated from." If there was "an honest intention to go by the contract, and a substantive execution of it," the court held, it would not decree a forfeiture. It should be noted that the Massachusetts court in Hayward v. Leonard expressly rejected Dane's view that the existence of an express contract barred recovery in quantum meruit. There was, Chief Justice Parker declared, "a great array of authorities on both sides, from which it appears very clearly that different judges and different courts have held different doctrines and sometimes the same court at different times." The result was that

1. 24 Mass. (7 Pick.) 181 (1828).

in Massachusetts and in most other states two separate lines of cases were developed, one dealing with service contracts, for which recovery in quantum meruit was barred, and another applying to building contracts, for which recovery "off the contract" of the reasonable value of the performance was permitted.

Few courts attempted to rationalize what Theophilus Parsons was later to call these "very conflicting" decisions. The leading explanation came from Hayward v. Leonard itself. In the labor cases the employee usually broke his contract "voluntarily" and "without fault" of his employer. Breach of building contracts was often "without intention" and compatible with an "honest intention" to fulfill the contract. Thus, it was not that courts had abandoned an underlying moral conception of contracts, but that the morality had fundamentally changed. The focus had shifted from an emphasis on the role of quantum meruit in preventing "unjust enrichment." The express contract had become paramount; denial of quantum meruit recovery was now employed to enforce the contract system. It was now regarded as just for the employer to retain the unpaid benefits of his employee's labor as a deterrent to voluntary breach of contract. But it was still unjust for the beneficiary of a building contract to enrich himself because of an honest mistake in performing the contract.

While the judges who adhered to the distinction between labor and building contracts never acknowledged an economic or social policy behind the distinction, it seems to be an important example of class bias. A penal conception of contractual obligation could have deterred economic growth by limiting investment in high risk enterprise. Just as the building trade was beginning to require major capital investment during the second quarter of the nineteenth century, courts were prepared to bestow upon it that special solicitude which American courts have reserved for infant industry. Penal provisions in labor contracts, by contrast, have only redistributional consequences, since they can hardly be expected to deter the laboring classes from selling their services in a subsistence economy.

Although nineteenth century courts and doctrinal writers did not succeed in entirely destroying the ancient connection between contracts and natural justice, they were able to elaborate a system that allowed judges to pick and choose among those groups in the population that would be its beneficiaries. And, above all, they succeeded in creating a great intellectual divide between a system of formal rules—which they managed to identify exclusively with the "rule of law"—and those ancient precepts of morality and equity, which they were able to render suspect as subversive of "the rule of law" itself.

NOTE ON PATERNALISM

The law of contracts recognizes many important limitations on what is often, and unhelpfully, called "freedom of contract." For example, two parties cannot create a binding contract to commit a crime (or a tort on a third party); nor can they by contractual arrangement alter established rules of evidence or certain substantive rules of law such as the formal requisites of negotiability in the law of commercial paper. A minor who contracts to do something is generally not bound by his promise unless he affirms it after maturity, nor is anyone bound by a promise extracted at gunpoint. Contracts in restraint of trade, oral contracts for the sale of land, penal clauses, promises unsupported by consideration, contracts for the sale of children (or, for that matter, adults) and a host of other promises are likewise unenforceable.

The limitations that the law imposes on an individual's freedom of contract assume different forms and are justified in different ways. For example, the unenforceability of an oral promise to sell land is a result of the *manner* in which the promise is expressed, and is most often justified in terms of the "cautionary" and "evidentiary" functions of the Statute of Frauds (see p. 64 supra). In contrast, the invalidity of a promise given under duress (or motivated by a fraudulent misrepresentation) is a consequence of the *circumstances* in which the promise is made and is usually explained by saying that the promise is in some sense involuntary (see p. 67 supra). In the case of a promise to commit a burglary it is the *content* of the promise, rather than its form or accompanying circumstances, that causes it to be unenforceable, and the reason for not enforcing a promise of this sort is that it is injurious to third parties.

At first glance, the existence of legal limitations on freedom of contract may appear to contradict a fundamental assumption of the positive economic analysis of law. However, although economic analysis does rest upon a strong conception of individual autonomy, not all limitations on an individual's freedom of contract are inconsistent with this conception. For example, the rule that certain contracts must be in writing to be enforceable, while in one sense limiting an individual's freedom of contract, is intended to reduce the risk normally associated with oral transactions and to protect the interests of third parties. If we assume that these advantages are especially great in the cases to which the Statute of Frauds applies, it is reasonable to view the Statute as an efficiency-promoting device whose constraints reduce the cost of contracting and thus facilitate rather than retard the voluntary transfer of entitlements. Consequently, although the Statute of Frauds limits freedom of contract, it imposes constraints which would in all likelihood be acceptable even to those whose freedom the Statute restricts if they were to deliberate about the matter in a rational and disinterested fashion.

However, while many limitations on freedom of contract may be consistent with even the strongest conception of individual autonomy, at least one class of limitations is not. These are limitations which may be called paternalistic. As we use the term, a limitation on an individual's freedom of contract is paternalistic if the sole justification for imposing it is to promote or protect the individual's own welfare (or happiness or good). If a particular limitation is imposed in order to reduce the costs of the bargaining process (for example, by insuring its procedural propriety), or to protect the interests of third parties, it can be justified on nonpaternalistic economic grounds.

Arguably, a number of the limitations the law imposes on an individual's freedom of contract are paternalistic in nature. For example, it has been suggested that the doctrine of unconscionability is often used in a paternalistic fashion, to protect poor and uneducated consumers from the consequences of their own bad bargains. This use of the doctrine is discussed, and criticized, in the article by Epstein which appears in Chapter 4. The special scrutiny given to releases of claims for personal injuries (at least where the injured party is relatively unsophisticated and the loss suffered far exceeds whatever payment he has received in return),[1] and the unenforceability of informal gratuitous promises, might be regarded as additional examples of paternalism in the law of contracts (but see p. 50 supra). It would be impossible, in a brief note, to consider every constraint on freedom of contract which is arguably paternalistic, and we limit our discussion here to three: the contractual incapacity of minors, the invalidity of contracts of self-enslavement, and the unenforceability of penal clauses.

I. The Contractual Incapacity of Minors

The rule today is that minors may make and enforce contracts but that their contracts may not be enforced against them—the one important exception being promises to pay for what are traditionally called "necessaries" (for example, food and clothing).[2] The rule has

1. Ricketts v. Pennsylvania R.R., 153 F.2d 757, 760–762 (2d Cir. 1946) (Frank, J., concurring).

2. 2 Williston, Contracts §§226, 240 (3d ed. 1959).

two effects. In the first place, it increases the risks of contracting with minors and therefore makes contracting more costly for minors themselves. Minors often discover that their promises will be accepted only if they are backed by adult guarantors. Second, the rule permits minors to withdraw without cost from contracts which they (or their parents) have come to regard as ill-advised or unprofitable.

The rule is evidently designed to discourage minors from contracting (by making it more costly for them to do so) and to protect minors from their own misjudgment when they do contract. The assumption is that minors need to be protected against themselves. The underlying—and intuitively plausible—idea is that very young people are less likely to appreciate the consequences of their promises and therefore ought not to be bound by them.

There are two related senses in which this might be true. First, from the point of view of an adult, a minor may have what appears to be a skewed or undeveloped conception of his own self-interest and therefore be unable to judge whether it is in his self-interest to make a particular promise. Second, and more important, a minor may often (at least more often than an adult) have only an incomplete and hazy idea of the obligations he is assuming when he does make a promise. When he signs the purchase form for his new automobile, he may have only the vaguest notion of the consequences of his signing. It might even be appropriate to say that he does not intend to commit himself contractually (having no idea of what that means).

Of course, the same argument can be made with respect to adults: some adults enter contracts without adequately appreciating the responsibilities they are assuming by doing so, and in this sense their liability-generating acts may be said to be involuntary. But if we assume that this happens less frequently with adults than it does with minors and that there is no convenient criterion (like age) to identify the few adults who have assumed their contractual liabilities "involuntarily," then administrative convenience and a desire to enhance the reliability of promises generally will lead us to deny adults the benefit of an incapacity defense (except in extreme cases like insanity).

Allowing a minor to enforce his contracts if he wishes is consistent with our analysis. The contract a minor makes may or may not be a beneficial one (in the sense that it promotes his self-interest). Therefore, if once the consequences of his promise have become clear a minor still wishes to go forward with his contract, the law permits him to do so.

To justify the contractual incapacity of minors we must, of course, assume that there is an identifiable and significant correlation between a particular natural fact about an individual (his age) and his ability to comprehend the meaning of his acts and thus to act freely. Although the connection between chronological age and good judgment is a complex one, it is a connection which is intuitively obvious. The contractual incapacity of minors represents a challenge to the libertarian assumptions of economic theory only if one is prepared to deny that a certain minimal intellectual capacity is a prerequisite for choice in any meaningful sense, and hence for freedom.

What of the exception that permits minors to make binding contracts for necessaries? The concept of "necessaries" delimits a class of goods and services that adult society judges to be required for (necessary to) the child's welfare. Normally, the child is supplied with necessaries by his parents or guardian—they have, indeed, the legal duty to supply them. If the child finds himself in the market for necessaries, there is a danger that he will be overcharged—but an even greater danger that if he is not permitted to enter into binding contracts he will be unable to obtain what society has judged to be essential to his welfare.

II. Contracts of Self-Enslavement

Our legal system does not permit individuals to sell themselves into slavery, or to pledge their personal liberty as collateral for a loan. Of course, even if contracts of self-enslavement were enforceable, few individuals in our society would make them. But what is the justification for disallowing even the rare individual who wishes to enslave himself, or to pledge his freedom as security, from doing so?[3]

The simplest answer would be that slavery—whether self-imposed or not—is immoral and must therefore be suppressed. When stated in this general form, the argument against self-enslavement is not (at least not necessarily) either utilitarian or paternalistic. For example, suppose one believes that slavery is immoral because it violates a divine command to treat all human beings as equals. On this view, the justification for prohibiting self-enslavement has nothing to do with the welfare of the would-be slave himself or even society as a whole: the prohibition is justified

3. John Stuart Mill argues that contracts of self-enslavement are prohibited because the would-be slave "defeats, in his own case, the very purpose which is the justification of allowing him to dispose of himself. He is no longer free; but is thenceforth in a position which has no longer the presumption in its favor, that would be afforded by his voluntarily remaining in it. The principle of freedom cannot require that he should be free not to be free. It is not freedom to be allowed to alienate his freedom." Utilitarianism, Liberty, and Representative Government 213 (A. D. Lindsay ed. 1951). Mill's argument is criticized by Gerald Dworkin in his essay, Paternalism, in Morality and the Law 107, 118 (Wasserstrom ed. 1971).

because it is required in order to satisfy an obligation owed to God. But since our principal concern is the conflict between paternalism and economic theory, we shall limit our discussion to paternalistic and utilitarian defenses of the prohibition on self-enslavement.

One intriguing explanation of the unenforceability of contracts of self-enslavement is offered by Tullock:

> The individual who would be willing to pledge himself in order to obtain additional capital the following year may this year think that it would be unwise. He knows that next year he would be likely to take a course of action which considered from the distant perspective of the present, seems undesirable. Under the circumstances, he would like to bind himself today not to make such a mortgage agreement in the future. . . . The situation is the same as that of a compulsive drunkard who hires private detectives to forcibly prevent him from taking a drink. When considered calmly, most of us would agree that we should not take the risk of enslavement and also that we might make a fatal mistake some time in the future. Thus, a prohibition on contracts containing clauses involving enslavement is similar to voting for prohibition because we feel that we are too subject to temptation.[4]

Tullock's general argument could be used to justify any conceivable limitation on freedom of contract. If the argument is convincing in the case of contracts of enslavement, it is only because we believe that the disadvantages of being a slave are so great that no one in his "right mind" would risk enslavement. The following line of reasoning lends some support to this view: Although human beings pursue many different ends in life, the achievement of any end—whatever it might be—can never constitute a good for the individual who achieves it unless it is accompanied by a sense of self-worth or self-respect. A feeling of self-respect is possible only if the individual in question regards the ends guiding his conduct as his own, as ends which he himself has chosen to pursue. A slave has few opportunities to pursue ends of his own choosing. In this respect, slavery may be distinguished, at least in degree, from other forms of domination—for example, that of an employer over his employee. A slave will therefore find it especially difficult to sustain a sense of self-respect, without which life has little meaning. Hence a person in his right mind would never choose enslavement.

Although this argument gives some content to Tullock's explanation of the unenforceability of contracts of enslavement, it is not entirely convincing. Tullock himself suggests an example which substantially weakens the argument from self-respect.[5] Suppose that in return for promising to be a slave, a father receives food to feed his

4. Gordon Tullock, The Logic of the Law 53-54 (1971). A similar argument is developed by Gerald Dworkin, supra n.3, at 120-126.

5. Tullock, supra n.4, at 52.

starving children (or enough money to finance their education). By sacrificing his own interest, the father advances the interest of his children in a way he might otherwise be unable to do. In this very act of sacrifice, the father may well attain his highest and most cherished good and provide the foundation for a lasting sense of self-respect.

A second justification for the unenforceability of contracts of enslavement attempts to avoid the paternalism of Tullock's approach by invoking the interests of third parties. According to this view, a contract of enslavement ought to be invalidated, even if it is in the best interest of the promisor, because the institution of slavery is offensive to most people in our society and its legal legitimation would cause them moral anguish. Private parties should not be permitted to enforce a contract which imposes these substantial (psychic) costs on others for the same reason that two people should not be allowed to make an enforceable contract to commit a tort on a third.[6]

This kind of argument is frequently made in order to justify the imposition of limitations on individual conduct in a way which avoids the embarrassments of paternalism. The problem with the argument is that it obliterates the line between what is sometimes called "self-regarding" and "other-regarding"[7] conduct and can therefore be used to justify virtually any limitation on individual freedom.

To be persuasive, an argument which rests upon an appeal to the interests of third parties must show, in any particular case, that the interests in question are sufficiently important to justify the limitation. In the case of slavery, there are two different ways in which this might be done. First, one might offer empirical evidence to show that most Americans are, as a matter of fact, deeply opposed to slavery and would be profoundly disturbed if contracts of enslavement were made legally enforceable. Even assuming that most Americans do feel this way about voluntary slavery (as distinct from enslavement by force), this first approach suffers from one important defect, at least in the eyes of many modern critics of slavery: it ties the illegitimacy of slavery to the shifting tides of public opinion.

This defect might prompt one to adopt a second, nonempirical, approach, according to which slavery is outlawed because it offends a conception of liberty and personal dignity which is embodied in the central provisions of our Constitution and to which we are

6. Compare the discussion of "moralisms" in Guido Calabresi & Douglas Melamed, Property Rules, Liability Rules, and Inalienability: One View of the Cathedral, 85 Harv. L. Rev. 1089, 1111-1112 (1972).

7. John Stuart Mill, supra n.3, at 176-179; James Fitzjames Stephen, Liberty, Equality, Fraternity 28 (R. White ed. 1967).

committed as a people. On this second view, every American has an interest in the maintenance of this conception and the institutions which reflect it, a permanent moral interest that is unaffected by the vagaries of public opinion.

It follows, from this second view, that voluntary enslavement is bound to have a deleterious effect on third parties even if public opinion vigorously approves such arrangements. Of course, it is now necessary to assume that the third parties whose moral well-being is threatened by contracts of enslavement may not themselves know what is in their own best interest. As a result, the most attractive feature of the appeal to third parties—its avoidance of paternalism—is lost. A proponent of this view must show that no person in his right mind would abandon the moral ideal embodied in the Constitution and that any expression of opinion to the contrary must be assumed not to reflect the person's true interests (just as Tullock's drunk is not asserting his true interests when he passionately insists that nothing could be better for him than a stiff drink). How this could be shown convincingly is unclear. One might argue, perhaps, that slavery means the loss of self-respect and that the loss of self-respect by some inevitably undermines the self-respect of others. But this argument is merely a more complicated version of the one outlined earlier and is subject to the same criticisms. It is subject to the further objection that it assumes the interdependence of different individuals' feelings of self-respect, something which is far from obvious. Why should my sense of self-worth be conditioned upon others' having a similar attitude toward themselves?

There is one other explanation for the unenforceability of contracts of enslavement that is worth noting. If people are extremely reluctant to enter into contracts of this sort, we may assume that almost every promise to become the slave of another has been given under duress or under the influence of misrepresentation (for example, a promise by the other party that he will not enforce the contract). If this is the case, then it is plausible to regard the rule prohibiting contracts of enslavement as a cost-saving presumption which achieves the same results as the more traditional, but also more cumbersome, ideas of fraud and duress. That it is an irrebuttable presumption is to be explained by the fact that the instances in which it is false are so few as not to justify the judicial costs that would be required to scrutinize each contract of enslavement more closely. Although this argument has considerable appeal, many opponents of self-enslavement are likely to find it unsatisfactory, merely because it rests on nothing loftier than the idea of administrative convenience. A deeper objection is that the argument rests on the same unproven assumption as Tullock's—that there are no strong (and morally respectable) reasons for people to enslave themselves.

III. Penal Clauses

The types of paternalism we have discussed so far are relatively uncontroversial, although for rather different reasons. The prohibition on private penal clauses is a more serious matter. Clauses of this sort have two important economic uses, and might be widely employed if they were permitted. First, as Goetz and Scott point out (p. 197 supra), a penal clause may be useful to a buyer who has reason to believe that his normal money damages remedy will be inadequate and who wants to force his seller to buy his way out of the contract before breaching. Second, for a seller who has not yet developed a reputation for reliability, agreeing to a penal clause may be the cheapest way to persuade his buyers that he is willing and able to perform (see Note 3 at the end of Chapter 6).

The economic analysis of penal clauses makes clear that a clause of this sort cannot simply be condemned as nothing more than a side bet between the parties which serves no useful social purpose. A penal clause may often perform a role, either as a risk-allocating or an information-conveying device, which increases the economic value of an exchange. There is therefore no reason to think that every clause of this sort constitutes what earlier writers called an economically "sterile" agreement. And in any case, since many jurisdictions enforce wagering contracts but forbid the use of penal clauses, the nonenforcement of penal clauses cannot be explained by a generalized hostility to gambling. (Query: is a wagering contract really economically sterile? How might it enhance the utility of the contracting parties?)

A second possible explanation for the hostility to penal clauses (although one which is rarely articulated) is that enforcement of such provisions would efface the fundamental distinction between punishment and compensation and give private parties the power to make breach of contract a crime. If private parties can create their own criminal law, one might argue, the power and authority of the state will be undermined.

This argument would have some force if, in addition to merely stipulating penalties for breach, the parties to a contract could also hire private protection agencies to enforce their bargains by any means necessary. Legal recognition of an arrangement of this sort would tend to weaken the state's monopoly on the means of violence and make it more difficult for the officers of the state to enforce even those agreements which fell within its jurisdiction. But legal recognition of penal clauses alone would not have this effect, so long as any private party wishing to enforce such a clause could do so only by invoking the power of the state through its judicial tribunals.

Furthermore, the economic utility of penal clauses makes it unreasonable to assume that almost all clauses of this sort are extracted under duress and that their flat prohibition is merely a convenient way of policing the bargaining process. Undoubtedly, some penal clauses ought to be invalidated because of duress, but an irrebuttable presumption is medicine which kills the patient. The important point is that even if courts were to continue to presume that every penal clause has been agreed to under duress, but to allow the introduction of evidence to rebut the presumption, it would be a doctrinal revolution.

Of the three paternalistic limitations we have considered in this note, the prohibition on penal clauses is both the most important, from a practical point of view, and the least defensible from an economic point of view—or any other. It is therefore not surprising that the rule has recently come under sharp criticism in the law reviews (see p. 194 supra). These academic stirrings perhaps signal, at least in this one corner of contract law, a retreat from paternalism.

NOTES AND QUESTIONS

1. Elsewhere in Law in Economy and Society (1967), Weber states that "voluntary agreements constituting the legal foundation of claims and obligations" have been "widely diffused even in the earliest periods and stages of legal history." Nevertheless, according to Weber, "contracts propagated by the market society" in which we live today "are completely different from those contracts which in the spheres of public and family law" once played a much greater role. Weber calls contracts of the latter sort "status contracts"; contracts of the former, market-oriented sort he calls "purposive contracts."

The distinguishing characteristic of all "status contracts," according to Weber, is that they aim to create, through "straightforward magical acts or at least acts having a magical significance," a relation between the parties which is political, personal, or familial. "By means of such a contract a person was to become somebody's child, father, wife, brother, master, slave, kin, comrade-in-arms, protector, client, follower, vassal, subject, friend, or, quite generally, comrade." "Purposive contracts," on the other hand, neither affect "the status of the parties nor give rise to new qualities of comradeship" but aim solely "at some specific (especially economic) performance or result."

In Weber's view, the "market community" constitutes "the most impersonal relation of practical life into which humans can enter with one another."

> The reason for the impersonality of the market is its matter-of-factness, its orientation to the commodity and only to that. Where the market is allowed to follow its own autonomous tendencies, its participants do not look toward the persons of each other but only toward the commodity; there are no obligations of brotherliness or reverence, and none of those spontaneous human relations that are sustained by personal unions. They all would just obstruct the free development of the bare market relationship, and its specific interests serve, in their turn, to weaken the sentiments on which these obstructions rest.[1]

For these reasons Weber concludes that the "absolute depersonalization" associated with the "purposive contract" is "contrary to all the elementary forms of human relationship," and must therefore represent "an abomination to every system of fraternal ethics."

But isn't the notion of individual autonomy on which our modern conception of freedom of contract rests also a moral ideal? And does its recognition necessarily entail the suppression of those "elementary forms" of comradeship which constitute the basis of social life in premarket societies? Does a developed market community deny *all* opportunities for "spontaneous human relations" sustained by "personal unions"?

2. Marx asserts that "[i]n every country in which the capitalist mode of production reigns, it is the custom not to pay for labour-power before it has been exercised for the period fixed by the contract, as for example, the end of each week." Although Marx recognizes that this "custom" may work to the disadvantage of the laborer (for example, if his employer becomes bankrupt), he deliberately chooses to ignore it in his analysis of the labor contract, stating that for "a clear comprehension of the relation between the parties" it is useful "to assume provisionally, that the possessor of labour-power, on the occasion of each sale, immediately receives the price stipulated to be paid for it."

Would it be relevant to Marx's analysis if the "custom" in question were—as Horwitz suggests—"an important example of class bias"? (But see Note 6 infra.) Does Marx regard the terms of the labor contract as unjust or unfair? In what sense is the labor contract

1. 2 Economy and Society 636 (Bedminster Press 1968).

exploitative? Marx asserts that labor-power, when "consumed," creates more value than must be paid for its use when it is purchased on the market. However, he goes on to say that "this circumstance is, without doubt, a piece of good luck for the buyer, but by no means an injury to the seller." Is this remark intended to be ironical?

Marx observes that for the "owner of money" to be able "to find labour-power offered for sale as a commodity," the laborer himself "must be the untrammelled owner of his capacity for labour, i.e., of his person." This constitutes the legal precondition of capitalist production. Does this precondition reflect a particular conception of what it means to *be* a person?

The "second essential condition to the owner of money finding labour-power in the market" is that the laborer be obliged to offer his labor-power for sale "instead of being in the position to sell commodities in which his labour is incorporated." In order for the laborer to be "obliged" to sell his labor-power, he must be "short of everything necessary" for its realization. Marx frequently expressed this same point by saying that the laborer must be "separated" from ownership of the means of production. Is this "separation" a legal phenomenon? A material or economic one? Does it have any moral significance?

3. According to Nozick, "[t]he general point illustrated by the Wilt Chamberlain example and the example of the entrepreneur in a socialist society is that no end-state principle or distributional patterned principle of justice can be continuously realized without continuous interference with people's lives." The suggestion is that a commitment to any patterned distributional principle (whatever its content) is incompatible with freedom of contract, and that one or the other must be sacrificed. But does this mean that a progressive income tax (which rests upon a distributional principle that can only be realized by "continuous interference with people's lives") necessarily conflicts with freedom of contract? If Nozick simply means that people's holdings would be different in the absence of such a tax, he is surely correct. But can't the same point be made with regard to any legal rule whatsoever? Consider the rules of contract law—for example, the rule that a promise unsupported by consideration cannot be enforced, that certain promises, to be enforceable, must be in writing, and so on. The holdings people have are affected by these rules and would be different if we had different rules or no rules at all. If this is so, how are we to distinguish nondistributive legal rules (like the Statute of Frauds) from explicitly distributive ones (such as a rule requiring every citizen to pay a variable tax based upon his wealth)? Isn't it true that Nozick's own idea of a "just" transfer requires a system of procedural rules for determining the propriety of any

particular exchange and that any such system is bound to affect (distort) the pattern of people's holdings? Would it be wrong to say that the idea of a pattern makes no sense apart from a regulating legal structure of some sort and that any structure is bound to alter the distributional pattern that would obtain in its absence?

According to Nozick, people should not be compelled to give up anything that they are entitled to under his so-called "entitlement theory." One important feature of Nozick's entitlement theory is the "principle of justice in acquisition." Elsewhere in Anarchy, State, and Utopia (1974), Nozick states that "[a] process normally giving rise to a permanent bequeathable property right in a previously unowned thing will not do so if the position of others no longer at liberty to use the thing is thereby worsened," and asserts that "any adequate theory of justice in acquisition will contain a proviso" of this sort. Could a theory offered in defense of a particular distributive pattern (for example, the pattern associated with a progressive income tax) be regarded simply as an expanded interpretation of Nozick's proviso?

4. In the well-known case of Hurley v. Eddingfield, 156 Ind. 416, 59 N.E. 1058 (1901), a physician was sued for his refusal to "enter a contract of employment" and treat a dangerously ill man, who subsequently died. The facts alleged by the plaintiff, decedent's intestate, were summarized by the court as follows:

> At and for years before decedent's death appellee was a practicing physician at Mace in Montgomery county, duly licensed under the laws of the State. He held himself out to the public as a general practitioner of medicine. He had been decedent's family physician. Decedent became dangerously ill and sent for appellee. The messenger informed appellee of decedent's violent sickness, tendered him his fees for his services, and stated to him that no other physician was procurable in time and that decedent did rely on appellee for medical assistance. Without any reason whatever, appellee refused to render aid to decedent. No other patients were requiring appellee's immediate service, and he could have gone to the relief of decedent if he had been willing to do so. Death ensued, without decedent's fault, and wholly from appellee's wrongful act.

The Supreme Court of Indiana agreed with the trial court that the facts, as alleged, did not support a cause of action against the physician, and dismissed the lawsuit. Would a holding in the plaintiff's favor have been inconsistent with the principle of freedom of contract? Evaluate the following argument: "The physician was licensed by the State, and thereby obtained the benefits of an artificial monopoly which he would not otherwise have enjoyed. Because it had conferred this benefit on the physician, the State is entitled to restrict his freedom of contract in whatever way it deems reasonable—for example, by requiring him to treat anyone with a life-threatening illness, whether or not the patient is able to pay for the physician's services."

Critics of the economic approach point out that willingness to pay is a function of ability to pay—that is, of a person's wealth. In a free market, doctors' services will go to the highest bidders; but are the highest bidders—those people who are willing to pay the most for the services—necessarily those who "need" them the most? What meaning, if any, can be assigned the term "need" in economics?

Bernard Williams, an English philosopher, makes the following argument in his essay, The Idea of Equality, in Laslett & Runciman, eds., 2 Politics, Philosophy and Society 121-122 (1962):

> Leaving aside preventive medicine, the proper ground of distribution of medical care is ill health: this is a necessary truth. Now in very many societies, while ill health may work as a necessary condition of receiving treatment, it does not work as a sufficient condition, since such treatment costs money, and not all who are ill have the money; hence the possession of sufficient money becomes in fact an additional necessary condition of actually receiving treatment. . . . This is an irrational state of affairs . . . it is a situation in which reasons are insufficiently operative; it is a situation insufficiently controlled by reasons—and hence by reason itself.

Is Williams' argument persuasive? Consider Nozick's reply.

> Why must [a doctor's] activities be allocated via the internal goal of medical care? (If there was no "shortage," could some *then* be allocated using other criteria as well?) It seems clear that *he* needn't do that; just because he has this skill, why should *he* bear the costs of the desired allocation, why is he less entitled to pursue his own goals, within the special circumstances of practicing medicine, than everyone else? So it is *society* that, somehow, is to arrange things so that the doctor, in pursuing his own goals, allocates according to need; for example, the society pays him to do this. But why must the society do this? (Should they do it for barbering as well?) Presumably, because medical care is important, people need it very much. This is true of food as well, though farming does *not* have an internal goal that refers to other people in the way doctoring does. When the layers of Williams' argument are peeled away, what we arrive at is the claim that society (that is, each of us acting together in some organized fashion) should make provision for the important needs of all its members. This claim, of course, has been stated many times before. Despite appearances, Williams presents no argument for it. Like others, Williams looks only to questions of allocation. He ignores the question of where the things or actions to be allocated and distributed come from. Consequently, he does not consider whether they come already tied to people who have entitlements over them (surely the case for service activities, which are people's *actions*), people who therefore may decide for themselves to whom they will give the thing and on what grounds. [Anarchy, State, and Utopia 234-235 (1974).]

5. According to Baker, "work, collective decision-making, and personal relations are among the processes of interaction which present situations in which people can and do value the mutual awareness of each other's participation and each other's concerns and needs." A market, in Baker's view, is incapable of allocating "processes whose value does not lie in satisfying an individual 'want' but in making connections in consciousness between different people's 'wants' and 'aspirations' and 'being.' " What exactly does it mean to say that certain values can be realized only in "processes of interaction"? Assuming that there are values of this sort, why is it that the market can't "handle" them? Suppose a worker is seeking employment. He has the choice, let us assume, of taking any one of five different jobs. In four cases, he feels no rapport with his would-be employer. In the fifth, he feels (rightly or wrongly) that he and his employer will share certain goals and perhaps even a view of the world. The fifth employer, for example, may be a corporation which invites its employees to participate in formulating the company's program of charitable donations. If he chooses the fifth job, it may be because only this one allows the worker to make a "connection in consciousness" with his employer and with his co-workers. The value of this "connection" may be large enough, from the worker's point of view, to offset a lower salary and less attractive fringe benefits.

Baker asserts that the defenders of the free market assume the market is neutral "vis-à-vis individual values," and he then challenges this assumption on the ground that the market itself actually creates values (for example, through advertising) rather than merely responding to them. Is Baker's objection simply that the market influences tastes, or that it influences them in the wrong way (by encouraging people to develop the wrong sort of tastes)? Does advertising promote or hinder an individual's ability to identify his own needs? There is a growing economic literature on advertising. See, e.g., Advertising and Society (Yale Brozen ed. 1974); Issues in Advertising: The Economics of Persuasion (David G. Tuerck ed. 1978).

6. Professor Horwitz's effort to infer an "important example of class bias" from contrasting common-law treatment of building and employment contracts is criticized in Richard A. Posner, Economic Analysis of Law 184 (2d ed. 1977):

> An obvious distinction is overlooked [by Horwitz]: the deferral of payment in the employment case was a device for assuring that the employee completed the agreed term of work, for if he were paid periodically and quit, the employer would have no practical legal remedy. To make the employer liable for accrued wages subject to

having to prove as an offset the damages that the employee's quitting caused him would reduce the effectiveness, and increase the cost, of the employer's self-help remedy.[2] The building cases expressly assume that the builder has completed the job contracted for, but that the completed performance differs in minor particulars from that agreed upon; here the owner is properly remitted to his damage remedy against the builder.

The author argues that the rule in the building cases fostered enterprise, while the rule in the employment cases did not discourage it because: "Penal provisions in labor contracts, in contrast, have only redistributive consequences, since they can hardly be expected to deter the laboring classes from selling their services in a subsistence economy." No evidence that nineteenth-century America had a subsistence economy is presented, and it seems strange that people living at a subsistence level could be induced to sign contracts under which they agreed to receive no wages for a full year. If the workers of the time *were* living at a subsistence level, no form of contract could redistribute wealth from them to employers since they would have no wealth. The entire discussion also ignores the important bearing of the Coase Theorem [see p. 6 n.6 supra] on the question whether rules of contract are likely to affect either resource allocation or wealth distribution.

A broader question is involved. Is contract law an effective instrument for systematically redistributing wealth, whether to capitalists or to workers? If an "oppressive" contractual provision is forbidden, won't this mean a higher price in future contracts? This is clearest in the case of a competitive industry, i.e., one where, in equilibrium, total revenues just equal total costs. If the industry's marginal costs (see p. 151 supra) increase, whether as a result of less favorable contract terms or of anything else, the market price must rise also. It can be readily demonstrated that a monopolist, too, will raise his price if his marginal costs rise. Thus, so long as the contract price is unregulated, it is difficult to see how changes in the (other) contract terms can bring about significant wealth changes. Of course, if the law forced contracting on nonremunerative terms—e.g., required physicians to serve the poor without charge—significant wealth redistributions, along the lines brought about by certain forms of taxation, would become possible.

2. Note the analogy to an installment sales contract in which title does not pass to the buyer until the good is fully paid for.

Index

"Add-on" clauses, 97-98
Advertising, 74-75, 237, 266
Alchian, Armen A., 3n, 36, 39
Altruism, 51, 54, 60, 101-102, 104-107
Arbitration, 6, 223-224
Arrow, Kenneth J., 36
Austin, John, 18n

Baker, C. Edwin, 266
Bankruptcy, promise to pay debt discharged in, 51
Bargaining power, inequality of, 79-81, 103-107
Barton, John, 34-35, 37, 64, 134n
Becker, Gary S., 46
Bentham, Jeremy, 38-39
Berman, Sidney, 37
Birmingham, Robert, 34-35, 64
Blackstone, William, 4n
Breach of contract
  and the fault principle, in a communist economy, 222-223
  and strict liability, 133-134, 229
  threat of, 68
Brown, John P., 229

Calabresi, Guido, 181, 258n
Capital and labor-power, 245-250
Carelessness, function of contract law in deterring, 4
Charitable pledges, 53
Cheung, Steven N. S., 33, 163n
Choice of contract, 12-13, 39
  in agriculture, 33-34
  contract and regulation, 39, 76-78, 93, 104
  labor contract, 31-32
  land-allotment contract, 12
  long-term supply contract, 32
  sharing contract, 11-12
Clarkson, Kenneth W., 224
Clay, Kenneth O., 225, 227
Coase, Ronald H., 6n, 39, 85, 110, 111
Coase theorem, 6n, 267
Collection costs. *See* Enforcement of contracts
Conceptualism, 104-105
Consideration
  function of as a formality, 40-45 passim, 52
  moral obligation as, 45, 65
  nominal, 44
  past consideration, 51
Consumer ignorance, 77-78, 83, 110. *See also* Advertising; Information
Consumer sovereignty, 233-239
Contract terms
  bargaining over, 72, 80-81
  construction of, 23-25, 30, 39
  degree of detail, 25-26, 38-39
  modification of, 43, 54, 57, 71, 108
  reasonableness of, 106
  standardization of, 72-78 passim, 108-109
"Cooling-off" period, 85, 96
Corbin, Arthur, 183n
Coronation cases, 132-133
Cost
  fixed contrasted with variable, 208-209
  inversely related to time, 3
Cross-elasticity of demand, 183

Dalzell, John, 107, 108

Damages
  in a communist economy, 220-223
  consequential, 30, 71, 99-100, 129, 133, 151, 164, 228-229
  contract and tort, contrasted, 66
  contrasted with return of goods, 168-170
  expectation interest, protection of, 19-21, 34-35, 64, 134, 154-155, 157, 160, 227
  and incentive maintenance, 154-155, 157
  liquidated, 194-207 passim
    as affected by changed conditions, 205-207
    economic rationale for, 194-197
    and insurance, 198-205
  mitigation of, 160-161, 205
  and nonmarket transactions, 155-157
  penal clauses, 194-207 passim
    as inducement to breach, 224-225
    informational role of, 224, 260
    and paternalism, 260-261
    traditional opposition to, 194, 224
    and unconscionability, 207
  recovery of profits, 161, 165-167
  reliance interest, protection of, 19-21, 44, 228
Danzig, Richard, 228, 229
Darby, Michael R., 113
Dawson, John P., 60n, 62n
Demsetz, Harold, 39
Disclosure, duty of, 116-121
Distributive justice, 240-242, 263-264
Duress, 67-72 passim
Dworkin, Gerald, 256n, 257n

Efficient rules, survival of, 6
Enforcement of contracts. *See also* Gratuitous promises
  costs of, 48-49, 85, 176-177
  and optimal allocation, 158-161
Enslavement
  and the Constitution, 258-259
  contracts of, 192-193, 224, 256-260
  and self-respect, 257-259
Entitlement theory, 240-242
Epstein, Richard, 111, 254
Error, legal, 23-24, 50, 64
Exchange
  as distinct from contract, 2-3, 7
  executory contrasted with half-completed, 41-42, 64
  and individualism, 102
  nonequivalence of values in, 87-88
  noninstantaneous, 3, 4, 10, 26, 175-176, 180
Extortion, 55, 57

Finders of lost property, 58
Firm. *See also* Choice of contract
  definition of, 32, 39
  reason for establishing, 31
Formalities, functions of, 40-41, 43
Form contract, 73. *See also* Contract terms
  reasonableness test for evaluating, 75-76
Freedom of contract
  and the allocation of social power, 230-233
  as characteristic of modern law, 230-231
  and distributive justice, 242-244, 263-264, 267
  and economic theory, 253-254
  and formalism, 231
  and paternalism, 253-254
  as a slogan, meaning of, 2
  and socialism, 231-232
Free market
  contrasted with political processes, 236
  and impersonality, 262
  justifications for, 234-239
"Free rider" problem, 111
Friedman, Milton, 36, 152
Fuller, Lon L., 49, 52, 64, 66, 156n

Garnishment, 177-179
General average, maritime doctrine of, 62
Goetz, Charles J., 223, 224, 260
Goldberg, Victor P., 38, 86, 110, 111
Gratuitous promises, 40
  economic grounds for, 46-48

Gresham's law, 74-75, 77-78
Grossfeld, Bernhard, 229

Hardy, Charles O., 35
Harris, Milton, 7n
Havighurst, Harold C., 37
Hobbes, Thomas, 247
Holmes, Oliver W., 19n, 35, 39, 56, 157
Horwitz, Morton, 262, 266

Implied contract, 59, 62
  implied in fact contrasted with implied in law, 62
Impossibility of performance, 54, 56, 122
  and agricultural contracts, 130-131
  and contracts for personal service, 125-126
  and contracts for specialized equipment, 129-130
  and forward contracts, 143-149
  and grazing contracts, 131-132
  and inflation, 138-139
  and loss-splitting, 135-136
  and partial performance, 137-138
  and prepayment, 136-137
  and risk bearing, 122-125
  and supervening illegality, 126-127
  under Uniform Commercial Code, 146-149
  war and transportation contracts, 127-129
Indexation, 152-153
Individualism, 100-101
  and capitalism, 109-110
  as distinct from egotism, 101
  and a market economy, 103-107
Inflation, 138-139
  and escalator clauses, 141-142, 148, 152-153
  and risk allocation, 151-152
  and unemployment, 152
Information
  cost of acquiring, 73-74, 83, 111
  deliberately vs. casually acquired, 118-121
  disclosure of, 84
  enforceable promise as way of conveying, 47
  and mistake, 114-121, 150
  property rights in, 119
  and resource allocation, 117-118
  supply of, 83
Injunction, contractual provision for, 191-192
Insurance
  contrasted with wagering, 204
  and moral hazard, 203-205
  self-insurance contrasted with market insurance, 124
Insurance contracts, 109

Joint tenancy, 62, 63, 63n
Joskow, Paul L., 153

Karni, Edi, 113
Kennedy, Duncan, 111
Kessler, Fritz, 108, 109, 110
Kronman, Anthony T., 151, 223

Labor contract, 31-32, 245-250 passim, 262-263
  contrasted with construction contract, 251-252
  historical conditions of, 246, 263
  in nineteenth-century American law, 250-252
Laissez-faire and freedom of contract, 93
Landes, William M., 49n, 52n, 58n, 66n, 224
Law-making by private parties, 73, 75-76, 110
Leff, Arthur Alan, 223
Legal rules, cost of particularizing, 120-121, 129
Legal sanction, economic function of, 4, 10-11, 18-19, 33
Libertarianism, 93
Liquidated damages. *See* Damages
Llewellyn, Karl, 40n
Lost-volume seller. *See also* Overhead, recovery of
  and perfect competition, 217, 219-220

Market power, concentration of, 80-81
Marshall, L. C., 27n
Marx, Karl, 262, 263
Melamed, Douglas, 181n, 258n
Mill, John Stuart, 256n, 258n
Miller, Roger LeRoy, 224
Minors
  and doctrine of "necessaries," 256
  promises of, unenforceable, 51, 254-256
Mistake
  and information, 114-121
  mutual, 148
  mutual and unilateral contrasted, 115
  and risk allocation, 114-121, 162
  in submitting a bid, 115-116, 121
Monopoly
  bilateral, 55-57, 62, 63
  as innate trend of capitalism, 109-110
Mortgage, foreclosure of, 62
Muris, Timothy J., 224

Need, economic concept of, 265
Nozick, Robert, 33, 263, 264, 265

Opportunity cost, 58, 60-61
Output contracts, 37-38. *See also* Choice of contract
Overhead
  and average cost, 219, 226
  and marginal cost, 214, 225-226
  problems of proof, 213, 219, 227-228
  recovery of, 208-220 passim

Parol evidence rule, 64, 83, 94-95
Paternalism, 52, 105, 225, 253-261 passim
Patterson, Edwin, 109
Peltzman, S., 78
Penal clauses. *See* Damages
Perdue, William R., Jr., 156n
Phillips curve, 152
Police discrimination, 82
Posner, Richard A., 5n, 39, 49, 52n, 54n, 58n, 64, 65, 66n, 107, 108, 111, 113, 133n, 150n, 151, 153, 224, 229, 233, 239, 266
Prisoner's dilemma, 16-17, 21
Promises
  as conveying information, 47
  economic rationale for enforcing, 22
  legal consequences of enforcing, 29
  nonenforceable, 22, 40, 47
    economic rationale for, 50-51, 64
Promissory estoppel, 65, 66, 107
Property rights, distinguished from contract rights, 3
Property rule, contrasted with liability rule, 181-182
Public goods, 84
Purposive contract, contrasted with status contract, 261-262

Quantum meruit, 250, 252

Raiffa, H., 112n
Raviv, Artur, 7n
Rejection of goods. *See* Tender, nonconforming or defective
Release of claims, 44-45, 69, 108
  and paternalism, 254
Remedies, inadequacy of, 56, 68-72 passim
Repossession, 177-179
Reputation
  and non-instantaneous exchange, 180
  value of, 179-181
Requirement contracts, 37-38, 159n. *See also* Choice of contract
  and good faith, 102
Rescission, contrasted with damages, 168-170
Rescuer
  nonprofessional, 60
  professional, 60-61
  promise to compensate, 51
Restatement of Contracts, 44, 53, 65, 66
Restatement of Restitution, 60
Restitution, 59, 63
Revocation. *See* Tender, nonconforming or defective

Reward
cost of publicizing, 58-59
knowledge of offer, 59-65
offer of, 58-59
Rights, concept of, 238-239
Risk
definition of, 26, 30, 35-36
and diversification, 124, 126
market risk as type of, 26-28
and standardization of contract terms, 109
Risk allocation. *See also* Choice of contract
administrative cost of determining rules for, 136
as affected by knowledge of the parties, 163
choice of contract as affecting, 13, 33-34
and inflation, 151-152
and insurance, 123-125
legal rules as standard terms for, 4
and mistake, 114-121, 162
and subcontracting, 27, 35-36
as subject of contract interpretation, 39
Risk aversion, 36-37, 87
and insurance, 123-124
and poverty, 112
Rosenfield, Andrew M., 54n, 151, 153

Salvage, maritime doctrine of, 58, 61
Schwartz, Alan, 111, 136n, 151, 152, 153, 175n
Scott, Robert E., 223, 224, 260
Seal, promises under, 53, 64
Slawson, W. David, 75n
Smith, Adam, 42
Social promise, 50-51
Specific performance, 181-194 passim
administrative costs of, 193
contractual provision for, 190-194
contrasted with damages, 29-30
and information, 185-187
ordered by an arbitrator, 223-224
role of in a communist economy, 220-223, 229
Speidel, Richard E., 225, 227
State, as a market phenomenon, 33
Status contract, contrasted with purposive contract, 261-262
Statute of Frauds, 64-65, 94-95, 253, 254
Statute of limitations, promise to pay debt barred by, 51
Stephen, James F., 258n
Stigler, George J., 126n, 183n
Subjective theory of contract, 151
Substitution effects, 88-89, 151, 183-184
and price rises, 140
Suez Canal, closing of, 128
Supply elasticity, and price rises, 140

Tender, nonconforming or defective
and efficiency, 168-170
rejection of goods because of, 170-175
and acts inconsistent with seller's ownership, 172-173
reasonable time for, 171, 172
substantive grounds for, 173-175
Tort, contrasted with contract, 66
Trebilcock, M. J., 111
Tullock, Gordon, 38, 257, 258, 259

Unconscionability, 94-96, 107
procedural, 82-87
standard of proof for, 94-95
substantive, 96-100
used to protect the poor, 95-96, 111-113
Unfair surprise, 83, 85
Uniform Commercial Code, 82, 85, 100, 131, 138, 143, 146-149, 153, 156n, 167, 170-175, 208-220 passim
Unilateral contract, 58
Unique goods, 169, 183-187
Unjust enrichment, 40, 43, 59, 62
Uranium market, 143-149 passim, 153
Utilitarianism, 93

Value
economic concept of, 2, 233-239
labor theory of, 247

Value—*Continued*
production of surplus value, 249-250
social values, 235, 266

Wagering contract, 260
Waiver
of defense, 98
of liability, 76, 99-100
Warranties, 75
and the poor, 111-112
Weber, Max, 110, 261, 262
Westinghouse Electric Corp., 143-149 passim, 153
Williams, Bernard, 265
Williamson, Oliver E., 39
Williston, Samuel, 254n
Will theory, 29, 67, 250
Wright, J. Skelly, 107, 128

Zoning, 78